The
Way
of
Suffering

A Geography of Crisis

The
Way
of
Suffering

A Geography of Crisis

Jerome A. Miller

GEORGETOWN UNIVERSITY PRESS
Washington, D.C.

Excerpts from "East Coker" and from "Little Gidding" in *Four Quartets,* copyright 1943 by T.S. Eliot; renewed 1971 by Esme Valerie Eliot. Reprinted by permission of Harcourt Brace Jovanovich, Inc.

Excerpt from "Journey of the Magi" in *Collected Poems 1909–1962* by T.S. Eliot, copyright 1936 by Harcourt Brace Jovanovich, Inc.; copyright © 1963, 1964 by T.S. Eliot. Reprinted by permission of the publisher.

On the cover: B-11106 GESCHREI (THE SCREAM), 1895, Edvard Munch, Norwegian, 1863-1944, National Gallery of Art, Washington, D.C., Rosenwald Collection

Copyright © 1988 by Georgetown University Press
All Rights Reserved
Printed in the United States of America

Library of Congress Cataloging-in-Publication Data
Miller, Jerome, 1946–
    The way of suffering / Jerome Miller.
        p.   cm.
    ISBN 0-87840-465-1. ISBN 0-87840-466-X (pbk.)
    1. Suffering. I. Title.
B105.S79M55 1988
128—dc19   88-4703
                                                                                CIP

Dedicated to
my grandfather
Alexander Richard Hampsey
1880–1965

"Old men ought to be explorers"

Acknowledgments

I want to express gratitude to John Breslin, the director of Georgetown University Press, for his eager backing of this expedition into unexplored territory; to Francis Kane, Tony Whall and William Zak, great friends and wise men who helped me to read the stars during many a dark night; to my children Thomas, Clare and Eileen, who, having no choice but to tag along, have put up with the discomforts of travel with wonderful good humor; and to Cathy, always my fellow pilgrim.

Contents

I had seen birth and death,
But had thought they were different; this Birth was
Hard and bitter agony for us, like Death, our death.

T.S. Eliot
"Journey of the Magi"

A Word on Mapmaking

What follows is an essay in the original but now almost forgotten sense of that term as a risk-filled venture, an exploration that is not guaranteed to reach its destination. It makes no pretense to finality and no claim that even its main theme is studied adequately. Moreover, its scope is less ambitious than its title might imply and it would be well if from the beginning the reader were resigned to its limitations.

The essay is about crisis. However, it nowhere mentions any of the particular "crises" which puncture our public life with such predictable regularity, or even the less dramatic but more profound crises affecting our basic political institutions and traditions. Little more than oblique references are made to what might be considered the crisis of modernity itself, the disintegration of culture as such, what seems sometimes to be the irreparable break in the chain which heretofore bound each generation to a long line of authority. Instead, this essay focuses throughout on the experience of crisis as it is undergone by the individual person, and on the pilgrimage which one inevitably undertakes if one allows crisis to uproot one's life. The individual is always inseparably bound to a world, to Others, and cannot be separated from the situation in which he lives and which, to some degree, he is. But throughout this essay we will see the world from the viewpoint of the private person, and whatever insights we are granted will be insights concerning the role of crisis in the spiritual destiny of the personal self, largely without regard for the particular cultural or political world to which he essentially belongs. Although there are no abstract persons, it is not improper to abstract the individual from his world to study his character as it is affected by crisis; but we must admit from the beginning that it is dangerous to extrapolate, from anything said in such a study, any conclusion about the meaning of crisis in cultural and political life. I would only note that my very restriction of this study to the private sphere is symptomatic of, and encouraged by, the disintegration of our public world in all its facets. Because most of us are only nominal members of any community, we are to a large degree thrown back on our private selves, especially when it comes to facing and understanding the kinds of radically disruptive experiences with which this essay is concerned. Having little or no faith in moral guides, each of us has little choice but to find his own way through crisis experiences. Generally speaking, our culture does not cultivate the kind of wisdom needed to make sense of them.

Envisioned as a pilgrimage, this essay moves from one terrain to another, each harsher and more dangerous than the one left behind. A word should be said here, perhaps, about these stages of the trip, whether each of them is necessary, whether the movement from one to the other is supposed to be inevitable. The essay attempts to describe and evaluate a series of different attitudes or modes of being, different "existential" approaches to life as a whole. Let me admit here at the beginning that there is, in all probability, no actual person who fits into these portraits perfectly. I hope that this is not because the portraits are stereotypes but because none of us possesses a perfectly consistent character; we do not at all times, or even perhaps at any time, act in accord with one single attitude. Nevertheless, underneath our daily inconsistencies, we espouse, in part consciously, in part unconsciously, some fundamental orientation or disposition; and we would, in fact, be the perfect embodiment of one of the attitudes depicted if we actually did live out this disposition in all its purity, down to the least details of our conduct. Portraits of no one, studies such as the ones essayed here try to portray what we would be like if we had, as it were, the courage to live out our deepest choices in the purest way.

To move from one such mode of being to another, to alter one's fundamental attitude toward life as a whole, is to undergo a radical change in character. The chapters of this essay map a certain sequence of such changes or, more accurately, a series of steps in the direction of the one truly radical change which, as human persons, we are capable of undergoing. These steps are not arranged haphazardly but in accord with a conviction that each represents a kind of advance, a maturation or deepening of character, over its predecessors. That the essay as a whole moves through a series of such metamorphoses to a culminating crisis makes it read, perhaps, like a far-fetched novel; and so the question arises again as to whether any actual person has, in fact, ever travelled the dramatic route I have taken pains to map. The answer to this query must be ambiguous. Each stage emerges from its predecessor and leads toward its successor insofar as it constitutes a distinctive attitude which the heart can adopt as it develops, haltingly, a deepness of character. The stages do not follow upon each other by virtue of a deductive necessity; nor is there any need to pretend that most people really go through the sequence of steps as here described. Indeed, we need not change at all; or we can move backward, resuming an old attitude more superficial than the one we are rejecting; or we can change more gradually, breaking up our journey into more distinctive stages than are portrayed here; or we can change in a less guarded fashion, without halting at intermediate attitudes on our way toward a radical metamorphosis. But what is claimed for the series of steps as mapped out here is that they are arranged in the morally proper order from superficiality to depth of character, and that they constitute the major options among which we must choose in adopting a fundamental attitude toward our lives. Beyond that, the sequence of steps presented here has only a kind of moral probability: it tries to describe the route we would all be likely to take if, in spite of our almost inevitable weaknesses, we kept heeding, though with much reluctance, the unrelenting demands of truth.

Some explanation must be given for the fact that this inquiry is conducted with little apparent regard for other treatments of its many themes. The essay contains almost no references to or discussions of classical or contemporary texts, a lack which does little to mend the break with tradition mentioned above with some regret. Nor does it refer except obliquely to historical or social circumstances. All of these lacks are at least partially accounted for, though not necessarily excused, by what I might call the relentlessly phenomenological style of the essay. It is a search to understand, without distraction or parentheses, the essential features of certain ways of living. I might have included historical illustrations and I might have compared my analysis of these ways of living with the interpretations developed by other thinkers. But such illustrations and comparisons would themselves occasion controversy which would deflect attention from what was intended to be an unbroken line of argument. From the beginning I have tried to allow the essay to follow its own unswerving path.

But direct quotation or explicit discussion is not the only possible testimony of indebtedness. It is not too much to say that those thinkers whose work I never mention I always have in mind. Indeed, this essay as a whole is a long, indirect reflection on the great works to which it is bound and indebted. So, for example, Nietzsche, especially the Nietzsche of *Thus Spake Zarathustra* and *Beyond Good and Evil*, is, as it were, the constant companion of chapter 4, just as Sophocles' Oedipus is the companion of chapter 5. On the other hand, certain aspects and sections of Heidegger's *Being and Time* are a preoccupation throughout the essay and have affected the entire argument in profound ways. Contemporary writers as different as Philip Rief and Mircea Eliade have had a dramatic impact on the thinking which goes on here, as will be evident to those familiar with their work. These thinkers whom I have mentioned are only the most obvious inspirations for the essay. While such sources are kept in the background, they are able to exercise from there the most subtle and decisive influence.

Having said all this, however, it would be disingenuous to deny that there is something out of the usual about the essay. However mindful of other voices, it has its own idiosyncratic ring. Once I get the solitary pilgrim I am trying to study into focus, I write as if nothing were more important than following, with unrelenting fidelity, the path that pilgrim opens in the wilderness of the heart. The whole essay is governed by that singular and abiding passion. Whether such single-mindedness is a blessing or a curse is not for me to judge. I can only admit that I am incapable of thinking through these matters in any other way.

Finally, I would like to say a word about what might strike some readers as the sexism of the language employed throughout this work. In the original version of it, the use of neuter pronouns proliferated. But given the highly personal nature of the experiences being discussed, such usage often rang false and gave many passages an abstract, impersonal tone incompatible with the substance of what was being discussed. In my view, the masculine pronouns subsequently introduced help to bring these passages to life and give them the personal flavor they require. There was a reason beyond sexist social convention for choosing the masculine rather than the feminine usage. The crises about which I write are crises which upset and undermine precisely those attitudes toward life which, in our culture at least, are deeply associated with masculinity. In that sense, the "will to control" about which so much is said in the following pages is profoundly phallocentric. If I refer over and over to the person undergoing crisis as a male, it is finally because it is the maleness in all of us that is devastated by it.

Point of Departure

Because God is so far removed from us, we are constantly approached by those who purport to be his oracles; it seems that as soon as the sacred disappears, instant prophets rush forward to take its place.[1] However curt one tries to be in dismissing them as hucksters of conversion, one's contempt for them is often only a way to silence their seductive appeal. Even the philosopher, suspicious of idols, is tempted to clutch at them when he lives in a void.

Indeed, no one is exempt from that appeal: for prophets preach in the public marketplace when culture as a whole is undergoing a crisis of identity. Only cults can give a culture the gods it lives for, and a culture whose gods have died should expect the contention of messiahs for its heart. Such messiahs sense that not just the individual but history itself waits upon their message and is anxious to know for which contending god—or beast—the time has finally come. When history itself is in labor, all of us, in part of our selves, want to be the parents of its new child and to christen it with our name. In such a situation, even the possibility of exempting ourselves from the dialectic of crisis and salvation attracts us as salvific.

But while it is true that the private life of the individual reflects the public crisis of the culture as a whole, it is also true that each person can see in the public crisis his own anxieties writ large.[2] Augustine's *Confessions* are to some degree the autobiography of an age, a private mirror of social disintegration with its swirl of circuses and cults. The fact that the gods have deserted the public altars is reflected in the fact that the individual finds a void when he turns inward; and when he leaves the city for the desert in search of the sacred, his apparently private pilgrimage is capable of having portentous public consequences.

In such a situation, what is occurring in both the private and public realm is the process of crisis, with its experience of dissolution and chaos, its unleashing of horrific possibilities, the sense it creates in us of being sucked into a yawning emptiness, of being carried along by dark undercurrents we cannot slow or direct. Even and especially then, the task of the thinker is to think, and to submit his life to the rigor of reflection and self-examination. For if the disintegration of tradition which both precipitates and results from crisis encourages one to be skeptical of every faith and even cynical toward believers, the emptiness of the present makes all beliefs seductive, but especially those which release one from the inhibitory power of real thinking.[3] Indeed, the two demonic rivals for a mind in crisis—the despair of nihilism and the Light of Perfect Knowledge—have a hidden affinity: they conspire with each other in the demonic refusal of thought. The vocation of thought is to resist these tempters and so to remain faithful to the radical tension which crisis involves. But, more than that, such a situation imposes on thought the possibility and even responsibility of thinking about crisis itself. Crisis, especially when it is a crisis in the thinker's understanding of his own life, demands of him that he think through the nature of crisis.

This essay represents an effort to meditate on the process of crisis, not in order to withdraw from it but in order to be more thoughtfully obedient to it. The reader can get some initial sense of the kind of crisis being discussed here by reflecting for a moment on the way we think of our own past in our most private reminiscences. Memory does not present us with a skein of nows succeeding each other anonymously and indifferently. My personal memory, my memory of my unique life history, is not reducible to a recollection of successive facts, none of which has priority over any other. Were it so reducible, I would see myself as a person who has never achieved anything distinctive and to whom nothing distinctive has ever happened. But then I would not be a distinctive person at all, and I would have no genuinely personal history. I would be living as a nonself, as an anonymous cipher. (And if personal memory is not the recollection of facts, a communal history is not the collection of historical data—it is the telling of a story.)

Rather, authentic personal memory enables me to return to those privileged experiences which have been decisive in some way for my whole existence. These are the experiences that profoundly seared and permanently altered my self, not because they overrode my freedom but because they involved a transformative exercise of freedom. In reflecting on my life, I realize that such experiences possess a kind of transcendent importance because during them my life as a whole was at stake in some radical sense. The whole of my life has the character of a drama in which every moment builds toward or flows from certain critical, life-shattering

experiences. Our social conventions encourage us to identify these experiences with specific events such as my engagement and marriage,
perhaps the birth of my children, or the final moments of some public
achievement, the reception of honors and accolades. But especially when
one's culture is in crisis, precisely those events one might expect to be
richest in dramatic import often seem strangely hollow and ordinary.
Perhaps even in normal times, the truly transformative experiences of
one's life will be more personal, more private, will take place in the hidden recesses of the heart. Perhaps even my recollection of them only occurs in my most private moments.

In short, the flow of time which constitutes my life as a whole is not
measurable by clocks or calendars, both of which level life off to an even
keel. Someone's adolescence may not end until middle age; another person might already be an old man in his youth. And I do not learn how to
tell time until I learn that the human self, which I am, lives most fully in
the interruptions when clocks stop and a plunge into the decisive time of
crisis breaks the even keel of its ordinary flow. When I think of my life in
this way, I date myself in accord with the decisive experiences of my life
and what I have become through them. And because such experiences
rupture the flow of the ordinary, they introduce the rise and fall of drama;
crisis events are, of their very nature, critical of the ordinary.

We can locate here the distinctive vocation of the narrative artist: he
remembers for all of us. He helps save from oblivion those ruptures which
break the hold of the ordinary. He disrupts facts with drama. It is possible
for each of us to make the privileged experiences told in his story part of
our memory of our own; for in stepping from the mundane time in which
I ordinarily live into the rise and fall of time which the narrative enacts, it
becomes possible for me to recollect and reflect on the critical moments
of my life. Of course, if I treated the narrative as no more than a catalyst
for my personal memory, I would only be using it for my private purposes
and not taking any interest in it for its own sake. I would then be reducing
the work of art to myself, instead of transcending my self by participating
in the drama it unfolds.[4] Precisely because it invites me to perform such an
act of transcendence, the work of art enables me to shatter the exclusivity
of my usually self-centered memory. It confronts me with Others and
what has erupted in their lives; it requires me to acknowledge the univer-
salizability of a drama that I can no longer think of as being only mine. Indeed, these Others, as characters, while distinctively human and not
anonymous, are not concrete Others actually living to whom I might respond when outside the world of the art work. Rather each character is
both unique and universalized, and in each of them a private experience is

transformed into something communal. The work of art is an epiphany of the essential human drama. Instead of remaining locked in the idiosyncrasies of memory, I can experience through the work of art the sharable nature of the drama of crisis.

But after the narrative ruptures the solipsism too often characteristic of personal memory, critical intelligence ruptures my participation in the narrative. The first project of critical intelligence is not to criticize; it is to make the work the theme of thought, and this means to think the drama it incarnates. This cannot be done without trying to speak what the work itself embodies but leaves unspoken, to call into question what the work itself only implies. Here, thought tries to appropriate for itself the insights incarnated in the images of art. When thought undertakes this project it tries to understand the nature of crisis in its very essence, irrespective of its specific content or who experiences it. The philosopher aspires to shift from the idiosyncrasy of memory and the sharable image of art, to the intellectual insight.

We might be tempted to accuse the philosopher of trying to move as far away as possible from the crisis itself not only to understand it but also to exempt himself from it.[5] Their sensitivity toward such an accusation at one point encouraged philosophers to personalize their thought, to demand existential involvement from an author, and even to make such involvement a criterion for the adequacy of thought. But does this not assume that crisis must be imported into thought, as if thought, when left to itself, always proceeds on an even keel, as if thought in its essence lacks the rise and fall of drama? Could we not say that such thought indicts itself and cannot be redeemed by our decorating it with existential fervor?

For, to take the present case as an example, we want to understand the nature of crisis. How are we to go about doing this? The very fact that we use the word and use it with linguistic propriety proves that we already understand the phenomenon itself as it is ordinarily understood. But such use also proves that we take our understanding for granted, since we use the word without looking at it or our use of it. And as soon as I begin to examine what I have unconsciously assumed, I rupture the flow of the ordinary and introduce crisis into thought. Thought which remains even-keeled has put all thinking behind it—it has levelled down the uprooting effect that questioning always has if it is authentic. Real thinking requires entering the rupture which questions create. In our case, to call into question the nature of crisis is to expose the shallowness of our thought to the depth of the phenomenon itself; to really think about crisis requires that one be willing to undergo the crisis of thinking. Only a thinking which betrays the nature of thought offers us an escape from upsetting experiences.

In short, by drawing on the sources of memory and art, the philosopher can critique the ordinary understanding of crisis and thus approach its essence. One tack he might take in trying to do so would be to enter into the controversies concerning the fundamental beliefs and alternative world views that contend for a heart in crisis. In doing so, he himself might become a partisan and carry the banner of an answer to the questions which crisis provokes. He would then try to articulate that vision, explain the rationale for adopting it, and try to show its power to transform our lives. He might be able to do all this without becoming fanatic and without imprisoning his thought in ideology. But if he is to articulate the meaning of that vision for human life, one of his most crucial tasks will be to interpret, in terms of that vision, the nature of the crisis experience itself; and when he does this, he will read back into the crisis a meaning derived from the vision which, in his view, resolves it, or ought to resolve it. Since he believes in the revelatory power of his vision, he expects it to illuminate the dread, the obscurities, the ambiguities which crisis involved.

But it is possible to reverse this whole perspective. That is, it is possible to interpret all possible Answers in terms of what a crisis is, instead of interpreting what crisis is in terms of one of the Answers whose effect is purportedly to end it. Instead of allowing an Answer to govern our understanding of crisis, it is possible to allow our understanding of crisis to govern our evaluation of all possible Answers. For if we could uncover the nature of crisis and what it reveals about the nature of human life, we would then have a truth to which every possible Answer would have to measure up if it claimed to contain not just therapy but wisdom. We would have a criterion for judging the authenticity of every conversion. Or, to put it positively, the truth about crisis is a truth every claim to wisdom must integrate, if it is to be congruous with the basic nature of human existence.

Now if this is to be our approach, it would seem that we are left on our own, without a vision to use as a framework for the development of the inquiry. We are forced to fall back on those ordinary prejudices and preconceptions which already, it would seem, prevent our uncovering what is buried[6] in memory and implicit in art. But while we are fated to start with these assumptions by using them to gain access to the phenomena under study, the rupture of real thinking enables us to transcend them— not, as Descartes wished, in one fell swoop, so that thought can begin with a clean slate; but through a patient, even delicate fidelity to questioning, at the end of which one expects to discover deeper questions.[7] Precisely that ability to ask questions, though no cornucopia of insight and no guarantee of inevitable progress, does enable us to disrupt our assumptions and so to transform our thought about drama into the drama of thought.

Moreover, just as the drama of thought begins in the disruption of ordinary prejudices, so the thought about drama must begin with the surface of the ordinary, with its even keel of routines, its secure, almost inviolable boundaries and the weapons it has ever ready at hand to protect them. An examination of those routines will lead us to reflect on those secret agents of crisis which somehow sneak inside the settlement and sometimes succeed in their conspiracy to undermine it. And then perhaps we will be able to look at the rupture which we so long avoid and which opens wider and wider like a fault in the geography of our hearts.

Chapter One

The Closed Home:

Ordinary Existence as the Will to Control

The ordinary is the everyday—what happens day in and day out. Whatever its more specific content, it happens over and over. Nothing memorable occurs. When I do happen to remember what I did two days ago, the very fact that I remember seems quirky and fortuitous. Why do I remember this triviality rather than that one, this forgettable event rather than any other? Nothing has occurred which *claims* memory and insists on its rights as something worthy of being remembered. My ordinary life is a skein of experiences, each of which disappears the moment it occurs into the anonymity of the past; today does nothing but repeat the day that came before it.

But this very reign of the ordinary is so complete that ordinarily I am unaware of it. I become conscious of how ephemeral my experiences are only when someone asks me about something that happened two days ago and I find that I can recall nothing. Only when an Other interrupts the flow do I realize that time slips away from me without leaving a mark. This means that I am so enveloped by everydayness that I am unconscious of my immersion in it; and, indeed, it is only for a moment that I realize I can remember nothing. As abruptly as it emerged, this bewildering recognition itself vanishes. I forget the fact that I cannot remember what I am doing with my life.

In that brief moment of recognition, I tend to blame memory—as if it failed in its duty to recall every event and action, no matter how lacking they are in any memorable quality. But perhaps this failure of memory represents a kind of covert rebellion on its part; and perhaps my memory is trying to insist that it will only be the guardian of what is precious. Memory occupies a site below the living flow of consciousness, and perhaps that depth (from which it surveys and examines the surface) makes it possible for my memory to be wiser than I am myself. Its refusal to recollect suggests that something in me protests the banality of everydayness. Though I do not do so consciously or deliberately, part of me objects to the absence of anything memorable from my life. On the other hand, in blaming memory for its blank spaces, I show that I am devoted to the triumph of the everyday even over the parts of my self still free from its sway. Instead of hearing memory tell me I have done nothing memorable, I rebuke memory for its failure to submit to the ordinary. I want to cure myself of transcendence.

Were memory submissive to that rebuke, I would memorize everything—which tie I wear each day, the food eaten at every meal, the products on every shopping list, the whole cluttered stream of everyday life. It is difficult but not impossible to imagine a person so completely immersed in and fettered by the brute data of daily existence. If a person were thus immersed, could we say in his behalf that he is obedient to the concrete reality of life? That he refuses to flee from the mundane but completely accepts it in its finitude and facticity? Indeed, no other mode of existence seems, at first glance, so perfectly submissive to the given and so immune to the appeals of illusion and fantasy.

But we wear clothes that "go together"; we have schedules of chores and well-planned lists of what to buy in the supermarket. The whirl of detail in which I am ordinarily immersed does not flood me like an innocent victim: it is the helter-skelter of my own projects, each of which aims at organizing life. Far from being a chaos of unrelated data, daily existence consists of a series of plans I myself impose on my world: if I am made dizzy by its frantic rhythm, I am made dizzy by my own obsessive busyness. Ordinary existence is the opposite of letting be what is. It is my attempt to subdue the totality of what is to the plans I have made for it. It is the will to repress anything that tries to interrupt the flow of my routines. The essence of the ordinary is control, and the essence of control is the will to dominate.

How, it might be objected, can such a characterization not be a caricature when ordinary life is identified, in all our minds, with placidity, the absence of disruption and terror, a tranquil uneventfulness, the quiet perseverance of mediocrity and ennui? Nothing would seem to be more foreign to everyday life than the violence implicit in the will to control.

But let us look at that placid uneventfulness which is assumed to be characteristic of the everyday: it is never as uneventful as we wish it to be. On the world's side, it is marred by accidents, the rust and breakdown of tools designed to be ready for use, the intransigence of things and persons opposed to our routines; and, on our side, it is marred by complaints and frustrations, by a thousand brief annoyances which eat away at the fabric of repose. Both the world and our own temperaments habitually throw us off the track of our routines.

That I experience an accident as interference, and my own anxiety as a disruption of the even keel of repose, indicates that I already have a blueprint I intend to impose on the course of events. If a day "proves uneventful," it is not because I accept whatever happens, nor is it because nothing happens. It is because everything has happened as planned. There is a placidity to such days but is that not because I feel during them an ease that is similar to that the despot feels when all conspirators have been silenced? "Everything goes smoothly" means that the world remains within the boundaries I have decided to assign it. To live without interruptions, to have nothing intrude upon or resist the smooth procedures of my schedule—such, indeed, is peace, but it is the peacefulness of a will which has first willed violence. If I go so far as to memorize every detail of the ordinary, if those details are nothing but data which get their meaning from my projects, if those projects originate in my plan for how I want my life to go, my fundamental purpose is to prevent the occurrence of anything out of the ordinary or upsetting.

But with what right do we disparage such a life, or even the violence of the attitude that underlies it, especially if it is only our willingness to impose a pattern on the world that makes it possible for us to be creators? Ordinary individuals have small projects; great individuals will to create a new world. Does not such creation require a radical transformation of what is, a refusal to let it continue to be as it is, an uncompromising will to make it what I envision? Must not the founder of a city be willing to lay waste to nature and direct the building of walls to exclude it? Is our ordinary will to control simply a lesser form of such heroic creativity?[1] Or is there some profound incongruity between the heroic and the ordinary which we have yet to appreciate? If we are eventually to answer these questions, we must stop to examine the nature of the ordinary with greater care.

1. The Closed World of Work

Let us begin this examination by focusing on the experience of work.

In work I set a task for myself to accomplish; I adopt a definite objective and deliberate over the means conducive to its achievement. The criterion used in this deliberation is efficiency: which action will be most productive but require the least expenditure on my part. In performing the act which deliberation has selected as efficient, I *use existence* to achieve my objective. I employ this italicized phrase in order to bring out the kind of totalitarian claim[2] which the objective tends to exert. In working toward it, I adopt a specific attitude toward the whole of reality: matter is viewed as raw material, things as tools, conversation as a distraction. Everything is evaluated in terms of its relevance to the project at hand.[3] Anything lacking this relevance is judged to be without use and therefore, in this context, without worth. Moreover, the act itself is not thought to have any value except insofar as it contributes to the end in view.

Both the deliberation preceding the act and the act itself require a particular disciplining of consciousness. I have to learn the rigors of calculation to measure the costs and benefits of possible acts; I have to acquire the know-how of techniques to perform the act well. Again, any knowledge irrelevant to calculation and production is considered worthless, and relevant knowledge is worthwhile only because of its relevance.

As the wielder of techniques I wrench the world into obedience. My success is measured by the degree to which I subordinate it to my purposes. But those purposes frequently are themselves pursued only for the sake of further purposes, and the latter again for the sake of still further purposes. Not only is the act a means but the goal is a means as well. In working, I entangle myself in a whole network of techniques and means, and the more complex the network the more distanced I am in my ordinary life from the ultimate objective that justifies the whole process. And the more immediately available objectives, precisely because they are themselves only means within a wider context, give no more than a short-lived sense of accomplishment.

Yet, despite the fact that work as such is only a means which naturally points beyond itself to its own cessation, and despite the insignificance of its short-term rewards and the distance separating us from its long-term consequences, we ordinarily succumb to work as if it were an enchantress. Indeed, there is usually something disorienting and unsettling in the experience of "having time on my hands" with no work in sight. I prefer the rigor of calculation and technique, with its prescribed sequence of acts, to the liberation which the completion of work makes possible. How can we account for this?

It has been argued that this fact only describes man now, in his current historical situation; that its remote cause is the discipline and self-repression long ago conditioned into our psyches by the practical necessities of survival; that its mediate cause is the process of industrialization which has mechnized us and drained us of our capacity for leisure; and that its proximate cause is the surplus repression of advanced industrial society, which indoctrinates an ethic of scarcity into an age of affluence in order to prevent the dissolution of the established socioeconomic system.[4] This argument suggests that it is only my cultural conditioning which makes me feel compelled to continue working long past the point where work serves any real necessity. It assumes that, if left unindoctrinated, I would prefer to be leisurely and to work only because and as long as a desired objective required it.

But this agrument overlooks the fact that, wholly apart from its beneficial consequences, the very process of work itself makes it possible for me to impose a direction, a sequence, and thus a pattern, on my life. The sequence of activities which, at first glance, seems to be instrumental for the imposition of a pattern, is itself already a pattern. If I never finish my work, that does not mean that I have to live in the chaos my work has not yet subdued. Rather, it means that I live in the sequence of routines which work itself prescribes. In this sense work, precisely insofar as it is a means to be used for imposing order, already achieves, as soon as it begins, its essential objective. Work always works insofar as its task is to impose an order on existence. And this means that, if I seek to maintain the even keel of my ordinary existence, I will seek to avoid the completion of work since this can only rupture the pattern of life which the routine of working has itself already established. To be "liberated" from work would be to rupture the order which keeps chaos at bay. Because work itself liberates me by enabling me to control my existence, to finish work is to be in crisis.

While, on the conscious level, I aim at an objective in relationship to which work is a mere means, it is really the process of work itself which gives me the sense of being in control. It is true that I keep my original objective in view, that I strive for its attainment, and complain of the obstacles which hinder my progress; for only my orientation toward a goal and my obedience to the discipline of technique gives my activity the orderliness which distinguishes it from random movement. But now I am in fact using the goal as an instrument to make work possible instead of using work as a means to reach a goal. The routine of work uses even the goals it seeks as its servants.[5] It is no wonder then that whatever leisure we have is usually justified as a means for enhancing production. The fact that we really enjoy our routines is revealed by the boasting tone that creeps into our complaints about how much we have to do; we like to demonstrate that we have made the whole of our existence a work project.

This analysis does not encourage us to view the reign of work as an idiosyncratic period of history. Rather, it suggests that there are no periods in history at all—no decisive breaks in the flow of ordinary time—except insofar as the ordinary, continuous tyranny of work is ruptured. And, in fact, at least in one sense every age in history eventually looks like every other insofar as practicality flattens every drama into the anonymous order of routines, and robs every revolution of its transforming effects. Modernity succeeds in making ordinary work its fetish, only because all along human beings have dreamed of and longed for just this utilitarian obsession.

2. The Promethean Dimension of the Ordinary: The Will to Control Out of Control

Every revolution in technique, every alteration in the processes of production, no matter how drastic, still takes place within the boundaries of the world defined by work. Even so, it would seem that such change still has the significance of drama since it at least ruptures those specific routines of technique to which we have grown accustomed. Does not a revolution in technique have, as its immediate consequence, an upsetting of the boundaries by which life is controlled? Seen in this light, our resistance to better ways of doing the same thing is far from irrational. The best way to control one's life, it seems, would be not even to undergo the disruption which a "better way of doing something" entails.

And yet, on the other hand, a passion for the perfection of technique is exactly what we might expect of a mode of life which has made work an end in itself. We might say that, since work has purged life of its drama—even that involved in the process of work itself—drama has nowhere else to go but into the rude ambition and Promethean feats of technical man. It seems that even in our ordinariness we cannot stifle the Promethean urge to do something great: confined to routine, it becomes the urge to magical prowess, the fascination with tools, the worship of technical excess. Once this urge takes hold, instruments are made without regard for their usefulness in producing benefits. The instrument is worshipped in and for itself. As soon as a machine is built, it becomes obsolete, not because of practical needs but because the god of technique mimics the older gods insofar as it too makes absolute demands. Once one has deified technique, no technique can quiet the desire to surpass it. And this means that, even in a world of pure work, even in a society which levels down everything to technique, the dialectic of ordinary and extraordinary can emerge, with its drama of stasis and disruption.

If one wishes to maintain the even keel of the ordinary even here, one must either refuse to be swept along by revolutions in techniques or devise strategies for robbing such changes of their psychological impact. In the latter case, one makes a routine of the very revolution in routines which technology is always introducing. Having tamed existence by confining it to work, and work by confining it to routines, and routine by confining it to adaptation, a person can settle into the serene security of everydayness. We cannot help but admire and even envy the imperturbable coolness of the person who is able to "cope with," "manage," "deal with" every situation that arises.

But even if one has tamed the Promethean urge in work, there still remains the urge to control which the practical world does nothing to restrain. The practical person wills to impose boundaries on everything, and to exclude from his life anything that promises to be uncontrollable. The paradox of this way of life lies in the fact that the very desire to control comes to dominate one's life completely.

The irony in this becomes apparent when we look at the way everything in our lives gets subordinated to the project of control: things serve this project by becoming tools, intelligence by submitting to the rules of technique, emotion by allowing itself ⋅ be confined to the habit of oscillation between comfort and complaint. To the degree that one thereby succeeds in managing everything, one feels like the master of one's situation. But this control has been achieved only by my allowing my desire for control to govern my attitude toward everything, including all aspects of my own self. It is clear that there is one experience I cannot handle: the experience of not being in control of whatever situation I am in. To prevent this loss of control from occurring, I cannot *let* anything *be*, including my self. Without realizing it, I subordinate my whole life to the project of being in control of it. I am thus the victim of my own obsession to manage successfully what happens to me. And this is the underlying reason why I often speak of the practical work as if it has a kind of autonomous power over me—even though work is nothing but my will to impose order on existence.

It is this need to control that explains the antireligious drive that is unconsciously at work in our lives. Insofar as we try to enclose everything inside the fixed boundaries of practicality, we seek to deprive everything we encounter of that Otherness that makes it potentially disruptive. In making a thing "manageable," we confine it and thus make it limited. Practical consciousness is, in its essence, this will to finitize.[6] And if by the "sacred" one means that Other whose Otherness has the power to overwhelm us, the purpose of practicality is to empty one's world of the sacred.[7] In that sense the will to control is the will to total secularity.[8] But this is also a will which intends to exempt itself from all management for its whole purpose is to set boundaries, not obey them. In our practical world, we desire to be the gods of all we survey. This Promethean urge gives our lives a certain grandeur and, at the same time, a certain pathos. The will to control, which tries to prevent anything tragic from happening to us, is itself tragic because in exercising it we end up confining ourselves inside a world from which everything Other than ourselves has been drained. We do not realize that we are ourselves the victims of our own desire to be safe. In control of everything, we live in the smallest and most narrow of all possible worlds.

3. The Other as a Problem to be Solved

Precisely because our ordinary lives are given over to the kind of practicality I have been describing, they provide evidence of the fact that, in the back of our minds, we live in dread of being upset. At the basis of our ordinary world is an unwillingness to be disrupted that would not be necessary unless existence in its unmanageable Otherness kept posing a threat to our ability to cope. The very fact that we cannot bear to think of losing control shows how determined we are to avert that possibility. But such aversion could not occur unless we knew all too well that what we are so intent on avoiding is capable of happening. But that possibility is always kept in the *back* of our minds.

In the practical world all we ever encounter are problems. Problems require solutions; to get solutions I must apply or divine techniques. Both the emergence and redress of problems belong to the process of routine—things "go smoothly" only if problems emerge as usual and call forth my habits of dealing with them. But what I am accustomed to treat as a problem is not a problem originally, even in my own experience of it. Initially, "something" disarms me by rupturing the pattern of routine I have established. A small but unmistakable resentment is awakened in me by the way this "something" spontaneously and unintentionally mocks my techniques. Because my feelings and intelligence are bound by the strictures of habit, I am at first unable to understand this disruption—it refuses to conform to my ordinary framework.[9] This is why it affords me, perhaps without my realizing it, my one and only glimpse of something Other than myself, something foreign and strange, an alien reality intruding upon the settled time and bounded space of everyday life. This "it" which

I cannot even name announces itself only as disruptive and thus breaks for a brief moment, whose memory I repress, the mesmerizing everydayness into which it too will eventually be absorbed. This "it" is precisely existence itself briefly tearing the shroud of practicality.

This nameless, intruding "it" seems first to come on the scene when it encroaches upon the boundaries I have already fixed for my life. But what drives us to erect boundaries in the first place? What prompts in us that will to finitize which is now confronted by this nameless intruder? We are incapable of remembering our original motive for making the universe a routine. Indeed, it might be that part of our original motive was precisely to silence our memory of it, to make our boundaries so fixed and secure that we will forget we made them. For if we can forget we made them, we can experience them as the limits of existence itself. Within those limits we can be irritated but not terrified; we can feel at home. Repression only does its work effectively when it is itself unremembered. But although we do not and cannot realize it, the nameless "it" which occasionally invades our boundaries is actually an emissary from the wilderness which it was the original purpose of our routines to keep at bay. In being confronted with such an "it," we momentarily (and without acknowledging it) reexperience the original situation we were in before we had our boundaries to protect us.

If the ordinary is to be preserved, this reexperience of the original must be only momentary. And I cope with this "it" first of all by defining it as a "problem." A "problem" is an interruption which, in principle, can be managed, an intruder which can be disarmed, even if the technique for doing so is as yet unavailable.[10] Even if I never find a solution, even if I spend the rest of my life figuring out how to deal with "it," I have already robbed the "it" of its power to rupture my life by imposing on it the role of a problem. For once the "it" is made into a problem, it can no longer call into question the structure of my life as a routine of problem solving. Thus, if I can treat everything as a problem, I can prevent anything that happens to me from being upsetting. And all I need to do in order to turn something into a problem is believe in its manageability. Moreover, if I am willing to admit into my life, without trying to avoid it, the whole horde of problems besetting me, it will be possible for me to believe that I have faced up to everything and not tried to cover anything up. I do not realize that the reason I can handle even the most upsetting experiences is because, even before I solve them, I have already domesticated them by treating them as problems.

Only now do we begin to realize how powerful the heart can be once it is determined to be in control. There is literally nothing that is able to hold out against it; for there is nothing it cannot turn into a problem to be solved. A human being can view every rupture in his life as no more than an interruption to be repaired. Nothing that happens is then able to cut through the shroud he uses to hide existence.[11]

It is true that, in spite of our interpreting all ruptures as problems, we usually continue to experience "tragedies"—radical intrusions that undermine our practical world. We even have some sense of the inevitability of tragic occurrences and thus some insight into the frailty of the human condition. But however destructive the consequences of such intrusions, we ordinarily still think of them as avoidable in principle. For we can always trace the intrusion back to a concatenation of causes and can conceive for each cause the real possibility of our preventing it. The evil results "inevitably" once certain causal conditions are realized; but the failure of men to take the preventive measures they should have taken is among those conditions. We *could* have devised techniques for avoiding what only a moment of despair exaggerates as unavoidable. And this "could" drives everything tragic out of tragedy. In fact, it reveals an essential feature of ordinary consciousness: it is, through and through, utopian,[12] not just in the sense that it is always working toward a better future, but in the sense that it already inhabits a world in which the most upsetting experiences have already been dealt with by our very success in thinking of them as manageable. But to live in such a world, one must exclude the whole totality of what is Other.

4. Avoidance of the Self and the Other

I think we are now in a position to understand why it is so misleading to compare those of us who live inside the practical world to the original founders whose actions in some radical sense created our public world. For the whole purpose of the will to control operative in the practical world is to keep us securely enclosed within its boundaries so that we will never have to face reality without an established way of coping with it. Insofar as the practical person protects himself from the dreadful experience of the Other in its Otherness, his productive life, far from being comparable to the heroic mode of being, is precisely a flight from it.

The more secure the practical person is in his world, the less chance he has of ever encountering that wilderness which confronts the heroic individual with so many upsetting ordeals. The practical person inherits a whole complex of habits which, by his very mode of appropriating them, are transformed into strategies of control: actions which were heroic ventures when first performed now belong to his ready-made repertoire of techniques; the way of thinking which the founders of his culture developed through dreadful exploration is used by the practical person as an ideology to silence questions; the veins of feeling which ran so deep at the beginning of his culture are in him no more than grooves of conditioned response; the imagination, once animated by such unexpected visions, is now stocked with clichés and stereotypes; morality itself is transformed into a set of social conventions which the practical person accepts as immutable, even though he has no inkling of the moral discoveries on which they are based. It is, I should emphasize, precisely the practical person's mode of inheriting them which insures that these "habits" will not be living traditions. Instead of being open to the ordeal of radical questioning without which insight never emerges, he accepts a "truth" as given and uses its obviousness as a justification for not thinking about anything beyond the practical sphere. Instead of personally consenting to a value whose moral demand has touched him, he simply accepts it as a convention and so silences its very power to discomfort him with its claim. He turns obedience into rote; his kind of discipleship is really a method of betrayal.[13]

But is it right to speak as if the practical person adopts this leveling process as his conscious intent and deliberate choice? There would be conscious hypocrisy involved if he pretended in public to believe in things which privately meant nothing to him. But if hypocrisy involves an incongruity between external behavior and interior motivation, a person cannot practice it unless he *possesses* an interior life, a private self which he keeps hidden below his outer surface. And it is just such a self which the practical person lacks; his superficiality prevents him from living the kind of double life the hypocrite practices. The routines of ordinary life prevent him from appropriating his life as his own, and thus, in a very radical sense, prevent him from *having* a self. And it is the awareness of this vacuum which must be avoided above all, since it would undermine the whole practical way of being.

But am I even justified in speaking of avoidance, implying thereby that in our practical lives we deliberately use our routines of thought and action to escape the crisis we would experience if we had to ask questions and make our own judgments? Is there really a conscious and deliberate avoidance here? Are not our ordinary selves simply the product, the passive result, of a socialization process we have no part in? All that I have attributed to the will of the ordinary self is really, it would seem, the outcome of conditioning. We ordinarily conform, in all dimensions of our lives, to the conventions of a world already given to us by others. That would explain why there is nothing in our ordinary behavior patterns that is distinctively *ours*.

But before we endorse this view, we should pause to reflect on all the little ways in which we cooperate with our conditioning. We might think, for example, of the silence, brief but agitated with embarrassment, which supervenes upon the initial exchange of pleasantries between new acquaintances.[14] After muttering a last cliché, an unnerving gap opens up between us; all words and thoughts seem suddenly and irretrievably to desert me, leaving me exposed and defenseless. The longer this moment lasts, and the more paralyzed I feel by it, the more desperate and determined I am to fill this silence, whatever the cost. The dread of this silence and its humiliation can lead me to say the most humiliating things.[15] In vignettes as trivial as this, we are able to recognize how desperately we squirm when we suffer even the slightest loss of control. When silence threatens the easy flow of conversation, my response is to use the weapon of speech to defend myself in any way I can from the dreadful Otherness of the Other which the silence allows to emerge.

In all unnerving situations, this sense of terror takes hold of the ordinary self, so that it has an instinctive desire to do something to regain control of its situation. But the terror and the instinct on their own do not accomplish this. In the example I have described, the very occurrence of the silence itself, the very gap in the routine of conversation, reveals how incomplete and vulnerable my boundaries are.

The silence teaches me that *I* must keep repairing and extending the barriers which protect me. My life is not so totally secure that gaps will not appear in my defenses. The behavior patterns I have been socialized to follow require my active endorsement. I have to put my full weight into protecting myself from interruptions of them. Only through my own agency will my life remain enclosed within those rules and roles which my very mode of choosing makes into routines. From the very first moment a gap appears in those routines, I myself become a willing participant in my own conditioning.[16]

But if we have justified saying that the ordinary self actively wills to avoid rupture and is thus to some degree responsible for its whole mode of life, we have still not examined the paradox at work in such avoidance. How can I avoid something without first becoming explicitly conscious of it? And how can I avoid it if I have already consciously encountered it?[17] This paradox is of central importance for the understanding of crisis. Is there, behind each deliberate decision to avoid, a conscious awareness of the thing to be avoided? Certainly, there must be: the voluntary choice to negate or annul something requires my consciously concentrating on the enemy to be repulsed. But in order to avoid, I need only to experience and acknowledge a moment of rupture in which routines are broken—I need not either experience or acknowledge whatever it is that would emerge if I allowed this rupture to be prolonged. The only enemy I need to encounter is the rupture itself, and the gap it introduces in my life. In the example discussed above, I have no idea at all of what might erupt within the unnerving silence—and it is just this feeling of being at the mercy of something foreign and unpredictable that makes me want to avoid any further exploration of it. The specific character of this foreign thing is not important; the fact that it is foreign is enough to make it evil in my eyes. I seek to escape not from the stranger himself but from his strangeness. And my determination to do so is conscious and deliberate—not in the sense that I know what I am avoiding but in the sense that I know I don't want to have the upsetting experience which the Otherness of this Other evokes in me.[18]

Now I have argued that we usually conform to our inherited traditions in such a way as to transform them into a set of conditioned routines. Because we are quick to heal every rupture in those routines, no rupture becomes upsetting enough for us to realize that part of what we are avoiding when we close it up is the emergence of our very selves. The paradox of avoidance results in our deliberately participating in what turns out to be the smothering of our own identities. But our avoidance of a disruptive crisis prevents our ever getting far enough outside our ordinary selves to realize that there is nothing to them.

One of the painful and ironic consequences of this avoidance is the effect it has on our relationships, especially those we think of as most intimate. In all my friendships I generally try to do nothing that will disrupt or unsettle the sense of familiarity they involve. This requires, on the one hand, that I resist any emergence of my friend as radically Other, since this would only puncture the usual hum of our talk with a bewildering and embarrassing silence. But it also requires, just as strictly, that I never, even in our most private moments, reveal myself as Other than I am ordinarily. I do not avoid such revelations simply because I want to avoid risking the loss of this friendship but because it would introduce a new and upsetting uncertainty about my own self. It is exactly such an unsettling occurrence which my will to control is intended to prevent. I want to have no well-kept secrets, no inner life hidden beneath the surface; I want there to be nothing more to me than what can be known of me by knowing my surface. I do not want to know my self as a self just as I do not want to know the Other as Other. And in all of this—in the active project of hiding all disruptive revelations both from others and from my self, in the strategies of avoidance which repress the extraordinary, in the refusal to let be in my self anything which would cause me to become Other for the Other—we see how we strive to be ciphers, how we struggle, in our uniqueness, to be anonymous.

5. To Have No Gods before Me

What am I then, in my ordinary life, if not someone who refuses to experience crisis of any sort, someone who keeps his life closed to every Other that threatens to disrupt it? I treat all of the upsetting things that happen to me as problems to be handled, managed, dealt with. I impose the boundaries of the ordinary on anything that tries to break through them.

And does this not mean that what I avoid above all is the boundless as such? Insofar as I want everything to be manageable, I want there to be nothing infinite in my life, nothing that surpasses or exceeds my power to cope and handle. If by the divine is meant something radically Other, infinitely beyond my capacity to control, then I must say that usually I will to exclude everything divine from my life. I intend to have no gods before me. But in order to be in control, I cannot give *any* Other the freedom to be itself. For in the Otherness of the Other lies its power to transcend the boundaries I need to impose on it if I am to insure it will not upset me.

That is why the will to control, which tries to deprive every Other of its independence, can never gain more than an empty victory. For every increase in control results in a shrinkage of one's universe, and absolute control means living in a universe where the only reality is one's will to be in control. It is true that then there are no gods before one; that one is, in fact, a god oneself—but the kind of god that is so terrified by Otherness that he can let nothing else be unless it is wholly subservient to his control of it.[19] The will to control is always motivated by a fear of vulnerability. It is what we feel driven to practice when we cannot bear to expose ourselves in our weakness to an Other who might wound us. What would a human being be like who took that risk instead of avoiding it? To answer that question we have to find a door that leads out of the room where we are perfectly safe and perfectly alone.

CHAPTER TWO

The Open Home:

Generosity as the Welcoming of Strangers

If we pause to reflect on the portrait of ordinary existence just drawn, we will be tempted to criticize it as one-dimensional. It can be argued with a great deal of plausibility that our description does not do justice to the richness which can, in fact, be found in every actual human life. And while it is not the responsibility of the philosopher, as it is of the artist, to embody the universal in individuals possessing real singularity, still the philosopher is supposed to explore the complexity of the human character, not to flatten it into stereotypes. Is there really anyone whose life is wholly dominated by the will to control?

If there *is*, as it is theoretically possible for there to be, someone who lives wholly and exclusively in the world of practicality, whose life in its totality is governed by avoidance, even such a person *is* what he refuses to be—a unique center of freedom and responsibility. If he wills to be wholly bounded by his roles, it is nevertheless he himself who personally wills this, and this will is his own and no one else's, even when he uses it to betray himself. In this sense, every human being is an individual. Nevertheless, insofar as our ordinary lives are based on the will to control, we are trying to impose a routine, a plan of our own devising, on reality as a whole. And what is a stereotype if not the enclosure of the singular, the elusive uniqueness of the concrete, within the fixed boundaries of a suffocating mold that robs the unique of its disruptive singularity? This suggests that it is not my description which has stereotyped our ordinary lives; rather there exists in ourselves, as we are ordinarily, a will to reduce everything to a stereotype. Were my ordinary will to have its way, nothing, including my self, would have any longer the distinctiveness that distinguishes it from the stereotypical. Whether, in fact, there is or ever has been an actual person who willed only this his whole life, who always avoided everything, is a question we could answer only if we knew everyone's deepest recesses and most private experiences.

But there does appear to be a type of experience in which all of us participate which is contrary to the will to control as I have described it: I am referring to the experience of leisure. That leisure is an important dimension of almost every human life seems to be an incontestable fact. And yet I have tried to argue that we all ordinarily operate inside the world of practicality governed by the will to control. But if this is true, then to cease working would mean to be in crisis—for how could the ordinary self allow any room in his life for leisure without ceasing to work at being in control, and how could he let go of control without being upset? On the other hand, how can we suggest that leisure involves a rupture of the ordinary when it appears to be a normal feature of everyday existence?

1. Running the Risk of Meeting

Clearly, these questions demand an examination of the experience of leisure. Let us begin with an example and then try to determine whether the example is idiosyncratic or representative.

I spoke before of the terror which almost paralyzes us when silence interrupts and threatens to rupture the flow of conversation with a stranger. I suggested that, ordinarily, we avoid this silence, no matter what this avoidance costs, and thus never discover what would emerge in the silence were it allowed to continue. But let us suppose that there are, in fact, however infrequently, conversations where I risk being *defenseless*. On these rare occasions I allow the silence to occur, and I allow to emerge, from within that silence, my address to the Other and his address to me. Such an experience has a dramatic character because of the vulnerability involved in such unplanned exposure of my self to danger. That the drama is completed in the unrehearsed, unforeseen *mutuality* of real conversation seems miraculous. I remember such an experience as a moment of grace, fragile and inexplicable, evanescent but precious.

If, in such an event, I am suddenly and momentarily my *real self*, who I really am, this can only mean that I momentarily *let go* of the roles which I habitually practice, and this in turn means that I *let be* the Other in his very strangeness, instead of trying to disarm him through the strategies of avoidance. In short, I stand at the edge of the boundaries which I have built to exclude every Stranger, ready to welcome what-is, to allow it entrance and give it hospitality: instead of aggression, I practice receptivity; instead of the will to control, the will to let the other be; instead of the arm raised in a gesture of power, the arm extended in the gesture of generosity.[1] The boundary is broken. But what ensues is not crisis but its opposite: what I feared would be a dreadful rupture is the miraculous communion of mutual speech. The Stranger is embraced and becomes my friend. If this example is representative of what leisure is, we should think of it as our making ourselves open and available for friendship, and therefore as a radical reversal of our ordinary compulsion to avoid everything strange and Other.

We need to emphasize that such receptivity results from a decision of the will to open my self to the Other as I see him approaching me; and in deciding to be available to the Other, I am also deciding to alter in a fundamental way the kind of person I am myself. Though I may not be conscious of doing so, I am radically changing my attitude toward the whole of what-is; for in opening my self to this one Other, I am really opening my self to Otherness as such. Implicitly, I am initiating a whole new way of life.

Given all this, we now need to face the question of whether it is justifiable to interpret this experience as paradigmatic of leisure as a whole. But first we must notice that the word "leisure" generally covers both a multiplicity of different acts—gardening, sports, dance, drama, intellectual inquiry, religious festival—and a multiplicity of different attitudes. I have chosen to describe one particular activity as expressive of a particular change in attitude. Is this choice arbitrary on either count?

2. Authentic Welcoming and Its Counterfeits

Let us consider first the multiplicity of attitudes usually included within the meaning of the term "leisure."

There is, first of all, the experience of having "free time" which I can use to finally get done all those things I have been wanting but unable to do, given the pressures of "work." But these "things," in fact, involve a list of projects which together fill every spare moment of my "free time." I discover all sorts of long-postponed chores and thus convert time free from work back into work. Ordinarily, I engage in these projects in such a way that I drain them of everything playful so that nothing in my manner or movement is "pointless"—everything remains pointed toward finishing the chore at hand. In this case, I am clearly not at all at leisure, if this term is taken to signify an attitude essentially different from the utilitarian single-mindedness of ordinary practicality.

But while there is a mode-of-being sometimes called "leisure" which in fact is indistinguishable from work, there is also a kind of "work" which really belongs to leisure: I can use tools to act upon what-is but without utilitarian single-mindedness. I can garden the earth but, unlike the wholly practical person, I can do so without willing the total submission of the hoe, the act of hoeing, the earth itself, to the routines of work. If my movement or manner includes any element which is not strictly utilitarian, the act so performed, to some degree, breaks through the boundaries of workaday existence: leisure as such is this release from the useful, and an act which is, in fact, productive is also to some degree leisurely if productivity ceases to be the exclusive concern of the person engaged in it. This occurs, for example, when in my very manner of hoeing I am open to the earth itself, irrespective of its yielding or not yielding me any practical benefits; when I am open to the hoe itself not just as a tool but as a being which deserves my attention in its own right; and when I am open to the very act of hoeing, not just as a means to a goal but as the interplay of hand, hoe, and earth. Who is it who is thus open? Not my self as worker, closed off in principle to every Other as such, but the self I let myself be when I let go of my desire to be wholly in control. In short, there occurs between the self and the world something very much analogous to what we spoke of in our earlier example—the communion of mutual speech. For in letting the earth be more than the means to its produce, I give it something like the freedom to speak to me.

Perhaps only now, under the impact of this analysis, do we begin to realize what it would really be like to live in a world of total practicality. An act of work, wholly unleavened by leisure, is an act of violence which robs everything of its power to speak and be spoken to: the total worker seeks a universe of absolute silence wherein he hears nothing but his own monologue. Only with the ingress of leisure into the closed world of work does the world cease to be a prison and become, to some degree, a home.[2] When the worker brings into his work something of the disinterestedness of the child at play, his work takes on some of the gentleness that belongs to love.

But we need to be cautious with our images. The leisure attitude I have described is a *deliberate attitude*, and a conscious act of love, if by love one means making one's self available to the Other and letting the Other be. As such, we need to distinguish it not only from the will to control but also from the experience of childhood. For the latter involves a *spontaneous* delight, a kind of fretless enthusiasm which lives each moment as a mira-

cle of song and movement. And this differs from the event of hospitality
where I let my self and the Other be in the communion of mutual speech.
For hospitality is a rupture of boundaries. It involves welcoming as friend
the Other whom I experience as Stranger. But I can experience the Other
as stranger only if I experience him *as Other*, different, independent, approaching me across a frontier which separates us. And this is exactly the
experience which puts an end to childhood, i.e. the state where we enjoyed an undifferentiated interplay between ourselves and the world. As a
child I did not have to open my self to an Other since, strictly speaking,
there existed for me only the play in which both my self and the Other
participated. Once this dance stops, I remember it as an extraordinary
time which was strangely timeless, an extraordinary space not yet sur-
veyed and divided by boundaries.[3]

Thus, when, entrenched inside the boundaries of my routines, I
nevertheless open my life to the ingress of a Stranger, it recalls but does
not repeat my childhood world. Here my daring is not fretless, my
generosity not spontaneous, the Other not already with me but approaching me from outside my settled world. Consequently, to be available to
the Other requires a deliberate turning of my heart, the running of a conscious risk; to be on the edge of the boundary which the Other approaches is to stand on the verge of something dreadful. And the communion of mutual speech which ensues involves an interplay of the self and
the Other, each of which is, nevertheless, a reality in its own right. It is
not the paradise of the child in which the difference between child and
Other is submerged. I may call it paradise regained but the end is different
from the beginning. The world which comes into being when the world
of work is ruptured differs from the world which existed before work
became necessary.

All of this is not meant to imply that we do not often seek to recreate
our childhood world. But we can see very quickly that when we attempt
such a return, we are really refusing to welcome the Other as Stranger.
For we are trying to abolish the necessity of experiencing the Other as
Stranger and the risk we have to run in welcoming him. A crude but obvious example of such avoidance is our use of intoxicants as a way to buf-
fer ourselves from the feeling of dread brought on by the approach of the
Stranger. I want to be relaxed with the Other without having to feel emotionally the risk involved in entering into relationship with him. I want to
pass over the very Otherness of the Other, as if it were of no import, as if
there were no reason to be defensive toward each other. My wanting such
immediate familiarity is really a refusal on my part to welcome or consent
to the real Other; instead, I will that he not possess precisely that Other-

ness which makes conversing with him a painful risk. The motive which governs such a desire is the will to control which wants, more than anything, to abolish the Other, not the will to welcome which dares to offer the Other its embrace.

Finally, we must distinguish the attitude of receptive letting-be, selected as our paradigm, from the experience of *desire* with all its modalities of thirst and possession. We might think, for example, of our experience of sensual craving, where I feel that even my will has been usurped by my appetites. In such an experience I "become" my body in the sense that I feel like I have disappeared into the urge which effaces everything from my consciousness except the object of my desire. But desire does not experience an "object"—it experiences the Other as a pure appeal to be consumed, eaten, rubbed. I experience the Other as something to be consumed by me, as existing only and wholly for my consumption. But the will which chooses to lose itself in this experience cannot be essentially different from the practical will to control which chooses to abolish the Other as Other. For in consuming the Other, what do I do if not transform it into my self?

This remains true when we move to a second and more subtle modality of desire—the craving of the decadent. The decadent does not crave the Other in the sense of wanting to consume her. Bored by this immediate form of satisfaction, he focuses not so much on the Other as on the experience of desire itself. Since being aroused has become an end in itself, he tries to delay indefinitely the fulfillment of its promises. The decadent is a kind of introverted voyeur who enjoys being the spectator of desire just as much as being a participant in it. Consequently, seduction becomes its own purpose, and serves no practical objective. But the caress of such a voluptuary is nevertheless no more than a grotesque parody of the communion of mutual speech. For the one who initiates it is only using the Other as a catalyst for awakening an essentially masturbatory fascination.

But there is a third modality of desire which is much easier to mistake as a real letting be of the Other. Someone who is in love with the experience of being in love, far from consciously using the Other, speaks of his empathy for the Other and treasures the wonderful moments of communion and attunement; he may even go so far as to center his life on such experiences and be disappointed if they do not occur. The person in love with love prefers the Stranger to the friend, because only the approach of the Stranger brings with it the feeling of risk, the promise of the unknown, the ecstasy of virgin communion—in short, an alternative to "friends" who have grown stale.

We are dealing here with a kind of spiritual concupiscence by virtue of which one uses the Other for communal experiences. I do nothing to the Other, I simply let the Other be—but, without my being conscious of it, I do so in order to experience an encounter with him. The Other is actually no more to me than the condition for having such an encounter. However intense the sentiment arising from this kind of experience, it is no more than a luxurious and self-deluded form of sentimentality. When I succumb to it, I am not so much engaged with the Other as I am aroused by the drama of my own feelings. I treat my relationship to the Other like a play put on for my benefit in the theater of my own consciousness. The gestures I make toward the Other are for this reason the perfect counterfeit to the gestures expressive of genuine communion.

We have good reasons, then, for adopting as the paradigm of leisure the willingness to risk speaking and being spoken to, the will to be generous. When I am eager "to get chores done" as soon as I have some leisure time at my disposal, I am preventing leisure from rupturing my practical world. When I want to be able to embrace the Other with the same fretless innocence I felt as a child, I am really trying to avoid the very Otherness of the Other which a real letting-be would require me to experience. And when I give myself over to any appetite, I am still trying to control the Other as I do when working, because I am hoping the Other will yield to desires which I think of as needs.

All these attitudes, though sometimes classified as leisurely, turn out to be at best analogies, at worst perversions, of letting-the-Other-be; and if leisure does not involve letting-be, it cannot be distinguished from work at all.

3. Examples of Hospitality

Now that we have some justification for saying that the will to be hospitable is the attitude characteristic of genuine lesisure, we can ask if it is appropriate to adapt, as our paradigmatic example of such an attitude, the communion which occurs in the initiation of friendship.

I have, in fact, already mentioned a different instance—the activity of gardening when done in such a way that I do not subordinate self, hoe, hoeing and earth to the tyranny of the results they may produce. But the fact that gardening is naturally productive, the fact that it consists of planting seeds which I hope will grow into produce, means that to engage in it as leisure I have to disregard, to some degree, the natural tendency of the act itself. And this means that no act which of its very nature tends toward the production of something external to itself can serve as a paradigm of leisure.[4] We need rather a relationship between self and Other which serves nothing but itself, a relationship released from the influences of anything external to its own playful mutuality.

This may tempt us to turn to the activity of sport, with its to-and-fro of mutual movement, enacted with a regard for the excellence of interaction but without regard for a practical objective. The fact that the goal scored in a game is not a "real" goal extrinsic to the game but only a playful goal within the game—the fact that the "goal" is, practically speaking, an absurdity—justifies us in including sport within the scope of authentic leisure. But that the game as a whole is structured into means and ends, however playful they may be, indicates that it is not exactly a parody of work but at least a transfiguration of work. It is work-made-play. While an example of authentic leisure, its very dependence on the structure of work prevents us from selecting it as the paradigm-example of leisure.

But it might be argued that the only act which of its very nature does not tend toward the production of something external to itself is the act of thinking, when thinking is freed from knowing-how and occurs only in relation to and for the sake of the Other which is the "object" of thought. In contemplation, one serves nothing except the Other to whom one opens oneself. One risks being radically receptive toward the world. Releasing itself and the world from practical concerns, the contemplative mind stops and rests in pure interplay with an Other.

All of this is true—and it shows us that contemplation is an example of the authentic leisure we have been discussing. But we should remember that there is no consciousness of any Other without my *situating* my self before it in some way. Embodiment is not simply a condition for the possibility of contemplation. An intrinsic part of contemplation itself is my stopping at a certain time, my standing at a certain place, my *gesturing* to the Other in this concrete way my willingness to welcome it. Contemplation is an example of the one act which does not point toward the production of something external to itself: the gesture of generosity toward the Other.

In short, the paradigm of leisure *is* the initiation of friendship in the speech of welcome: only when I speak the welcome and do so for the sake of the Other, to make the Other welcomed—only then do I give the Other its freedom and let it be. Moreover, it becomes clear now why the classical triad of art, thought and religion has, from antiquity, been intimately associated with leisure.[5] We know that all three have their origin in festivals which occurred in a sacred space and a sacred time set apart from the ordinary, festivals in which the community risked the act of addressing its gods and being addressed by them. Art, thought and religion are languages which institute letting-be.

Let us look, for example, at the painter who paints because he is "inspired" and is "inspired" only because he lets himself be carried away by something Other than himself. The act of painting is not an excrescence which gets attached to the painter's prior experience of receptivity and inspiration. In fact, the Other which the painter allows to take hold of him is nothing but the painting itself. And the finished painting, although it can be treated as a product extrinsic to the act which created it, offers itself to us not as a thing to be consumed or possessed nor as a tool to be used, but as an incarnated conversation in which we are invited to participate. It is the painter and what-is-painted gesturing to us to share their dialogue. Only one who is unwilling to risk exposure to the Other experiences it as an object to be merely looked at, and fails to realize that it beckons him.

We can use the same terms to describe what occurs between the thinker and that to which his thought is turned. Is not every inquiry the risking of a question which may go unanswered, every insight an embrace which fulfills and completes an inquiring gesture, every text the incarnation of a dialogue to which we are encouraged to add our voice? And might we not also say that the worshipper gestures to the Sacred by his very silence before it; that revelation, if and when it occurs, fills that human silence with a divine word; and that the text or liturgy thus instituted is the incarnate gesture of god-and-man inviting us to join their fellowship?

The real friendship of human selves, of artist and painting, of thinker and theme, of worshipper and divinity—all involve that letting-be of the Other by the self which occurs only when the self chooses to welcome the Stranger, in his very strangeness. In willing to do this, I leave myself unguarded; and in that sense I consent to the possibility of being wounded. I place my dreadful and groundless trust in the Stranger who approaches as wholly unknown. The heart consents to the Other before it knows anything at all about it—except that it is Other. What then does its gesture say to the Other if not "I consent to your presence without qualification"? Leisure is this gesture of welcoming consent to the Other in all its dreadful strangeness.

4. Welcoming as Suffering

We seem, then, to have good reasons for claiming that leisure of its very essence requires opening one's self to the Stranger—which practicality works to exclude. But we have not yet examined with sufficient care what is involved in the passage from work to leisure, from control to generosity, from practicality to love. It is clear that we encounter here the

first instance of what I have called the fundamental event of human life—
the event of crisis.

Perhaps no concrete instance of communion is more revelatory than
the experience of falling in love: if we briefly explore the nature of this
experience, perhaps it will open up to us what always occurs, even if not
so dramatically, in the passage from control to letting-be. That I "fall" in
love means that it *happens* to me; I find my self falling, turned "head over
heels," dizzy, off balance, no longer in command; something strange is
happening to me which I cannot account for. When I am with this other
person, I lose my "cool" because I feel my control over the situation slip-
ping away from me. I feel myself drawn precisely by the strangeness of
the Other, the uncanny wonderment of her which is disarming and impossible to define. The very Otherness of the Other beckons me out of
my self.

We can see how falling in love differs fundamentally from sensuality,
where my experience of the Other is subordinate to my experience of the
desire she arouses in me. In falling in love, I am carried out of my self
toward an Other who opens up an infinite world to me. On the other
hand, we can see how easy it is to misinterpret what is, in fact, love-for-
the-experience-of-being-in-love as love for the *Other* who is experienced
as mystery. The counterfeits of romantic love are more difficult to detect
than plain sensuality. But neither involves the deep loss of poise and self-
possession, the potential for humiliating embarrassment, that are characteristic of falling in love. Sensual craving becomes embarrassing only
when I am discovered by an Other whose presence makes me ashamed of
my craving. When I fall in love with love, I am not caught up in the Other
but in my experience of her, and that narcissistic attitude enables me to remain enclosed within myself. But when I fall in love with an Other, the
fall is a real loss of control. I find myself incapable of "handling" the
situation; I feel suddenly and inexplicably awkward; I become acutely
self-conscious, as if I were naked before the Other. Insofar as I allow
myself to remain in that condition, I am giving up my will to control. I
become, instead, an ego without weapons, without defenses, and no matter how the Other treats me, this very defenselessness, this moment of
frailty and fragile availability is already a rupture which wounds. The
transformation of my will to control into a willingness to be open to the
Other cannot occur without my undergoing the crisis of becoming
vulnerable. To become a self capable of being wounded is itself the undergoing of a wound.

In short, falling in love does not occur without one's consent to the
Other in its elusive Otherness, and this consent is not given without the

suffering of the ego. It is just this condition of suffering which distinguishes falling-in-love from its counterfeit and its perversion.

Now this consent does not *cause* one to fall in love. Indeed, the consent is precisely a consenting to not employ the tactics I am equipped with as a controlling agent. I allow the Other to be itself and to establish its relation to me without my infringing upon it through my action. This is why the lover cannot account for his fall, just as the artist, the thinker and the worshipper cannot account for their inspiration. They necessarily and rightly attribute their participation in the Other to the Other whose Otherness operates on us with a mysterious power and bestows on us an unearned grace. But, while I am incapable of causing myself to fall in love, the experience cannot occur without my consent. And, in fact, we are required to say that consent itself is an act—indeed, an act with a kind of redemptive efficacy. But to appreciate this paradox, we need to examine more carefully the nature of suffering.

If it is true that letting the Other be in its Otherness involves suffering, does this mean that suffering itself always involves the letting-be of the Other? At first glance, there *seem* to be modes of suffering which involve no such letting-be. When another person insults me, and that insult wounds me in a mortal way, it seems that I cannot avoid suffering but I certainly do not accept the insult which causes it. Rather, I would like to erase the insult and thus restore myself to the condition I was in before it wounded me. Indeed, I would like to be able to prevent such insults from "getting to me"; I would like to be rid of my very vulnerability, the very possibility of being the victim of others' criticism. But is it not clear that in responding to the wound in this way I am refusing to be the sufferer of it? If, for example, I hope to seek revenge for something said to me, that very hope transforms me from victim into a seeker of vengeance. And the will to get revenge is successful the very moment I will it insofar as it immediately ends my condition as sufferer. In that sense, anger never fails: it always succeeds in reestablishing us in our will to control. We let our wounds be only as long as we allow ourselves to suffer them. And we can be wounded in the first place only if we have allowed ourselves to be vulnerable before the Other, only if we have allowed ourselves to listen to his speech and be affected by it. Whenever we suffer, we do so because we have permitted the Other to rupture our boundaries. If "suffering" is to be distinguished from the strictly sensory experience of physical pain, if by "suffering" we are to mean an experience that affects us in the core of ourselves, then suffering occurs only when we consent to undergo a wound.

In short, I suffer when the Other ruptures my boundaries, but this rupture cannot occur without my permitting it. And this means that I suffer only when I will to undergo this rupture. Suffering is a *human act* and thus, in a sense, an accomplishment. But it is an act which accomplishes nothing for the self who "does" it. In "doing" it, I undo what would have been accomplished had I exercised my will to control. I give in to that dimension of the Other which I am usually bent on avoiding—its Otherness. The only alternative to ordinary action is the act of suffering, where I open myself to utter defenselessness to an Other over whose Otherness I have no control.

Consequently, there are good reasons for saying that in leisure I open my self to the advent of the Other in my life; but there can be no such advent without letting-be, no letting-be without consent, and no consent without suffering. The passage from ordinary work to genuine leisure cannot occur without crisis. I cannot let the Other be without letting go of the will to control; and this letting-go is precisely my consenting to suffer.

If I have focused on the experience of being in love, it is because it gathers all these motifs together into one concentrated and poignant image. It is no accident that love is represented, traditionally, as a *playful* figure who persuades the hard-hearted to join in its child-like game; but to let one's self be so persuaded, to let down one's defenses, is precisely to suffer, *to be wounded*, to become the hapless victim of an arrow tipped with a deadly poison. Such an act of letting-be lets the Other captivate me so that I fall under the sway of her disruptive and irresistible agency.

5. The Original Wound

I would like now to consider a criticism that might be lodged against the whole interpretation of leisure I have been trying to develop. It might be objected that, instead of interpreting leisure as a crisis which ruptures our practical world, I should have interpreted work as an intrusion upon the self-at-leisure. Had we taken this approach, the objection continues, we would have realized that openness to the Other is the natural human condition: before being paralyzed by inhibitions, we were spontaneously open to the Stranger and willing to offer him our embrace. According to this view, alienation between oneself and the Other exists only because one violates at some point one's own natural accord with the Other by seeking to control it; one's will to control causes one to institute boundaries to protect one from an Other which is experienced as an enemy only because of one's desire to dominate it. In this view, leisure, while in a real sense the rupture of those boundaries, is, at a more fundamental level, the restoration of the original and natural human condition. While the reopening of oneself to the Other involves that one risk being vulnerable, the risk, it is argued, evaporates as soon as it is felt: for the Other appears as a threat only as long as one is determined to control it. On this account, it is only because of the will to control that the Other is ever seen as a Stranger. As soon as the self renounces this will, the Other reemerges as friend. Suffering, far from being essential to leisure, would then be seen as antithetical to it.

I do not think it is hard to understand the perspective from which this alternative view emerges.[6] There is something in us that would like to believe that the will to control is a mere aberration, an absurd and inexplicable mistake which causes us to view as an enemy a world that should never have ceased being our friend. For if the will to control is a mere aberration, we can eliminate it and thus return to the world of our childhood, where self and Other were bound to each other in unbroken play. Such childhood rapport differs from the kind of leisure we have been discussing because in it the difference between my self and the Other has not yet emerged. But the alternative theory suggests that the Other is experienced as a Stranger in the first place only because I will to subordinate it to myself. Thus the crucial question it raises is this: is it my will to control which causes me to experience the world as an Other, or is it my experience of the world as Other which causes me to want to control it?

If we are to unravel this issue, we have to recognize in the first place that if the counterproposal is correct, the Otherness of the Other is no more than an illusion in which I become entangled when I start asserting my self as a separate reality. In such a view, to have a distinct self at all is to be egocentric. When I let go of the will to control, as I do in leisure, I would, in this theory, cease being a distinct self, and would exist instead only in the once again undifferentiated interplay of self and Other.

But the mortal flaw in this account is precisely its inability to account for the initial passage from interplay to the egocentric will to control. What causes or motivates the original rupture of our childhood? Why would we disrupt our innocent rapport with the world by choosing to control it, even while it was still presenting itself to us as our friend? The will to control, on this account, is a sudden, arbitrary upsurge of pure egocentricity for which there is no explanatory motive or cause. The position I have been arguing, rooted as it is in a reflection on our everyday lives, does not suffer from this failure to account for our obsession with finding ways to "cope with" and "handle" the world. It suggests that we try to control the world because we are fleeing from the Otherness of the

Other. Far from being an irrational whim which inexplicably disrupts our childhood rapport with the world, our will to control what happens to us originates in our desire to restore the untroubled simplicity that we enjoyed before the emergence of the Other as Other. In that sense, the will to control is precisely the effort to recover childhood. It is the attempt to get back to the situation where the Other was not differentiated from our selves. And insofar as the counterproposal encourages us to believe our childhood rapport to be retrievable, it is itself motivated by the same will to abolish the Otherness of the Other that underlies the will to control.

Our consideration of this counterproposal has not been a detour. For it now enables us to understand the painful rite of passage from the will to control to authentic leisure in terms of the structure of our lives as a whole. What makes us nostalgic for childhood is the same impulse that makes us crave, as adults, to be coolly in control: adulthood is ordinarily the attempt to continue childhood by techniques we did not need when still innocently unaware of the Other in its Otherness. Our will to control did not put an end to childhood. The end of childhood gave rise to the will to control. We can all find what caused the end of childhood if we look far enough underneath the cool self-possession we practice in our everyday world: we will find hidden there, just where we buried it, the primordial terror, the kind of terror one feels when one's naked defenseless self is exposed in all its radical vulnerability to an Other which overwhelms one with its Otherness. We have become adults precisely because we were unable to bear this wound, to suffer the anguish of being thus exposed in all our frailty. We could not bear to exist so vulnerably. Caught in such a defenseless position, we did the only thing that seemed reasonable: we chose to do whatever we could to handle this Other whose Otherness put an end to our childhood repose. The anger and resentment and malice, which we now direct against any disruption of our lives, is also directed, though we are ordinarily unaware of it, at our own frailty. We still cannot bear to be defenseless selves.

Whenever one opens oneself to the Other, as one does in every authentic experience of communion, one has to put oneself back in that original position of defenselessness and naked exposure. Every communion runs the risk of reopening the first wound. Why else would we be so afraid of enjoying the very leisure we work for? If we cannot bear to experience the Other in its Otherness, it is because we cannot bear to be ourselves in our frailty. We would rather there be no world at all than one we have to be in defenselessly. Leisure, when it really occurs, is made possible by a kind of miraculous willingness to be open to hurt. Is it too far-fetched to say that the dread we feel when risking such exposure is akin to the dread one feels in the face of death itself? Is leisure in its very essence a kind of dying?

6. The Will To Be Generous and the Avoidance of Horror

Now if we follow the intimations of these last questions, I think we will be led to the surprising conclusion that the kind of communion experience we have taken as our paradigm of leisure does not actually undo our deepest avoidances. Even in an experience as apparently open-hearted as being in love, the will to control has not been completely surrendered.

I do not mean to deny that, in opening one's self to the Other, one has to some degree broken the sway of the will to control. In risking such openness, one makes one's self in a very real sense available and thus vulnerable. As I walk toward the person whom I have never met before, readying my introduction, I know that after I tell her my name, she might say nothing—and I know how *annihilated* this nothing will make me feel. Were I unwilling to suffer, I would never run the risk of such annihilation. In speaking to the Stranger, we reopen, even if only for the briefest of moments, the wound that is buried so deeply in us that we are ordinarily unaware of its existence. No one determined to be wholly in control of his life would take such a step.

But what is it that motivates me to run this risk, reopen this wound, reach out to the Stranger in her very strangeness? What gives me the courage to speak to her is precisely the hope that she will find my words *disarming*. My revealing myself to her is also my invitation to her to reveal herself to me. My words are intended to make her feel that there is no need to be defensive with me. And what can this mean except that, by saying them, I hope to give her, in her Otherness, an intimation of our sameness? I welcome the stranger because I desire to dissolve the very strangeness that separates us. But this means that, no matter how quickly one opens the door, no matter how generously one welcomes the stranger into one's home, no matter how disarming one's conversation is, one has still not taken the one crucial step that alone would prove one's willingness to reveal one's self to the very strangeness of the stranger. For to do that one would have to do something radically different from welcoming the stranger into one's home: One would have to leave one's home and go disarmed into the territory of the stranger.

If an example is needed to help us understand how dramatic a difference there is between these two experiences, we need only to think of what happens when someone with whom we are on intimate terms suddenly discloses something that we find horrifying—that she has been raped, for instance, or that she has terminal cancer. I pull back from such a revelation as from a physical blow that temporarily incapacitates me. As I recover from this initial shock, I make my first effort to show the other person that our intimate relationship has not been affected by her revelation. I try to demonstrate, in fact, a more radical solicitude than I have shown her before. But no matter how successful I am in hiding it, not just from the other person but from myself as well, a feeling of revulsion that I am powerless to prevent springs into being as soon as I hear her words. I want my embrace of the other person to provide her a kind of sanctuary where she will feel relieved of her anguish. But with regard to the tumor itself, I recoil from it as from a horrifying reality that has the capacity to upset my life as a whole. I am more receptive than ever to the other person but the closer I come to her wounds, the more I feel repelled by them. My very solicitude for her makes me want those wounds to be erased, perhaps more than anything else in the world. This desire of mine is given concrete form in my making every effort I can to help her get her life back into its ordinary routine, even perhaps in my talking to her as if the horrible thing had not happened to her. Perhaps at a conscious level I am convinced that I am doing this for her benefit, "to help her take her mind off it." But my very solicitude for her betrays an underlying incapacity on my part for responding to what has befallen her. The deepest part of her is precisely the wounded part, the part that is now and always will be inseparable from the wound that horrifies me. In recoiling from her wounds, I recoil from the experience of sharing in her suffering of them. The part of her most in need of solicitude is the part I could only reach by going outside and participating in her destitution. But to be destitute is to have no home at all; I myself would have to suffer the very wound from which my compassion makes me recoil.

Now it might be that this other person from whose most intimate wounds I recoil, has the exact same attitude toward them that I have: it might be that she, too, cannot bear to be the sufferer of them and is doing the best she can to remain exactly the same person she was before they happened to her. Indeed, her need to get rid of her wounds may be all the more urgent precisely because she knows much more intimately than I do how devastating an impact they would have on her if she completely abandoned herself to them. Must we not admit that the response of the victim, like the response of those friends who are desperate to console her, often moves back toward the ordinary world that the crisis has disrupted? The other alternative—the alternative of moving toward the edge of the abyss which the disruption of one's ordinary world has suddenly made accessible—is not just not thought about; it is, usually, not even thinkable.

But in refusing to think that possibility, are we not, at the most critical moment, closing ourselves off so that nothing radically Other will ever reach us? The will to control, it turns out, is not given up as easily as we think it is. We are willing to suspend it only as long as the strangers we are ready to welcome do not reveal something horrifying. Intimacy may come so easily to us that we may wonder why in the world we ever felt the need to be defensive, or worried about our ability to "handle" relationships. And then, without warning or preparation, one of our best friends tells us something about herself that opens up that wound in ourselves that the will to control was originally devised to tourniquet. We need only an inkling of such anguish to make the thought of fully abandoning ourselves to it unthinkable. At such critical moments, the will to control takes control again and in so doing, reveals its true nature. The will to control is simply the will never to be devastated, never to have my life as a whole undermined and overturned.

Does this mean then that my desire to be receptive to Others, my willingness to risk revealing myself to them, has actually been governed all along by a will to control that operates so deeply in me that I am not conscious of it? Our reflections have been leading us to acknowledge that there is a painful, even excruciating irony at work in our ordinary way of letting the universe be and welcoming it with open arms. We really do want to be generous. Instead of willing to control the Other, I run the risk of welcoming her; instead of refusing the Other, I make myself receptive toward her very Otherness—these "insteads" are genuine. But generosity does not usually go beyond the risk of inviting the Stranger to be open, to come forward, to surface. I fail to realize that when I invite the Stranger into my life, I am hoping that she will leave behind the very things that have the capacity truly to devastate me. My generosity lets me venture to my own front door but no further. I cannot get beyond that point because to do so would require nothing less than my losing control of my life as a whole. Generosity ordinarily congratulates itself far too early on its courage. Its very failure to be suspicious of itself, its taking for granted how radically it differs from the will to control, its inability to doubt its own innocence—all these become apparent once a crisis situation reveals that underneath the surface the will to control has remained operative all along.

Now the more unconscious a person is of this underlying will to control, the more unaware he will be of any lack of receptivity in himself. The most extreme version of this would be the person who does not even have an inkling of the fact that others have wounds whose painfulness he is incapable of fathoming. Such a person does not understand why some of those to whom he is so receptive seem reluctant to disclose themselves. He suspects, perhaps, that they have not yet found the courage to risk being vulnerable; he fails to consider the possibility that, having suffered much more deeply than he has, they recognize in the very innocence and affability of his hospitality evidence of the fact that he is profoundly closed off to any real communion with their wounds. Is it necessary to emphasize that the kind of generosity and open-heartedness we are dissecting here become offensive precisely when they motivate us to ask others to talk openly about their suffering? To invite someone to talk about being raped, to invite her to be open and not defensive about it, to tell her that there is no need to keep such a wound hidden—all this is itself another violation of her when it is done in a way which (unintentionally) implies that being raped is an experience toward which it is possible to be open-heartedly receptive. One asks the Other to disclose her wound without realizing that to do so would require her to treat what is horrifying as if it were something ordinary. I may think there is nothing inappropriate in my making such a request because my conscious motive is to make the violated person feel welcomed. And yet it is the very innocence of the questions I put to her, my very unawareness of how they aggravate the evil done to her, which makes my way of embracing her a kind of violence. My ignorance does not exonerate me, for it is an ignorance that derives from a pattern of ignoring that has become so deeply ingrained that it usually operates in me unconsciously. The very innocence with which I open myself to Others shows how unaware I am of the wounds they harbor. My ingenuousness is, in a sense, its own ulterior motive: it is my not wanting there to be anything in the Other that has the potential to horrify me.

What is true of our attitude toward the Other is equally true of our attitude toward ourselves. Ordinarily we do not admit that there are secrets about ourselves which it would be devastating for us to unlock because they would undermine our whole way of being. The thought that it may be necessary to experience such realizations is profoundly foreign to us. We find it inconceivable that there might be truths about ourselves which will not become accessible as long as we continue to live as we are now. We want there to be no more to ourselves than appears on the conscious surface of our lives. We wish there were no unconscious depths to ourselves, because we all know that such depths are beyond our control. In willing to be in control of life, we will to not have an unconscious because, precisely by virtue of its being unconscious, it defeats the effort we make to control it.

It is in this context, I think, that we have to understand our fascination with therapy and the therapeutic mentality which it fosters. For what draws a person to therapy is ordinarily the desire to "come to grips" with, or "find a way to handle" the deep-set anxieties which up to that point he has had no success at managing. The willingness to enter therapy certainly suggests a new receptivity, a willingness to encounter one's anxieties instead of repressing them. Such openness represents a genuine breakthrough insofar as it shows a genuine acknowledgment of unconscious realities whose very existence was previously denied. Real avoidances have been severed by this readiness to talk to someone about the very things which one had always carefully avoided mentioning. And yet, one's motive for opening the door to one's deepest fears is precisely one's desire to disarm them and prevent them from interfering with one's control of one's life. The purpose of excavating the unconscious is to make it conscious and thereby deprive it of its power to resist one's welcoming embrace.

It is not surprising, then, that someone who enters into this kind of therapy will feel like he is making enormous strides in becoming a healthier, more whole person. Am I not finally getting to the bottom of the insecurities that have always bothered me? Am I not finally mastering the sense of inadequacy that has always undermined my self-confidence? My anxieties and self-doubts, once brought to the surface, seem so easily disarmed that I can't help but smile at the fact that I have been afraid of them for so long. I never realized how easy it is to change one's life, once one learns to express one's fears instead of repressing them. When my therapist cautions me about the long-term nature of the therapeutic process, I may be momentarily hurt or discouraged; but then I realize that the more I unearth from the unconscious, the more control I will have over my life.

Now, however open such a person manages to be, there is one possibility to which he remains as closed as ever: the possibility that when he uncovers his deepest anxieties he will find hidden inside them certain horrifying truths which his whole effort to control his life has been designed to keep repressed. He remains convinced that whatever he brings to the surface will thereby be brought under his control; he never suspects that the process of exploring the unconscious might lead him to realities he is impotent to handle. No matter how great the strides we think we have made, the very moment we have even a slight inkling of such realities, our impulse is still to pull back from them in horror. For all our readiness to talk about what we used to repress, it turns out that the real reason for such receptivity is that we thought it would enable us to prevent forever the one thing we have always dreaded most: to be the victim instead of the master of our deepest anxieties, to be devastated by them instead of being in control of them. What I remain unreceptive to is the experience of crisis itself.

It is only now that we begin to see just how relentless the will to control is. The person who approaches his own emotional life with a therapeutic attitude remains caught in its stranglehold even when he thinks he is making great breakthroughs in his efforts to transcend it. The will to control controls, without our realizing it, the very efforts we make to break free of it. Indeed, is it not the will to control, operating in me without my consciously adverting to it, that makes me want to believe I can change myself radically without being devastated? The very superficiality of my life makes me believe that the power to deepen it is readily accessible to me. But none of the realizations I reach, however profoundly I take them, are allowed to affect me with their full gravity. For I understand them in such a way as to deprive them of the very upsetting impact they would have to have if I were fully open to them.

How can we expect it to be otherwise? The will to control, which we might like to think is easily undone, has done its work effectively. We are, far more than we can bear to admit, the prisoners of our own avoidances. Even when we try to sever them, we do so in a way that is designed to enable us not to be upset by the surgery. If the will to control originates in my desire to protect myself from something devastating, the only way to become truly receptive to the world is to open myself to that devastating experience and do nothing to interfere with it. The only way to stop avoiding is to suffer. As long as the will to control is treated as if it were itself a problem we can learn to deal with, any of the cures we invent will only contribute to the disease. There is, in short, nothing a human being can do to transform himself radically. For radical transformation cannot be brought about through one's accomplishing it, but only through one's suffering of it. It is not something I can *do*, but rather something that occurs by virtue of my being wholly *undone*, by virtue of my succumbing to my own disintegration, my being overwhelmed by the very things my will to control was originally designed to keep repressed.

When we decide to explore our hidden selves, we never glimpse the abyss we will have to plumb if we are to be radically changed; but the fundamental self-transformation which we seek can, in fact, occur only when we let go of all the things we have devised to keep from falling into it. We can only stop exercising the will to control by losing control of our lives. Such a loss of control cannot happen, of course, without our consent. But in giving our consent, we do not master it: we only say yes to our suffering it.

7. Recoiling from the Abyss

All of this leads us to conclude that while the will to open oneself to the Other seems to be a radical departure from the will to control, it ordinarily turns out to be no more than a perforation of our avoidances, a brief breakdown of our defenses which is easily repaired. It hints at a deeper, more uprooting form of anguish; it points toward an original, irreparable fault in the geography of the heart. But it does no more. A person whose actions are grounded in the kind of transparency and generosity which I have been describing exudes a tenderness which can quicken and leaven the lives of those who are touched by it. His daily life may be governed by solicitude for Others, a sensitivity to their welfare, an ongoing project of discovering and responding to their needs. But, however diligently he searches out the needs of Others, this kind of generosity can never find the wound they keep hidden under the surface. For it never motivates one to be open to the horrifying itself in its very capacity to devastate one.

How should we evaluate a life lived in this way? It is a mistake to describe it as hypocritical. For while the hypocrite only pretends to be generous this kind of generosity is genuine—even though it unconsciously refuses to be open to those things our avoidances were originally designed to repress. It is precisely this ironic incongruity that gives such an attitude its almost tragic character. In practicing such generosity, I continue to exercise the very will to control which my generosity purports to reject. Moreover, the overt good which I accomplish through such generosity actually makes me even more oblivious of my covert avoidances than I might otherwise be. But blindness does not excuse if, in the final analysis, it is self-blinding.

Can we not bring this all into focus by acknowledging that such a life contains innumerable hints of those terrible realities that we are all powerless to control? But such hints do no more than point to a depth of generosity and suffering which could be reached only if one's deepest avoidances were served. In refusing to be open to that devastating experience, we betray the very impulse to be vulnerable which has brought us so close to horror. Ordinarily, we retract our gesture of welcome at the very moment when we realize we have offered it to a reality that has the capacity to wound us mortally. The only alternative to such a retraction is to consent to one's own radical disintegration. But as soon as we glimpse this possibility, we recoil from it as from a crevasse which endangers our very being. We pull back to the geography of the ordinary, but in that abyss from which we have retreated we have already glimpsed awful realities that, no matter what we do, will never cease haunting us.

CHAPTER THREE

Beginning the Journey:

The Experience of Dislocation and Homelessness

Someone who runs the risk of being generous and is hurt as a consequence may afterward decide never again to leave himself in such a vulnerable position. Such a person does not realize, when he makes this decision, that only suffering makes our lives real. Comfortable as we are inside the world our techniques create for us, we are, precisely because of such comfort, incapable of experiencing anything as a reality in its own right. For we do not let its Otherness make its disturbing claim on us. The will to control keeps all its doors shut and its windows boarded up.

On the other hand, the person who has been hurt once can choose to risk it again. We can end our solitude. Even though one's mouth is dry with embarrassment, one can initiate conversation with an Other one has never met before; one can open oneself to the world of Otherness as a whole, with all its unexpected variety and unpredictable vicissitudes. Then other people become real Others whose very Otherness one welcomes, and before whom one reveals one's awkwardness and vulnerability. The person who opens himself to the world in this way is subject to ecstasies and anxieties, hopes and disappointments, embraces and scars, which the person who wills to control reality never experiences. The monotony of routine is transformed into the drama of encounter. And yet even as we acknowledge that such a person lives in the world of real Others and pays the price, we have also been led to say that he remains on its surface. There is in every Other he confronts an abscess whose existence he never even suspects. Everything that happens before his eyes has a deeper significance of which he remains oblivious. And one of the unalterable truths about our lives is that when they do not become deeper, they become more shallow. In our most serious moments of reflection, when we look upon our lives as a whole, we somehow sense that the most important experiences are the ones we did not have because whenever we got close enough to them to realize how upsetting they would be, we sealed up as quickly as we could the rupture they might have caused if we had allowed ourselves to suffer them. We prefer our lives to be ordinary because we know the only alternative is to let them become tragic.

However open-hearted a person may be in living this way, he remains unreceptive to the radical suffering of crisis. His universe is never turned upside down. But just as it is possible to risk opening the monotonous anonymity of one's life to real Others, it is possible to break through what has become the shallow melodrama of one's life to the eschatological drama of fundamental crisis. If most of us never make this breakthrough, it is because to do so costs not less than everything. We must now try to understand what is involved in this travail which is simultaneously a fall and a descent, a fate and a choice, an overwhelming experience that happens to one and a mortal rupture that does not occur unless one chooses to embrace it.

1. The End of the World

The disintegration I will try to describe is the disintegration of the person whom generosity has already drawn outside the narrow world occupied by a wholly uninhibited will to control. I will begin by trying to indicate what seem to me to be the mortal vulnerabilities just underneath generosity's surface.

The melodramatic person takes himself too seriously because he has no suspicion that there are realities far more dreadful than those he is open to. Generosity inspires him to set up societies for the preservation of . . . everything and to embrace every "cause" that calls for his service. If he tries to do too much, it is because he believes there must be a way to heal every wound. Why do we hesitate to criticize such a person, if not because we recognize in his enthusiasms a magnanimity we lack insofar as we still will to control the world instead of loving it? His ingenuous enthusiasm provides a dialectical contrast to the cynicism and skepticism of the will to control which respects and believes in nothing. And yet just as the will to control is itself governed by a hidden terror of its own vulnerability, the desire to be generous is governed by the illusion we unconsciously want to have about our own goodness.

The generous person has no pretensions or conceit. The last thing he would ever suspect is that he himself might be deriving some benefit from his altruism. But his positive concept of himself derives from the experience of generosity and from the sense it gives him that his life is, in the most profound way, responsive to the world's needs. Because he is willing to bring every needy person inside the affectionate haven of his home, it is natural for him to think that there really are no limits to his hospitality. But it is this very sense of self-satisfaction which ought to give him pause. For while it comes from succoring the violated, it is also the proof of his inability to identify with them to the point of making their suffering his own. Indeed, it is this very self-satisfaction which prevents the generous person from realizing that to open himself fully to the Other he would have to give up the comfort and stature associated with being the one who succors, and become instead as humiliated and destitute as those who have to beg for succor.

More often than we suspect, the illusions of those who think themselves receptive to everyone bring about their own painful and ironic undoing. Perhaps an example will help convey the impact of that irony and enable us to illustrate the kind of devastating experience that finally breaks a person out of the ordinary world in an irreparable way. What means the most to the kind of open-hearted person we have been describing are those familial relationships which offer the opportunity for the most intense and long-lasting intimacies. What makes his home a haven for strangers is the perfect rapport that seems to exist among those who already live in it. But it is precisely because such rapport seems so perfect that those held fast by its affectionate bonds would never want to do anything to shatter it. Can I assume that no lengthy argument is needed to show that the oldest son in such a family might be very likely to have an especially acute sense of dread about failing to emulate his father, whose goodness is so publicly evident? Perhaps some of us know from our own experience how such dread has a way of paralyzing the person who suffers from it and thus makes him fear that he is incapable of resisting the very thing he dreads will happen. Let us say, for instance, that for reasons we need not explore, the son is subject to homosexual urges which he ultimately finds himself helpless to resist. He knows that while his father would be hospitable to a stranger who had done such acts, he would be utterly devastated if he found out that the person whom he thought he knew better than anyone had always been a stranger to him. Such a realization would turn his father's world inside out. He would not be able to welcome this homosexual as a stranger into his home. For he would suddenly realize that the home he had worked all these years to make a haven of intimacy, had never in fact existed; all along, it had been an abode of strangers who did not know each other.

Shall we imagine that the son cannot bear to shatter his father's world in this way, and for that reason feels like the one stranger who does not deserve to be the recipient of his father's generosity? Shall we imagine that, feeling that all doors are closed to him, he goes to his room in that house that is now more a prison than a haven, and that from the ceiling of that room, filled with mementos of old birthdays, his father finds him dangling the next morning like an excruciating question mark? If he has seen previously a look such as he now sees fixed forever on the face of his son, he has never before been pierced all the way through his heart by the kind of final, unalterable horror which those eyes petrified in despair now convey to him. His world is ended, just as surely as it would be if the noose were wound around his own neck. The very room that was the sanctuary for so many of his most precious intimacies now harbors a horrifying reality which he cannot welcome into his life because it puts an end to it. Precisely because, until that day, he took such pride in his son and was so flattered by his admiration, he feels immediately, even before having the chance to think about it, that he has been, for some mysterious reason he cannot fathom, his son's executioner.

The dead body of his son is flesh of his flesh and, at the same time, the very incarnation of something horrifying and totally foreign to him. It is the one thing in the universe he cannot embrace without being totally shattered.

If I have labored over this example, it is because it is illustrative of the kind of horrifying experience that we are profoundly unprepared to accept, no matter how open-hearted and receptive toward life we have tried to be. For such experiences deprive us of the very world which provides us the stable order into which we integrate the events that happen to us.[1] Such experiences cannot be "accepted" and integrated into one's world because the more open one is to them, the more completely they shatter the world which has always provided one the stable perspective needed to integrate things. In the example I have developed, the father has taken great pride in practicing what he thinks is an unprejudiced hospitality toward every stranger that enters his life. But the son knows what the father is incapable of realizing—that there are horrifying realities which have the capacity to undermine the very foundation of the home that makes all hospitality possible. And is not the reason why his father wanted a home in the first place because his deepest need, like ours, is to keep such realities at bay? What we work so hard to avoid is the shattering of our lives by horrors we know we will be helpless to control. No matter how many strangers we have welcomed into our homes, our habit of hospitality does nothing to prepare us for the mortifying experience of becoming homeless and destitute ourselves.

Now to speak in this context of the end of the world might seem to be a rhetorical exaggeration. After all, even when one's child commits suicide, the other relationships in one's life remain intact and may even be strengthened by the ordeal. Indeed, whenever someone experiences a devastating event such as this, those closest to him will most likely do all they possibly can in the ensuing days and weeks to prevent him from "falling apart" because of it. Extraordinary efforts will be made to help him resume his ordinary routine. And, in fact, we know all too well that it is possible to turn even an excruciating rupture like this into an interruption that is only temporarily devastating. There is no crisis, however horrifying, that cannot be "dealt with" in such a way as to permit one to resume living the way of life it threatened to undermine. The tactics needed for such crisis management are precisely the ones we practice day in, day out, in our ordinary exercise of the will to control. The world we live in never has to fall apart because we can always find a way to repair the rents that are made in it, even when they tear the most delicate membranes of the heart. We can find ways to put even the deaths of those we love in parentheses.

But we cannot do so without violating whatever generous impulse we have to open ourselves to those who suffer and to the experience of suffering itself. The father in our example might find a way to stop thinking about all the dreadful questions that are punctuated by his son's dangling body. He might find a way to forget the paroxysm of horror he felt when he first opened that door and saw that face eyeing him with its vacant stare. He might be able to find a multitude of causes for his son's act, none of which points to himself. He may, in short, succeed in covering up the whole devastating experience before it has a chance to do its devastating work. But he could not do so without shutting out of his life everything that might remind him of the questions he does not dare ask, everything that might evoke that original feeling of irreparable horror. And how could he do that except by refusing to open his door to any stranger? The only alternative to being devastated is to will to be in control.

This shows, I think, that generosity is not to blame for our failure to be receptive to the devastating experience of crisis. In fact, it is only those who have risked being receptive who are open enough to be momentarily horrified by the realities which they would have otherwise wholly avoided. Generosity has, in a sense, a dynamic of its own; if left to itself, it would motivate us to open ourselves not just to the strangers looking to us for haven, but to all those undomesticated horrors from which our homes usually shield us. In that sense, generosity would lead us, if we let it, to our own disintegration. That is why, as we shall see, a human being cannot undergo the complete process of crisis except by constantly opening himself to it in an attitude of generosity; for only through such consent does he make himself available to, instead of trying to prevent, the ordeal of suffering it entails. And while in saying it I am anticipating a great deal, perhaps it should be mentioned that only when someone reaches the very heart of the crisis experience does he allow generosity to become what it is in its essence—a pure fire that transforms the one who suffers it into a holocaust.

Avoidance, on the other hand, keeps blocking the route in order to delay the pilgrimage into horror that generosity tries to make us take. If generosity keeps beckoning us forward to a new form of suffering we have not anticipated, the will to control keeps making us recoil from realities which we know can make us impotent. That impulse to recoil is never stronger than when the reality to which generosity has exposed us has the capacity to shatter our world as a whole. That is why our responses to such shattering events are the decisive choices of our lives: we decide in such moments whether to allow ourselves to be irreparably devastated.

That is the only alternative which the father in our example has available to him. The dangling body of his son does not terminate simply one relationship, or one dimension of life; it calls into question his whole way of being by suddenly confronting him in an excruciatingly intimate and personal manner with horrific realities whose existence he never suspected and whose effect on his life he is impotent to control.[2] Those dead, despairing eyes convey to him in one penetrating, unmistakable glance the superficiality of all his generosities. Their riveting darkness opens up to him a whole underground universe which is not just different from the world he has lived in, but undermines its foundation. That is why, in the weeks and months that follow, if he does not recoil from the reflections which this devastating event will evoke from him, all the things he used to take seriously will lose their significance. They will seem not just less and less important but less and less real, the more they are dwarfed by the horrific realities to which this dead body has already begun to expose him. Crisis precipitates nothing less than an undermining of one's sense of reality as a whole.

It will require the rest of this chapter to follow this faultline in our ordinary sense of reality that a crisis event widens into an abyss. But before doing so, I need to address a suspicion that the example of crisis I have used may have raised in the reader's mind. Not everyone's son commits suicide. Not everyone has his world turned upside down by this kind of sudden, uprooting ordeal. Whether one's whole sense of reality is put in crisis seems therefore to depend on chance, on accidents of fortune whose occurrence we do not cause and cannot prevent. We would then have to say that crisis affects some of us and not others, and that therefore it has nothing to do with what is universally and essentially human. There would be some people for whom the whole theme of crisis would be irrelevant.

But these claims overlook the fact that, even if a crisis of the type used here as an example never happens to us, it is nevertheless ever present in our lives—*as that which we spend our lives avoiding.* The person whose son commits suicide seems at first glance to be compelled by a quirk of fate to confront dreadful realities which the rest of us have the good fortune to be unaffected by; but in fact, the real difference between us is simply that nothing sufficiently upsetting has yet happened to us for us to realize that these dreadful realities have held us all along, without our knowing it, in their implacable sway. All we have succeeded in doing is keeping ourselves unaware of their grip on us. Death and evil are no less real, and no less horrifying, for our having found ways to deceive ourselves into thinking of them as problems to be "dealt with." A devastating event, such as the suicide of one's son, precisely because it has the capacity to rupture one's ordinary life in an irreparable way, gives one a way of access to an entire universe that the will to control works to keep us shut off from. There is no other way of access to that universe except through suffering, and in particular, through the kind of suffering we associate with crisis. In that sense, we can say that it is through crisis and crisis alone that the deepest realities are discovered. Suffering is our only avenue to those realities because there are so many layers of avoidance that need to be severed before one gets to the bottom of them. The richest truths are the ones it is most excruciating for us to uncover.

What we must now try to understand is the shattering process one goes t...ough in discovering this other universe, keeping in mind as we do so that those who endure this process are brought by it to the same basic wrenching realizations we would all have if our most intimate and personal avoidances were severed. Each heart has its own unique faultline, but when the faultline ruptures, it opens up for all of us the same abyss of horror.

2. In the Throes of Tragic Reversal

The first thing that someone entering this universe realizes is that it *is* another universe, one which no one is aware of except himself.[3]

What do I mean by this? The person in crisis begins to realize that the whole world in which he used to live was unreal in a fundamental way so that it now seems like a play put on by actors who were no more than shadows. He used to resent the events that disturbed the surface of that world for their irritating disruption of what was truly important; now he realizes they were intrusions of reality itself into a world designed to keep everything upsetting repressed. He knows now that the upsetting things always catch up with us, no matter how effective we think we have been in dealing with them. The terrible realities we keep hidden might allow us to delude ourselves about the importance of our ordinary world; but all the while, without realizing it, we are allowing these realities to prepare our downfall. The person who finally realizes this discovers it too late to prevent it. His conscious acts have been used by the terrible realities of which he was ignorant to bring about the very horrors he most dreaded. Now he realizes, as we do not, that these realities have their residence inside our very selves; we cooperate with them without even being conscious of their existence. Is it any wonder that these powers which hold us in their awful sway and undermine the meaning we ordinarily assign to our lives, these powers we cannot comprehend and before which we are helpless, which seem to possess a terrible wisdom that outstrips all human cunning, were once called gods?

Though, unlike primitive man, he does not call them gods, the person in crisis realizes that these terrible realities which have the capacity to undermine our lives are much more real than anything accessible to our ordinary powers of observation. Those of us who have not been shattered by them might dismiss belief in such realities as superstitious and delusional. We may think that only those unable to deal with upsetting experiences in a rational manner believe in an underworld inhabited by horrible powers which science is helpless to verify. But what prompts our modern obsession for subjecting everything to rational techniques, for reducing all mystery to formulas, if not the obsession to wrest control from those realities which terrify us so much that we refuse even to believe they exist? We feel driven to find remedies for the most trivial breakdowns in our lives—colds, headaches, flat tires, accidents of any kind—because even the slightest puncture can become a rupture too upsetting to seam up. Too sophisticated for superstitions, we nevertheless find ourselves unable to get rid of our neuroses; too secular to believe in inexplicable powers, we are nevertheless terrified of going anywhere without a full repertoire of disarming techniques. Secretly, we suspect that the terrible realities we refuse to believe in lie in wait for us just over the horizon, ready to spring on us.

Perhaps my discussion of these realities and their capacity for undermining our conscious intentions will be brought into sharper focus if I pause to contrast a crisis of the type I am describing with that brought on by an accident or a natural catastrophe. The father in our example would be devastated to know that his son had cancer but he would not be devastated in the same way that he is by his son's suicide. The difference is crucial for understanding the excruciating poignancy that is characteristic of those crises that we ourselves have had a part in bringing about.

To begin with, we experience chance as simply the collision of vectors of force. This would not have been true of primitive people, who thought even the natural world was held in the sway of mysterious and terrible presences. But we view the natural world as merely matter in motion, dumb and indifferent to our desires. For that reason we cannot help but feel it is inferior to ourselves because it seems to spend its terrible power thoughtlessly and to no purpose. The person who falls victim to chance always continues to feel superior to it. He cannot take chance seriously, even when it triumphs over his plans and intentions. Brute matter, conceived of simply as moving quantity, can never *humble* us. For we never cease believing that it *ought* to conform to the plans we make for it.

In fact, there is always an element of apparently justifiable resentment in our response to accidents. When a tire, in itself only a trivial instrument made to serve my purposes, wrecks my whole schedule by going flat, my immediate reaction is that it has no right to do so. It simply does not deserve to have such influence over my life. As a human being who originates action, who in fact has the power to organize a world, I have an intrinsic dignity, a natural superiority to this piece of rubber which, left to itself, does nothing except exist in its brute facticity. It is against the injustice of its interfering with me that I hurl obscenities. To call this thing "shit" is not just to call it a worthless excrescence, a piece of waste, unusable and discardable—it is also a moral judgment and a refusal to recognize its right to trespass on the order I am trying to give my life at that moment. This helps to bring out the fact that we experience chance events as intrusions of the material universe on our human purposes.

This whole attitude (of righteous indignation) ordinarily remains operative and is, in fact, intensified when the accident is a drastic one, e.g. one which results in the death of someone important to me. It is even possible that, under the impact of such an accident, my attitude will develop into a conscious metaphysical attitude.[4] That these chance microbes do not just interrupt schedules but have the power to upset our very being, that the human person who, by his very nature, has the power to organize a world is himself reduced to an excrescence, to an obscene, absurd mass, means that the pettiness and stupidity of chance is finally triumphant over us. This fact can lead one to the absurdist's view that it is an insult to our dignity to have to exist in such a universe; or it can lead one to blame God for creating a world that is designed to devastate his highest creature instead of being designed to serve him. If God is all-good, why didn't he make the world respectful of us? If God is all-powerful, why didn't he do a better job of controlling matter's arbitrary impulses?[5]

Now it should be noted that this attitude of resentment toward God does not differ essentially from the kind of devotion to him which presumes that his primary purpose is to fulfill our prayerful requests: it is simply that same attitude . . . after having learned its painful lesson. But it is even more important to recognize that this attitude of resentment, whether it takes the form of absurdist indignation against the world or religious indignation against God, is itself the result of a refusal to accept the experience of suffering. It expresses, in fact, a kind of moral defiance so that, in adopting it, we keep intact our sense of our own importance. Indeed, it enables one to feel morally superior to God himself, who does not recognize the fact that the world he created ought to be designed to serve its highest creature.

At a later point we will have to examine this kind of attitude in greater depth; at the moment I want to return to the question of how the experience of an accident (which can lead to such resentment) differs from the kind of crisis I have been trying to describe. The father whose son has committed suicide feels that the terrible realities which have shattered both his son's life and his own are realities which he himself is to some degree responsible for setting in motion. His son's death is not something that intrudes upon his life from the outside, like an accident that happens to him without his cooperation or permission. It is more like the work of subterranean powers within himself and his son which they set in motion and yet were helpless to resist. Before a crisis experience such realities seem profoundly foreign, indeed unreal; but to the person in the crisis experience they are more real to him than he is to himself. For what he has always thought of as his self is nothing but a shadow, compared to these realities that hold him in their merciless and crushing grip.

Of course, as I have already said, the father in our example is not directly responsible for his son's death. Indeed, at the level of direct responsibility no one is more innocent, more generously devoted to the son than the father. As long as we stay at this level, we can admit that, to do justice to his son's death, the father need only respond to it as if it were an accident in which he played no part. The father is not consciously a murderer; nor am I suggesting that the father had an unconscious desire for his son's death. Indeed, the reason it is so devastating to him is primarily because it is a horror that he never even dreamed to be possible. For this father, as we have imagined him, had not the slighest inkling that anything was upsetting his son. But he realizes, as soon as the look in those dead eyes penetrates his own, that *that* was the reason his son could not speak to him. Even after months and years of trying to identify the devastating realities that led to his son's suicide, the father may remain ignorant of just what they were; he may never know more than he knew in that first paralyzing moment when he realized that they were things his son could not bear to talk to him about because of the shattering effect he felt sure they would have on him. And why could his son not bear to have that conversation except because, having been raised in his father's world, he found those realities too devastating to acknowledge, too shattering to accept?

That is why the father must finally realize that his son's death is the consequence of his own hidden terrors, indeed, the very incarnation of his own avoidances. The awful realities which eventually tormented the son into suicide found their first hiding place in the father's own failure to face them; he could not have known that in giving his heart to his son, he was passing on to him the very realities which he himself had so deeply repressed as to be wholly unaware of them. What his son inherited was precisely the part of his father that could not bear to experience those realities. It is not simply that his son's death causes them to reemerge; the son's death is their vengeance. The terrible realities which have engulfed the son have been able to do so precisely because of the father's refusal to suffer them.

I hope this example illustrates that it is precisely the intruders which we are most desperate to exclude from our settled lives that secretly take up residence within them and gain ascendency over us. As their culpable but unwitting accomplices, we set them in motion and are also their prey. We are not the innocent victims of an accident that happens by chance; we are victims of a tragic reversal which our own avoidances call down upon us. An accident is, in itself, something trivial and without importance; when its consequences have a decisive impact on human affairs, one is struck by the disproportion between the triviality of the cause and the seriousness of its effects. On the other hand, a person suffering a tragic reversal feels that he has been overcome by something superior to himself, an awful and implacable power which he is incapable of controlling, even though his own acts have unleashed it. That power looms over everyone affected by it; no matter how shattering its consequences, it never seems to have spent the full measure of its fury. Even after it seems to have finished its work, its brooding presence continues to hang over one.[6]

And yet, lest we miss the horror of its paradox, we have to remember that while we have no control over this power and are incapable of standing up to it, the whole reason why it undermines us in a way that accidents do not is that *we* are the ones who have unwittingly handed ourselves over to it. Only our doing so has its power set in motion with regard to our own lives. We elect our destiny by the very things we do to escape it. The realities which seal our fate are only able to hold us in their sway because, in refusing to face them, we set up a residence for them in the cellar of our homes. Having relegated them to the cellar of our selves, we think we can keep them hostage and strip them of their importance. Reality always seems to be powerless in the face of our techniques for coping with it; it lets us exile whatever we do not want to suffer into the cramped quarters of our unconscious. But all the while reality remains what it has always been: tremendous, unvanquishable, sovereign over us, waiting patiently for its infallible retribution.

3. The Avoidance of the "Gods" in Ordinary Religion

The reader may wonder why, in speaking of these powers that seem so similar to ancient gods, I have made it sound like they are always the bearers of doom who transform an apparently happy life into a tragic one. After all, were not the gods thought of as benefactors as well as avengers? Can not destiny be a privilege as well as a curse? Might it not be that my life possesses a fullness of meaning which the gods will gradually unfold for my benefit? Why have these possibilities not been discussed?

As the ancients would have put it, the discovery of the gods, the realization that they actually exist and have a bearing on our lives, is always *horrible*.[7] For it always involves a radical experience of suffering which one cannot anticipate or prepare for; it requires falling off the edge into what must seem like an abyss. Of course, long before events bring a person to that vertiginous edge, he might very well believe in the gods in the sense that he prays for their protection from intruders who threaten to disrupt his ordinary life.[8] One would not say such prayers if one were not to some degree convinced that the gods were capable of intervention. But what preoccupies the person who says them is his own safety, the security of his boundaries: he is asking the gods to serve as his guardians, to insure his routines against interruption. An elaborate mythology, according to which the gods, as the founders of the cosmos, retain their power over it, might seem to justify such prayerful appeals. But in fact, a true understanding of the myths themselves is not compatible with worshipping in this way. For if they portray the gods as the founders of the cosmos, they also portray them as *Powers outside its boundaries*—powers from whom one is always tempted to flee in terror. When we pray for divine help in dealing with the upsetting realities we are helpless to handle on our own, are we not actually praying for protection from the awful power of the divine itself? Ordinarily, religion is blasphemy. And, indeed, if all of ordinary life as a whole is based on the avoidance of upsetting realities, religion of the type just described will naturally be needed as its consummating illusion.

But, besides the attitude of the will to control, there is the attitude of receptivity. The person who has adopted that attitude consents to the advent of the Other, consents to welcome the Other into his life. Such generosity would lead one to *welcome* the presence of the gods, and would convert the prayer of self-centered appeal into a prayer of praise and gratitude; it would recognize the gods as the *highest beings*, as beings who stand above all other beings in power and value. The gods would no longer be viewed as hired protectors but as guests deserving the highest honors and most servile homage. We do not find here the self-serving, if unconscious, presumption underlying the prayer for protection. But can we not detect a continuing presumption in this readiness to welcome the gods into the ordinary world, as if they could be enclosed within it without being deprived of the dreadful sublime stature that distinguishes them so radically from mortals? The gods are welcomed in the sense that they are escorted inside our boundaries, but in this process they are robbed of that very power which makes them the creators and destroyers of all boundaries, the power which makes them gods.

The experience of crisis, on the other hand, i.e. the experience of being handed over to powers which upset one's whole world and before which one is helpless, brings about the realization that the gods can never be domesticated. The real gods are not the ones we welcome as guests inside our homes; they are the very realities from which our homes are meant to secure us. In the end we feel like their helpless, unimportant playthings; it is the divine powers we prayed to for protection which turn us into homeless beggars. Exiled from home, there is no place we might go to escape the wasteland their work has left. Everything familiar has disappeared. Our discovery of the divine is always devastating. For it does not consist in our bringing something out of obscurity into the light of day where we can get a handle on it. Rather, it involves our being plunged into a darkness that extinguishes the light of day itself. The suffering we undergo when we allow something strange to enter our life is superficial; for before it enters our life, it comes out of hiding, presents itself to us, shows us its face. But in undergoing a tragic reversal, we are handed over to underground powers which we cannot see and are incompetent to deal with. Those powers give us nothing to hold onto; they do not have faces we can recognize and name. What primitive man meant by the divine is encountered only by fully suffering crisis instead of avoiding it.

4. Moral Horror and the Experience of Doom

But why is it necessary to bring any reference to primitive man's experience of the divine into our description of the crisis experience? In addition to the fact that this manner of speaking evokes outdated superstitions, psychoanalytic theory provides another way to speak and think of such powers. If Freud employs mythic images and figures, he evidently does so only to make more imaginatively vivid his science of psychic processes. And, indeed, it would not be difficult to recast all I have said so as to situate it in a psychoanalytic framework. I have claimed that the self (ego) avoids (represses) forces which threaten to disturb its normal existence. Such forces disappear but do not cease to exist; they go underground (the unconscious). The more severe the repression of these forces, the more certain it is that they will reap their vengeance and make me their victim; inadvertently, I precipitate my fall into their power. But if one is willing to participate in it, the process of psychoanalysis can lead the ego to the anguished discovery of these repressed forces and of one's unintentional complicity in setting them in motion.

Underlying both the psychoanalytic and my own account is the same fundamental insight: despite all our efforts, we are not in control of our lives. Even our best attempts at being receptive are ordinarily under the influence of forces which do their work mercilessly and of which we are unconscious. The discovery that this is so involves a dreadful recognition of foreign powers which govern one's life. These powers are experienced as foreign insofar as they radically undermine one's self in one's ordinary existence. But in developing a scientific account of such an experience, psychoanalytic theory typically interprets such powers as instincts internal to the self; and it portrays the drama of human life as primarily the drama of their vicissitudes. The question we must ask is whether such an account explains experiences of the type I have been describing, where human beings feel undermined by horrifying realities which they themselves set in motion.

Our most direct acquaintance with our instincts occurs when they make a claim on us and demand its fulfillment. Especially if we have reasons to resist them but even when we are their eager ally, the instincts seem to possess a kind of autonomous power that is under no obligation to follow the directions we might try to give them. Because of this autonomy, we are often engaged in a kind of civil war with our instincts;[9] they prevent us from being whole and undivided because we always have to contend with their alien and unpredictable presence. But this war is a civil war, because my instincts are mine, and belong to me by virtue of my very existence as an embodied self. They are independent of me only in the sense that they seem to come from a part of my self that is not spontaneously or naturally obedient to my rational control. Moreover, even when they overpower me, my instincts remain inferior to me in the sense that, in and of themselves, they lack the stature which belongs to me as a rational agent, responsible for my actions. The instincts are irrational forces which for that very reason are beneath me and ought to be subservient to my governance. The passions may sometimes be stronger than the ego, but their brute force does not make up for the fact that they lack the dignity the ego possesses simply by virtue of its capacity for making deliberate decisions.

But psychoanalytic theory makes us aware of a complex and devastating irony that is at work in our relationship with our instincts. It makes us realize that just when we think we perfectly control them, they subtly undermine our governance. They are always busy behind our backs, devising strategies for their fulfillment and vengeance. The instincts win not just overt but covert victories; not only do they occasionally overrun the ego but, more importantly, they have the ego working on their behalf even when it thinks it is acting solely in its own interest. No theory of human nature seems quite so mortifying, such an insult to our will to control, as this theory according to which unconscious forces subvert the meaning I think my decisions have. To realize that the instincts govern us even when we seem to be in control of them undermines our whole sense of being the master of our lives.

That is why such a realization would be an example of the kind of crisis I have been describing. Our own unconscious is *one* of the realities which we are ordinarily unaware of that has the power to shatter us. And in fact, the example I have been employing throughout this chapter might benefit from psychoanalytic interpretation. In all likelihood, the son's inability to discuss his homosexuality derives in large measure from his father's own deep-seated anxieties and ambivalences about sexual matters. But I do not think that psychoanalytic theory, as traditionally articulated, is able to do justice to the particular sense of horror the father feels when the repressed returns to haunt him in the form of his son's suicide. In portraying him as an ego outwitted by instincts whose influence he is helpless to control, the psychoanalytic perspective gives him the status of an innocent victim. For there is no essential difference in moral stature between the will victimized by internal natural forces whose devious vicissitudes he is not responsible for, and a person who is the victim of an accident caused by external events. What psychoanalysis does not help us understand is the *moral* character of the horror we feel when a crisis shatters us into realizing what our avoidances have wrought. Indeed, the primary therapeutic purpose of psychoanalysis is to provide us a way of understanding the unconscious motivations that have shaped our actions and often undermined our conscious intentions; the logical effect of such therapy would be to *relieve* us of or at least diminish the sense of horror we have about how we have lived, and alleviate our sense of being responsible for the upsetting experiences that have devastated us.

What leads psychoanalysis in this direction is the fact that, in its view, the avoidances which lie at the origin of our failures are themselves the effect of influences over which we have no control and for which we are not responsible. Its "talking cure" does not culminate in any horrifying realizations of how we ourselves set in motion through our very avoidances the upsetting realities (such as sexuality) that have now returned to undermine us. It culminates instead in the liberating realization that our avoidances were themselves the work of psychic forces which we could not have known how to outwit. Therapy conceived in this way, even if it helped a person realize how gravely mistaken he has been in thinking he was in control of his life, would not wring from him the realization that his very effort to be in control of it is what led to his undoing. It leaves unaffected the one crucial thing that a crisis of the type I have described shocks one into questioning—the will to be in control itself. Psychoanalysis tries to strip us of the illusions we might have about ourselves, but only for the ultimate purpose of strengthening the ego's ability to "deal with" its life. For that reason its therapy, no matter how painful it may be, leaves the most fundamental presuppositions of our ordinary world undisturbed. While it might strip us of our vanity, it leaves our pride intact.

Now, in the experience I have been struggling to portray, it is precisely the pride we take in being able to control our lives that is undermined. Here too, certainly, there is a fall: my whole ordinary existence is pulled out from under me. But this fall is something I have brought upon myself. I have set in motion my own disintegration insofar as I am responsible for grounding the whole structure of my life on avoidances which the very realities that I excluded from my life are now undermining. It is far more upsetting for me to be the victim of my own avoidances than it is to be the innocent victim of my instincts. It is not that my will to control is undermined by instincts which, because of their inferior stature, have no right to get the better of me. Rather, my whole effort to avoid being upset is itself responsible for setting in motion the crisis that shatters me.

Such an experience upsets the ego in a profoundly intimate and humiliating way. For instead of merely confronting one with the limits of one's control over one's life, it requires one to realize that one's lifelong effort to be in control has all along been a flight from the realities that matter. That realization does not sink all the way into a person until it wrings from him the acknowledgment that he has lived his whole life *wrongly*. It is only the acknowledgment of such wrongness that is able to devastate us in our very capacity as rational agents, in our very character as persons. It is only this feeling of having lived wrongly that can break a person in his very subjectivity.

This is why a person undergoing the kind of crisis I have been describing has the sense that the ground is being pulled out from *under* him, but that this is being done by powers which are *superior* to, i.e. *above* himself. For unlike the physical world which interferes in human life without regard to the moral character of its victims, the tragic reversals we experience shatter the *meaning* of our worlds while leaving us physically intact, and they do so in such a way as to expose in an excruciating light our most personal weaknesses and failures.

Such reversals must seem, to those who suffer them, to be the work of powers that cannot be located in the physical world. When others ask the person who has been shattered by them what has happened to him, he finds it impossible to point to any observable object as the cause of his collapse. In that sense, the power responsible for our tragic reversals has no place of residence except inside that private sphere of our subjectivity which is not directly accessible to observers. But we nevertheless experience this power as overwhelmingly real and titanic, and as capable of overturning the very things we have concentrated our lives on accomplishing. Such power is able to destroy one's ordinary presumption that one's plans ought to be followed. It is not surprising that someone who has been shattered in this way seems to carry an infinite weight, seems to have been struck down by an unbearable sorrow; even in a crowd of his own friends, he seems like a solitary vagrant who has been overcome by a secret, individual doom. We cannot do justice to the power responsible for his ordeal by equating it with any natural forces or causes with which we are familiar. The experience we are describing is precisely the discovery that there is a power capable of undermining our moral structure which even the most violent natural disasters leave unaffected.

Now someone might persist in asking how I can affirm something to be real if it never makes itself present in the observable world, and in that sense never appears in the light of day. But what prompts those of us who have not been subjected to such a reversal to ask this question is precisely our spontaneous identification of reality with the familiar world where nothing is real except what is subject to our control. In exercising the will to control, we adopt, whether we are conscious of it or not, the ontological perspective implicit in it.[10] We assign things a meaning by situating them within the world generated by our projects. But the experience I have been describing is above all the experience of being judged by a reality which wrings from me the humiliating acknowledgment that the most important realities are precisely the ones I never acknowledged. Such an acknowledgment requires radically revising one's very understanding of being—so radically that it is one's own existence and the reality of one's familiar world that is thrown into question. One cannot take any of the beings of one's familiar world seriously now because none of them retain their importance in the face of one's fundamental horror. That horror gets its power to horrify precisely from the fact that it is not a thing alongside other things; it does not present itself to one for inspection like a being within one's world; it draws one's world as a whole into the void it creates. If we must say of such a power that it exists, we must also say that it is experienced as the nothingness that subjects all beings to its horrifying sway.[11]

With what justification have I compared our experience of this power with primitive man's experience of the gods? Our mistake, in trying to understand those gods, is thinking of them as persons in the familiar sense of that term. If this is what primitive man meant by the gods, then the gods were simply imaginary figures he used to domesticate the power that he knew could pitch him into the void. But even apart from all the evidence produced by the modern study of religion, we know from Aeschylus himself that originally the gods were infinitely more than this—that men wished, above all, to escape their reign, and to silence the "unbidden and unwelcome" song of the Furies which they heard within themselves:

> Ah! to some end of fate, unseen, unguessed,
> Are these wild throbbings of my heart and breast
> Yea, of some doom they tell—
> Each pulse, a knell.[12]

The original response to the gods is always foreboding, which differs from anticipation, even the anticipation of something painful.[13] Anticipation awaits the arrival of some *thing*, perhaps something threatening, e.g. the arrival of the hurricane which happens, by chance, to be approaching me with all its natural force. But I am possessed by dreadful foreboding precisely when I sense that something horrifying is about to happen and yet am incapable of anticipating what it might be. It is no accident that the masks which primitive man used to represent the gods were not ordinary human faces—they were always precisely grotesque distortions of the human face which were designed to evoke horror, not assuage it.

In short, belief in the gods does not make the experience of being engulfed by terrible realities more palatable; it makes that experience more concretely upsetting. That primitive people preferred to speak not of power as such but of power as exercised by the gods tells us that they experienced this power neither as an abstraction nor as a natural force, but as an implacable agency which finds a uniquely appropriate way to devastate each individual. The gods are representative of the way doom is apportioned in a multiplicity of directions so that it will catch up with all of us, no matter in what direction we try to flee. The god who overturns my particular life is precisely reality visiting its fury on me in an excruciatingly appropriate way.

However, have we not spoken throughout of this power in *personal* terms—when we describe it as furious, and talk as if it possesses a terrible wisdom which outstrips human cunning? Should we not admit that these are mere metaphors used to accentuate the powerfulness of what is experienced? Is this nothing but analogy, or is there something not just appropriate but even necessary in our adoption of such language? These questions bring us to perhaps the most intractable aspect of the experience I have been trying to describe.

I have empasized, again and again, that this reversal of my life, my being subject to a power which overturns my conscious intentions, is radically different from a mere accident. For I myself set this power in motion by my own acts of avoidance, my refusals, by repeatedly ignoring whatever had the potential to disrupt my life radically. When such a disruption does occur and the whole meaning of my life is reversed by the very reality I had tried to avoid, my experience is very different from what happens when I am the victim of an accident. In the latter case I may very well say to myself, "After all, you deserved it. This accident somehow makes up for all the blameworthy acts which you got away with." Such a verdict reveals something of the moral sensitivity of the speaker but it betrays a curious logic. The speaker here is obviously reading a moral significance into a natural event. If he were religiously inclined, he might go so far as to conclude, as primitive man did, that the gods were using this natural event to balance the scales of divine justice. But the event in itself has no moral meaning; it does nothing but accidentally disrupt my life, and I am the one who has to invest it with meaning.

But in the situation we have been speaking of, the exact opposite is the case. I feel that events themselves are bearing down on me with an inescapable irony which suggests that they have been devised as a kind of pitiless instruction—so that I might learn from them and their excruciating irony, what a folly my life has been. It is as if this and only this course of events can teach me how completely unaware I have been of the true meaning of things. But it teaches me this not by revealing to me some broader plan or higher meaning, but only by undoing the very plans I had made for my life as a whole. It is as if life or reality itself has had it in mind all along to unravel the very design I have been trying all along to impose on it. It is as if I were born precisely in order to be taught, by this humiliating reversal, how wrong I can be. All my plans have pointed toward and prepared for this very undoing of them. And all this suggests that whether I want it so or not, my life is subject to the power of a terrible wisdom I cannot outrace or comprehend, a wisdom which, with endless patience, works at exposing me in my ridiculousness. Harmful accidents may be appropriate occasions for edifying discourses. But doom is wisdom itself striking me down with those pitiless truths which I have spent my life trying not to realize. The fact that doom seems, to the person who suffers it, to have been devised by some terrible wisdom does not indicate that he is anthropomorphizing it; his calling it wise does not make it at all like himself. Its wisdom is precisely its power to make the meaning of his life unfathomable, its power to withdraw itself from all his attempts to understand it. He has to call it wise because it shocks him into realizing how unwisely he has lived his whole life.

5. Tragic Reversal as the Confirmation of Freedom

One of the paradoxes of such a tragic reversal is that no one can suffer it without consenting to do so—for suffering is precisely this consent to be overwhelmed by an Other. But this does not mean that the person who refuses to suffer thereby exempts himself from a tragic reversal; it only means that he exempts himself from the *experience* of it, from the anguish and disorientation such an experience involves. He never realizes the fact that his life does not have the meaning he assigns to it with such self-assurance. Kierkegaard would say of him that he is doubly lost because he is lost and does not realize it.[14] Does this not suggest that the person who begins to suffer is on his way to waking up, and that the person who never suffers sleeps the sleep of the dead? And if the experience of crisis brings suffering to its culmination, must that not mean that we are fully alive only when we allow crisis to devastate us?

We must try to appreciate more fully what is involved in this act of consenting to a tragic reversal of one's life. And the question which immediately arises is whether it any longer makes sense to speak of consent, now that we have introduced the idea of doom, fate, destiny, the power of the gods. Is not the realization that my life is in the hold of such powers precisely the discovery that I have no freedom, that I am whatever such powers predestine me to be? It is certainly true that modern determinists, such as the behaviorists, portray the rule of fate in such a way as to make it incompatible with human choice. But such determinists invariably equate fate with either chance or natural necessity, and usually neglect to discuss the wrenching experience of tragic reversal I have been trying to describe.

I have suggested that we live, in fact, deterministic lives insofar as we ordinarily avoid exercising our power to choose, since such an exercise would be disruptive of our everydayness. But this means that ordinarily we will not to will, and suffocate our freedom in the routines that have been conditioned into us. The philosophical doctrine of determinism can be used to rationalize such avoidance. For it enables me to think of myself as wholly the product, the passive victim of, physical or social forces to which I have been subjected. If I am an aggregate of atoms tossed here and there by accidental collisions and fortuitous commotions, my acts are not self-originated but predetermined by past events which are themselves predetermined. Such a view leads to a radical denial of subjectivity as a reality in the world. It results in our viewing ourselves as things, indeed, as playthings.

Now the self I have been trying to describe does experience himself as, in a sense, a plaything—but as a plaything in the hold of powers which he himself has set in motion. It is my acts, my deeds, which have brought on their own reversal. My own acts of avoidance have given fate its power over me. Because of this complicity, I am a victim who yet is responsible for having put himself in a helpless position. And the cry in which I finally acknowledge this is both a *lament* and a *confession*. If I lament my "fate" without acknowledging as my own the fault which sets it in motion, I am not allowing the ordeal to upset me in my very status as a responsible agent; indeed, I continue to think that I am innocent of complicity in my own downfall. On the other hand, if I not only lament my fate but acknowledge my role in it, I open myself to the humiliating realization that I am responsible for my own doom—and only then do I fully open my self to the upsetting experience of it. And this means that, far from excluding freedom, a tragic reversal not only presupposes freedom but requires my acknowledging its reality in a way I never have before. The experience of doom occurs when one freely chooses to recognize one's responsibility for those acts of avoidance which have set in motion the reversal of one's intentions. Such an act of acknowledgment is not simply an instance of free choice: it is one's realizing for the first time the dreadful import of one's decisions. Far from teaching us that we have no choice, the experience of tragic reversal teaches us how portentous our choices are. This lesson is perfectly expressed in that outcry of horrified amazement and recognition: "What have I done!" With this brief exclamation, I express how unaware I have been of the doom which now engulfs me and, at the same time, I confess my responsibility for giving it its momentum.

But who is the "I" here? In this experience of horrified recognition one realizes that one is responsible for having brought about something completely contrary to one's conscious intentions. Does this not mean that one is not the person one thought one was? There lies, beneath the surface of all my projects and intentions, a whole series of unacknowledged avoidances; but my self-image has always been drawn exclusively from the conscious surface of my life. I avoided thinking about the possibility that there might be an underside to myself of which I am wholly unconscious. But when a tragic reversal opens my eyes, I have to acknowledge this long practice of self-deception. Such an acknowledgment is always humiliating for it entails discovering not just a hidden fault but the set of avoidances that one has used to delude oneself about the meaning of one's life as a whole. It turns out that I am not at all the person I thought I was; I no longer know *who* I am. Bereft of any clear identity, I no longer feel comfortable in any of my relationships and therefore find it impossible to resume my ordinary life. I cannot bring myself to participate in my customary daily projects. Those who function with such aplomb in the ordinary world do so, I now realize, only because they delude themselves into believing in their own avoidances. It now seems both ridiculous and amazing that I believed so long in the reality of this ordinary world, that I succumbed to it so naively and unquestioningly. But while I see through the self-delusions of the ordinary, I have nothing to put in their stead except the void created by my loss of them.

In short, the person who has fallen prey to a tragic reversal resembles an old man whose very self has been shattered and rendered useless. He has nothing to live on but his memory of what he has ceased to be. The final horror of this tragic reversal is precisely the fact that it has not killed him. That he exists—precisely this is the horror; that he has not died; that he must go on being himself although his life is already over. Hence the feeling that his very being in the world is superfluous, that he is point-lessly prolonging something that has no purpose or meaning, a life that is only a caricature of living.

But even as a tragic reversal causes one to lose one's ordinary identity, it sheds a new and horrifying light on one's past. From the perspective which the tragic reversal makes possible, one begins to realize that decisions which made one's avoidances operative had a horrifying weight one was never aware of. Neither innocuous nor ordinary, they rever-berated far into the future with unmanageable consequences. And what does this reveal if not that even when we are unconscious of doing it we ourselves possess the terrible power to ruin and create, to set doom in mo-tion and bring about its awful effects. We ourselves are capable of un-leashing the power that undermines the ordinary world. When, at the culminating moment of tragic reversal, I say "What have I done!" I am recognizing my self for the first time and realizing the terrible power I have to set the forces of life and death themselves in motion. For the first time, with this admission, I break through my superficial consciousness of myself and recognize my own upsetting role in the tragic drama. The hid-den I which I acknowledge in exclaiming "What have I done!" is the "I" in its very subjectivity, the ego in its very activity as a choosing agent, the self at its most intimate and personal level. It is the very self I am that all along I have not wanted to know.[15]

Thus, the experience of tragic reversal I have been describing has little to do with discovering one's unconscious, if the latter is identified with the id and if the id is thought of as being distinct from our selves as rational agents responsible for our own acts. The psychoanalytic frame-work encourages us to think of the ego as the always embattled center of ourselves as persons, and it tends to identify the ego with its conscious in-tentions. In this view, the ego is beset primarily by enemies other than it-self. But what we avoid above all is realizing the terrible power we exer-cise by virtue of being selves. We avoid becoming conscious of the depths of our own subjectivity. In the psychoanalytic framework, the ego can discover its heretofore repressed id; but this localizing of the repressed in the id allows the ego to avoid facing up to the moral horror of its own deepest avoidances. Even if the ego has to confront what it does not wish to see, it remains intact and secure if it does not have to acknowledge its own role in its reversal. The anguish that is associated with undergoing psychotherapy is ordinarily the anguish of lament, not of confession. The subject confesses a hidden sin—but one which he himself, in his very character as subjectivity, cannot be held responsible for. One might have to discuss one's most embarrassing desires, but one does not have to undergo the humiliation of realizing that what led to crisis was not these desires but the decision one made to avoid facing the questions they should have raised. In the end, the I, equated with its conscious intentions, remains innocent.

But in the kind of self-discovery I have been describing, the ego does not emerge unscathed. It undergoes a real and radical change. For no one can admit being responsible for setting in motion forces that lead to his own disintegration without losing forever his sense of innocence, and without realizing the terrible burden we bear because we are accountable not just for our acts but for our avoidances. It is exactly in coming to these realizations that one falls out of the shallowness of one's ordinary self-image, and into one's own nausea-inducing depths.

But if it is a mistake to disburden the ego of its culpability, it is just as mistaken to go to the opposite extreme of thinking that a tragic reversal results from a conscious intention to do evil. This too is an attempt to simplify the basic paradox involved in the fact that we hide from ourselves—the paradox of avoidance. The real evil of our ordinary lives lies in the fact that their superficiality permits us to believe them innocent. We are the victims of our avoidances in the sense that we do not consciously intend to cause the ironic reversal that shatters our world. But we are the perpetrators of that reversal by virtue of our having chosen to exclude from our lives the very realities that return to haunt us. Throughout our ordinary lives we have hints and intimations of those realities and presentiments of the mistake we are making in ignoring them. Such intimations are forebodings of insights to be reached in a future moment of crisis; but they are also the vestiges of insights long available to us that we have chosen to ignore. Those insights never failed to pursue us: haunted by them, we still try not to believe in their existence—until the moment comes when we have to acknowledge them as the confession which from the beginning has deserved our signature.

6. Vicissitudes of Horror

There remains one final and crucial aspect to the experience of tragic reversal that I have not yet discussed. From all that we have said, it has become clear that the critical moment in the ordeal of such a reversal occurs when the individual undergoing it has to acknowledge what until then he has avoided. What has not been discussed is how the outcome of the ordeal depends on the attitude one adopts in that moment of acknowledgment. For instance, I have repeatedly referred to the horror and dread, the sorrow and depression, that characterize such an experience; but I have not explored what these emotionally weighty terms signify.

Perhaps it will help if we begin by simply examining how a person undergoing this kind of crisis is likely to appear to others. Inevitably, he will seem to have turned away from the world and inward to himself. Events no longer seem to affect him. He appears, in fact, to have "no affect," as psychologists would say—to have lost his capacity for being emotionally engaged in the ebb and flow of daily existence. He seems "dead." Perhaps he simply sits and stares without blinking, as if light no longer has the power to bother his eyes, once they are fixed on emptiness. His refusal or inability to speak makes him seem insensitive to everything except himself; he appears to be self-absorbed in an enervating way, like the motionless victims of depression. Such a person may continue to perform his routine activities or he may physically remove himself as much as possible from the world, sitting day after day in the same chair in the same room; but in either case, whether moving or sitting still, he seems completely detached from the present and removed from what is happening around him.

Are the symptoms of crisis therefore the same as the symptoms of psychosis? We must realize, first of all, that observers who themselves operate in terms of the ordinary will to control will be unable to specify significant distinctions between these two conditions. Psychosis and crisis alike cause the one suffering from them to disappear from the surface, and those of us living on the surface use it as a criterion of sanity. But that paticular criterion loses its binding force, once one realizes that the ordinary world is itself grounded on self-delusions. Madness and crisis have in common the fact that they cause us to leave that world behind, although we may sometimes look back to it with nostalgia. If we are to appreciate the difference between these conditions, we must move beyond the similarity of their symptoms.

The person whose ordinary world is shattered experiences that ordeal as both horrifying and dreadful. To be horrified by something is to be repelled by it; what horrifies me evokes an immediate urge to turn away from it, to avoid it at all costs because of its upsetting character. But we need to distinguish being horrified from being scared or frightened.[16] I am scared of the thief, the airplane accident, the mouse scratching in the attic; but no matter how intensely the fear of such things assails me, it does not threaten me in the very center of my subjectivity, because it does not affect me in my very character as a moral agent who is responsible for having fashioned his world. I experience fear as an urgent but impersonal impulse which warns me of some danger to my security; but it leaves all the deepest sources of personal insecurity untouched. There is nothing individualizing about fear; in being frightened we are indistinguishable from each other because fright does not touch us in our very identity as unique moral agents. Fear is never more than a disturbance of my outer world; it springs on me with the immediacy of an instinct to which I am free to give or withhold my consent. "Horror" is something essentially different from this. When, for instance, I stare at my son's dead body dangling in front of me, my immediate impulse to turn away, to cover my eyes, springs from the deepest source of my self, from the very center of my being; for what I see disturbs the avoidances that lie hidden in the deepest, most intimate places of the heart. Moreover, while fear disappears as soon as I escape from what threatens me, horror does not disappear unless I devise a way of forgetting what has so upset me. This is why horror is, in a real sense, voluntary: one is horrified only if one opens oneself, in one's very subjectivity, to what has the power to be horrifying. I can always avoid the horrifying by treating the realities capable of evoking horror as things that are merely frightening. Fear is a self-protective reaction motivated by the desire to prevent injury. Horror, on the other hand, is my recoiling from an unbearable reality, the very sight of which has already started to devastate me. The reactions horror urges us to make are always too late. For we have already started to suffer the wound it would like to prevent, in the very experience of being horrified.

Now for me to experience something as horrifying in this sense, it cannot be a thing in the ordinary sense—it can only be "something" absolutely Other than what I am familiar with, "something" that, instead of being integratable within it, subverts my world as a whole, "something" which I experience not as a being at all but as an abyss that . . . horrifies. It is not an event to be placed beside other events, but the end of my world as a world. Horror is the drawing back, the recoil of the self, as subjectivity, from this nothingness which it has already begun to experience.[17] It is the heart's urge to protect itself from a radically disruptive Other which has already and irrevocably subjected the heart to a shattering impact.

Now if the heart obeys this impulse to recoil from nothingness, it will flee in terror from what horrifies it. But the terror felt in the heart is not an involuntary biological panic; it involves the horrified revulsion of the heart itself, its attempt to protect its world of meaning from what has the capacity to shatter it. We are accustomed to think of terror as being simply a sign of weakness; in fact, it originates in our desperate desire to remain in control of our existence. The terror of the heart is precisely its attempt to escape from an experience of being overwhelmed which it senses is imminent. It is not a simple weakness one yields to, but our last unyielding refusal to be vulnerable. Dread, on the other hand, is the heart's trembling consent to undergo what is horrifying, to suffer the end of its world, to surrender itself to the very truth from which it would like to recoil in terror. In dread, the will surenders itself to horror for the sake of what horrifies it—that is, for the sake of finally acknowledging the very horror that it has tried so long and hard to avoid. That is why, unlike terror, which gives rise to a restless inventiveness, dread brings with it into the center of horror a terrible, speechless serenity.[18]

Now the question we must ask is: does this anguished surrendering and serenity in fact amount to *resignation*, to careless indifference, a sealing off of one's self inside one's private abyss? This is certainly what it looks like from the outside. Does "disappearing from the surface of life" really mean ceasing to live at all—sitting numbly inside the cocoon of one's renunciation, motionless, immune to the "interesting," staring at life as if it were a charade in which there is no reason to participate? Since I have argued that ordinary life is such a charade, do I have any right to object to someone preferring despair to its pointless busyness? Is not such despair guided by an uncompromising lucidity which sees through all illusions and by a courage that dares to live without them? In short, have we reached here not just the heart of crisis but its only authentic catharsis? How can there be any more stages to crisis if one has got to the bottom of despair and realized the absurdity of all our worlds?

Advancing with dread and horror into a depth which undermines the surface of life, one despairs of the surface; one no longer puts any hope in it whatsoever. And since living on the surface means precisely avoiding what lies in the depth, anyone who despairs of the surface is on his way toward truth. The person living in dread and the person who despairs have this despair of the surface in common and for that reason they should be able to share their darkness like brothers. For they are both exiles displaced by a courage and lucidity that others lack. But the person who is in despair holds himself aloof from even this kinship of anguish. Even if he recognizes this other sufferer as inexplicably akin to him, he still lets him pass by as if he had not noticed him. For only so can he maintain his attitude of despair toward everything, even the possibility of sharing his anguish.[19]

The person who commits himself to total despair crosses over the boundary which separates darkness from ordinary existence, but once in that darkness he covers his eyes. He remains there at the edge of the world, his face in his hands, completely absorbed in his own hopelessness. But is this not a refusal to look *into* the darkness, and a refusal to surrender to it? Genuine surrender means allowing oneself to be drawn ever more deeply into the encounter with what horrifies. Dread is obedience to the power which empties my life of its ordinary meaning. It responds to the beckoning of what horrifies. Despair, on the other hand, gives up—it is the heart's refusal to be open to anything any more, the will's refusal to let anything matter to it now that it has given up all hope. But that means that despair itself is a kind of tourniquet for the open wound that causes it. Despair is dread introverted and transformed into an end in itself—and thus it provides me a way to protect myself from everything outside myself. Hence, this motionless depression—which offers precisely the comfort of being motionless, the security of being fixated on one's own absurdity. No one is more invulnerable and secluded, more immune to crisis, than the person who lives in that deserted sanctuary.

But it seems that few can live in such a condition of severance, disassociated from the community of ordinary people and concerns by one's willingness to suffer, disassociated from one's fellow-sufferers by virtue of one's very despair—few can live in such complete despair without the help of madness. It is as if the human mind, now secure inside a darkness it cannot bear to leave, is nevertheless compelled to *function*, to think, to occupy itself; and nothing exists for it, now that it is so disassociated from the ordinary world, except the figments of its own imagination. The mad begin to live again but on the stage of a completely private theater. Ironically, there is a tragic similarity between the esoteric drama of madness and the mundane drama of ordinary existence: in both, one strives to achieve absolute control over one's life and often succeeds. Madness is not the opposite of our ordinary sanity but its mirror-image, and the tragedy of the madman is not that he differs from the normal but that he resembles it so perfectly, with its arbitrary, self-centered rule, its rigid closedmindedness, its intoxicating hubris; indeed, madness does not merely resemble the characteristics of the ordinary but carries them to their extreme, so that it offers us not a contrast to the normal but a caricature of it, a burlesque.

And this is what leads us to conclude that motionless depression, and the madness which is sometimes its outgrowth, are precisely the ordinary modes of being-in-crisis. They deflect dread away from its desolate pilgrimage and rob it of its natural impetus. Left on its own, dread would never abate its journey into exile, its obedience to the power of darkness which holds it in thrall and beckons it to explore its desolate landscape. Ordinarily, the heart cannot bear to continue, once it has been broken by crisis. Exhausted by its wound and drained by its ordeal, its simply halts and takes shelter inside the only haven available: its own dereliction. It dreams of healing its wound by disappearing inside it. Irrevocably estranged from ordinary routines of control, one cannot escape the apparently indefinite and endless suffering which an ever-deepening crisis involves except by using suffering itself as an escape.

Madness is the most dramatic version of this escape but I should not neglect to mention less shocking examples of the same desperation. There is, for instance, the implacably stubborn ennui characteristic of those displaced persons who, uprooted from their ordinary worlds, refuse to suffer the agony of a new beginning, preferring instead to meditate on their loss and to harbor their resentment. Or we might think of the sense of forlornness and uselessness felt by those who, once busy, are suddenly unable to do the smallest tasks or, once well-off, are suddenly destitute; they come to cherish their very forlornness, devoting the long hours of each day to self-pity's quiet reverie and voluble complaint. In these and all cases of static suffering, what we might call the natural momentum of anguish is reversed; its power to generate ever deeper levels of crisis in one's life is lost. Utterly cut off from the ordinary world, one begins to live off the suffering this estrangement entails; one uses one's own suffering as a technique for being in control. Self-pity's requiem, resentment's curses, despair's speechless stare: all anticipate the soliloquy of madness. For all are introversions of suffering, which make suffering serve the very ego whose egocentricity it would rupture if allowed its natural efficacy. Strangely enough, these introversions of suffering can eventually transform the sufferers themselves into extroverts who look to the universe itself for an apology. When its every tactic to avoid loss of control fails, the will-to-control tries to use its very despair over losing control as a refuge from further, unpredictable horrors. The more totally one succumbs to one's suffering, the more one succeeds in approximating the dead, whom one envies because nothing more can happen to them.

The only real alternative to all these avoidances is to let crisis uproot one's life, to obey its unsettling summons with no reservations. To do this requires that one allow suffering's unpredictable and pitiless demands to impinge on one's life at every moment. One promises to follow dread wherever it leads, even if this costs not less than everything. But in doing so, one converts one's exile, one's homelessness, into a pilgrimage on behalf of dread's dark and elusive truths; one becomes the pupil of its harrowing lessons.[20] One allows suffering time and time again to disrupt one's self-absorption. Although his own acts have set in motion the powers to whose sway he is now subject, such a person nevertheless invents no excuses to rationalize his past conduct; doomed to wander in indefinite exile, he is nevertheless without self-pity. Having had to give up all he ever hoped to attain, he is nevertheless determined to earn in its place, from the very powers whose dreadful summons he obeys, some modicum of honor.

If we are to follow him, it seems that we must leave behind both ordinary existence and the ordinary ways of being in crisis. For the latter are simply tortured versions of ordinary avoidance and as such still involve our turning our backs on crisis and turning a deaf ear to its compelling intimations. Ordinarily, we will do anything rather than be in crisis. Indeed, ordinary existence is, in its essence, the avoidance of the radical suffering crisis involves. If we, as inquirers, are to follow where crisis leads, we must ask what occurs when, rare as it may be, someone embraces its most demanding ordeals instead of fleeing from them.

We know already that this entails succumbing to powers over which one has no control, not praying to such powers for exemption from their awful sway. If ordinary existence is my leveling everything, my robbing every Other of the Otherness which makes it threatening to me, extraordinary existence is my willingness to encounter in everything its dimension of terrible mystery and sacral power. The ordinary self reduces every Other to a problem; the extraordinary self feels himself surrounded on all sides by Others too dreadful to be called anything but gods. We have just begun, not finished, trying to describe his heroism. Is he, after all, the enemy of the powers which preside over his life, or their compatriot?

CHAPTER FOUR

Heroism and the Will to Greatness

A moment's reflection will suggest that our exploration has reached not simply a new stage but something of an impasse. It is not so difficult to follow the journey of an adventurer who has a compass to guide him, even if he has no familiar landmarks; but how are we to get a bearing on the explorer who has lost not only his way but also the ground under his feet? Were we to find a way to locate him on our usual maps, we would be rescuing him from the very condition of being lost which we want to describe.

This impasse is not one we can slide by nimbly. For it raises a question about our whole enterprise which we have heretofore neglected to address. We assigned ourselves the task of hunting down the nature of crisis. And the tendency of the hunting intelligence is to grasp, to make the Other its quarry and surprise it with traps, to wrest the Other out of its Otherness. Even when intelligence tries to release the Other from its grasp and allow it to reveal itself as it is, intelligence has not yet completely renounced its will to be in control: for it still tries to keep the Other within the scope of its vision. But at the point in our inquiry which we have now reached, has not crisis plunged us into an obscure depth which the light of our inquiring intelligence can only distort by trying to force it to reveal itself? How are we to locate the individual who has left behind all of the territory for which we have maps? Are we not required to admit, under the impact of the present impasse, that our whole inquiry is itself an example of what it has criticized? Have we not been trying to make the experience of crisis obedient to our desire for insight into its meaning?

A person is rarely his own best critic, but one can at least testify to one's intentions. If this inquiry does, in fact, try to make crisis obedient to its demand for insight, then it sets in motion its own tragic reversal. But I have not intended to make crisis obedient to my inquiry; I have tried to make my inquiry obedient to the demands of crisis. To be faithful to those demands, our examination of crisis must become, at certain crucial junctures, a self-examination, a rupturing of our inquiry by crisis itself; crisis must be given the opportunity to undermine whatever we have said about it. Unless we give it this opportunity, our thinking about crisis will not be exposed to the crisis of thinking.

Still, this suggests that there may come a moment when we will have to fall silent—when crisis will finally dumbfound our best efforts to understand it. Up till now we have been on our way toward the experience of crisis, but now we seem to have arrived. We have moved from the will to control, both overbearing and terrified, the victim of its own desire to be invulnerable, to the half-crisis of generosity, with its receptivity and unconscious unwillingness to be radically ruptured, to the horrifying experience of having one's life undermined by subterranean powers which one's own acts have set in motion. With this third mode of being we reach, it seems, a radical inversion of the first: the person originally secluded inside the safety of his boundaries, after becoming the gatekeeper who welcomes strangers, becomes a homeless traveler, himself without compass or passport, a refugee who has lost all hope of returning to his homeland. The dialectic which began with the total avoidance of crisis and its anguish has reached completion in the destitution of the vagrant.

Nevertheless, if one dialectic has been completed, another is emerging. For radical as are the transformations which I have sketched, all of them occur within the context and from the point of view of the life disrupted by crisis. This becomes apparent as soon as we examine more closely the language we have been called upon to use: "the vagrant," "the homeless traveler," "the loss of a compass," even "falling into an abyss"; all these phrases describe experiences from the vantage point of *home*, with its sedentary life, its familiar landmarks, its firm ground. I have sought to describe crisis as it is experienced, and the entrance into crisis is experienced *as exile from the familiar*. But a person who thinks of himself as exiled is still viewing himself in the light cast upon his life by the homeland from which he has been uprooted. He is continuing to orient and locate himself by understanding his position as a dislocation from his original settlement.

This is no semantic quibbling. It goes to the very heart of our description of falling into crisis. For I argued that this involves leaving the ordinary world behind; but even during the experience of leaving it behind, the person undergoing crisis continues to equate his homeland with the universe, the surface of his life with life as a whole, the familiar things he is losing with being itself. But this very way of viewing crisis cannot be true since it looks at the crisis experience from the perspective which is undermined by it. But what looks like the end of the universe is, in fact, only the rending of the illusions one had been using to equate reality with the ordinary. And this means that the feeling of losing everything must eventually be transformed into the realization that crisis enables one to discover a whole new universe of being whose very existence was not previously suspected.

Perhaps I can give this argument more impact by returning to the example discussed in the last chapter. The father, who up until that moment had felt secure about his way of life and especially about the pattern of paternal generosity he thought it followed, discovers his son's suicide; this crisis leads him to realize that, in some way he cannot decipher, his very generosity contributed crucially to his son's despair. The encounter with this horror differs radically from the recognition of a specific error, from shame felt for a particular act, even from the painful confession of habitual vices and inadequacies; the very structure of meaning which made his life seem intelligent and intelligible now stands revealed as an illusion he has been using to protect himself from horrifying realities he could not bear to experience. This buried horror is not a single thing; it is not a specific truth hidden by a specific error; it is not a specific reality left unacknowledged by a specific avoidance; it is the whole of reality from which he has protected himself by imposing upon it a pattern of meaning he willed it to have. The person who encounters the horrific is not simply discovering a new dimension of reality which complements and deepens his former structure of meaning. For the horror is such that it radically undermines the old structures and overturns them; it confronts him with a radical unintelligibility that lies at the very heart of his life. It is not simply that his former way of living revealed only one aspect of reality and left the rest undisclosed; rather, he pretended that his viewpoint was comprehensive and exhaustive and thus robbed it of even the partial truth it would have had if he had confessed its limits. This is why the image we have used for this reversal is the image of a traveler who has been enveloped by darkness and lost his bearings.

But the person who loses his way inevitably finds himself in a radically new world whose existence he was unaware of because his old maps did not show it. The lost man sees what is hidden from men who are still imprisoned in and by the illusion that they are on the right path. The person who has undergone radical crisis has stepped out of ordinary history; he loses interest in all everday busyness; he is no longer engaged by or caught up in the small dramas that we ordinarily act out as we clamber forward with our ambitions. But this does not mean that he "lives in the past" in the sense that he yields to the seductions of nostalgic self-pity. Someone who "lives in the past" in this way uses it as a place in which to hibernate from the ordeal of time itself. We can imagine the father in our example doting over old photographs, rereading his son's grade school compositions, as if by poring over these mementos of his shattered world he might find a way of reentering it. He would be trying to repress what he knows not, like the madman, through delusions, but like the sentimental poet, through the falsifications of romantic reverie. In trying to live in the past, he would be trying above all to forget what he had discovered about it: that the very things he did to love his son led to his undoing.

In order truly to leave ordinary history behind, an individual has to despair of it in its very essence and without reserve. In so doing, he has to leave ordinary life without baggage, without memorabilia, with nothing but the passport of his destitution. Then ordinary events lose their power to affect him, not because he has become invulnerable, but because he suffers the kind of wound which ordinary life as a whole exists to prevent and refuses to acknowledge. The ordinary world might look upon such a person as aloof, insensitive to everyday worries, indifferent, self-absorbed, depressed, a victim of psychic disorder. He seems older than death itself, he seems not to belong to the same planet. Were the father, in our example, to follow the experience of horror where it leads, he would be both pitied and resented by his friends for his unwillingness to resume ordinary existence. His son's suicide has already been superseded, in their minds, by other events and distractions.

Alone in his continuing obedience to the reality of his son's death, the father can discover the magnitude of its horror, a magnitude which the ordinary world's way of reckoning cannot help but demean. The father would then be undergoing an initiation into a whole universe from which we in the ordinary world are always excluded because we level every crisis down to a problem with which we must learn to cope. We can imagine the father in our example discovering, with a horror ordinarily avoided, the magnitude of death and at the same time, the awful sacredness of the human life which death extinguishes. Gradually, over months of reflection, he might realize that, all along, he allowed no dimension of his world—his marriage, his friendships, his career—to be affected by the terrible gravity of meaning which life as a whole now has for him. But his very consenting to this shocking truth is precisely the beginning of his fidelity to depths of which even his wife and friends remain stubbornly ignorant. No one else, we may suppose, has taken his son's death or their complicity in it seriously enough to recognize, under its shocking impact, that their actions have an enormous, often terrifying significance which they are unaware of when they commit them. He alone, initially through his obedience to his son's death, and then through his fidelity to all the radical questions it prompts him to raise about everything, becomes a participant in the deeper drama of human existence—the drama that is punctuated by terrible truths and horrifying realizations. His many months of apparently morbid obsession culminate with his realizing that the one crucial fault for which he was responsible was not his complicity in his son's suicide but his willing participation in ordinary existence as a whole, his consistently shrinking back from any awful realities that threatened to disrupt any dimension of his existence. The only genuine way to make amends for that basic fault is to reverse it by embracing the Awful instead of fleeing it.

Of course, none of this is meant to deny the fact that in leaving the ordinary world we inevitably feel like we are leaving the world of meaning and entering an unintelligible chaos. But if the ordinary is in its essence a flight from reality—the reality of everything—then, in fact, to leave that world is to move from illusion to potential meaning, from folly to the possibility of wisdom, from hollowness to the possibility of substance, from nothingness to being. The reversal involved in undergoing crisis cannot be complete until we reverse the ordinary interpretation of crisis itself so that the crisis that is touched off by some horrible occurrence nevertheless is itself viewed not as a terminal event but as a radical beginning, not as an interruption to be avoided but as an opening to be explored. If what darkness extinguishes is the false light of illusions, being enveloped in it is the condition for the possibility of finding something real. The person who is ostracized like a homeless vagrant by the community of ordinary men because he does not take their worries seriously is for that very reason prepared to live his life for the first time in relationship to those ultimate realities which we all usually spend our lives avoiding. Expelled from the ordinary, he is ready to risk living among the terrible powers which the ordinary world ignores out of terror. Those who dismiss him as the victim of morbid obsessions have no suspicion of either the horrors or the ecstasies he is now open to experiencing. The individual who breaks through the ordinary world to the underworld inhabited by the awful realities we ordinarily repress is transformed by this process into something like a companion to the gods. Although from the perspective of the ordinary he might seem to be a homeless beggar, this wanderer who has left behind his desire for home, who ventures into the underworld without any way of defending himself from the gods who reside there, is, in fact the only one among us who deserves to be called heroic.

1. The Heroic Individual and the Herd

Our task has therefore been set for us. We have broken off, in a decisive way, with ordinary existence; we are done, hopefully, with its self-protective avoidances and strategies of control, all motivated by an unconscious fear of being wounded. We must try now to imagine its opposite, the extraordinary way of being which is properly called heroic. What constitutes, precisely, the heroic manner? How would a person live if he were wholly faithful to the heroic ideal? What does this ideal demand and what are the distinctive traits of the person who lives it out with unreserved passion and so acquires the kind of sublime stature we associate with greatness? By exactly what criteria do we distinguish the heroic way of living not just from its opposite but also from its counterfeits?

I do not think we have to seek far to find the clue we need to begin responding to these questions. For the distinguishing feature of ordinary existence is precisely the avoidance of crisis, the belittling of its radical disruption into an interruption. Ordinary existence is essentially flight. Therefore, its opposite can only be the kind of will to greatness that would welcome crisis even as it recognized the dreadful disruption which crisis requires one to suffer, the kind of will that seeks to do justice to the radical demands that crisis makes on an individual.[1] Only in our rare best moments do we break free enough of our avoidances to admire such a heroic attitude instead of ostracizing the person who lives it out. Nevertheless, we will try, first, to understand the nature of some of its most important virtues, and, second, to imagine some concrete embodiments of it.

However, as we proceed in this essay on heroism, we must remember continuously to mistrust our *ordinary* assumptions about what heroism involves. Insofar as we operate inside the ordinary world, we most admire the person who can manage things, cope with them, handle them. We like the fact that such a person is not upset, as we are, by petty annoyances and disruptions. Nothing ever seems to upset his equilibrium; his poise makes us think he is able to master every situation. Nothing that happens ever gets the better of him. In such a person we see what we ordinarily think of as our own best virtues developed to a state of perfection where they are exercised with casual ease. But the self-assured nonchalance characteristic of such "coolness," the studied avoidance of any kind of discomfort, the refusal to let anything affect one—all these are, in fact, evidence of a profound lack of heroic character. Precisely because we are ordinarily not offended by such a person but envious of his invulnerability, we can be sure he shares our own ordinariness of spirit. The master of all situations is, by virtue of that very fact, more expertly resistant to and more perfectly unaware of the heroic possibilities presented by a crisis situation. The master of control never risks anything. The genuine hero is ready to risk everything. The former is so successful at controlling existence that he never has to suffer, like the latter, the dread visage of an enemy whose power is inhuman and horrifying. The real hero hopes he will be able to prove himself worthy of such enemies.

But this means—and our portrait of his traits might well begin here— that the relationship between the genuine hero and the community of the ordinary will inevitably be ambiguous and unstable because of the fundamental incompatibility between their modes of being. Indeed, the real hero will be set apart from the multitude by the multitude itself as soon as its common sense discerns in the hero something out of the ordinary. On the surface the hero may be granted a place of honor and looked up to; his virtues may be held up as the ideal to be emulated, his deeds may become a legend that is told and retold—he may be set apart by being elevated. But that his deeds are radically different from our ordinary repertoire, that admiration of his virtues means acknowledging that they are in some sense the opposite of our own, that he acquired his heroic stature precisely by radically rejecting ordinary life as a whole—all these facts that constitute his greatness are ordinarily repressed. Were we to have a real inkling of what sets the hero apart from us, we would not elevate but expel him from our midst, rendering his status not significantly different from that of the criminal, the insane, the destitute, the Stranger, all of whom we usually cut off to protect ourselves from contamination.

If this ambiguous response to the hero is interpreted in the light of our previous reflections, we can recognize the will to be generous operative in our emulation of the hero and the will to control operative in the desire to cast him out. But it should be noted that we are inclined to expel the hero only because we accurately discern in him a rupture of the ordinary; on the other hand, we want to emulate the hero only because we do not discern the anguish and suffering which real emulation would involve. We ordinarily identify the hero with *our version* of his virtues, his deeds, his legend; we leave out of our account of his heroism his rejection of what we ordinarily embrace, his passion for the very things that terrify us, the destitution he feels on account of belonging to no established community—all the experiences without which the hero would, in fact, be indistinguishable from those who pretend to emulate him. We welcome the hero into our midst, but our very welcoming of him is a way of trying to bring him within the boundaries of the world which he heroically leaves behind. Underneath our adulation for the hero is an unconscious desire to expel him; at the bottom of that desire to expel is a grudging acknowledgment that we center our lives on avoiding what he suffers.

Now the hero cannot always avoid noticing either the applause of his adulators or the suspicions of those who would reject him. Both these groups trivialize his ordeals and among neither can he find companions. From his point of view, no one is more self-deluded than the celebrity who is ambitious for the applause of the multitude except perhaps the outcast who is in despair over their insults. Insofar as he searches out the very realities which the ordinary world is designed to exclude, the hero cannot help but be contemptuous of the whole ordinary way of being. Expulsion from its world, far from causing him despair, actually confirms his sense of being set apart from it, and of belonging to a world that Others are not even aware of. We must think here of the kind of contempt which Nietzsche practiced toward "the herd" and Kierkegaard no less than Nietzsche.[2]

Heroic contempt differs from malice insofar as it treats its object as being unworthy of its attention. The hero refuses to belittle himself by taking either the criticism or the applause of the "they" seriously. He will not let himself be lowered to the level of resentment's small-minded vengeance. His relationship with the herd is, strictly speaking, irrelevant to the axial concern of his life; he may not even care if the "they" are deluded into thinking that they are in some sense his equals. The hero need not begrudge the herd its delusions; he may even hope they will be sedated by them.[3] He is tempted to resent the existence of the herd only when their envy and their craving to belittle him make them treat him as an inferior.

All this suggests that there is a strict analogy between the multitude's attitudes toward the hero and what I have described as the ordinary attitude toward the gods. The will to control is ordinarily too busy controlling its existence, learning how to handle and cope with all situations, to pay any attention to the gods; we usually take the gods seriously only when we find ourselves losing control of our lives, at which point we appeal to them as a strategy of last resort. The will to be generous, on the other hand, seems to welcome the presence of the gods and even renders them homage; but we are usually hospitable to the gods only when we do not realize what horrifying realities their presence portends. The same holds true for the hero whose heroism is either ignored, until an impending crisis prompts the multitude to appeal to him as a savior, or acclaimed, under the illusion that his virtues are not incompatible with the whole ordinary mode of being.[4] What is at the basis of this analogous attitude on the part of the ordinary toward gods and heroes, if not a similarity in their identity—a similar power, a similar awfulness, a similar contempt for ordinary fears which the ordinary must find terrifying?

2. Counterfeits of Heroism: Psychosis, Nihilism and Despair

Before exploring these suggestions further, it might be helpful to explain why other apparent analogues to real heroism—madness, violence and despair—have, in fact, only a faint resemblance to it.

The psychotic, as we have already seen, is a caricature of the ordinary: if more open to suffering the horrors which are ordinarily avoided, he unconsciously and tragically mimics the ordinary by constructing a world inside which he can be secure from any upsetting ordeal. He stops just short of being the hero we are seeking, even if the multitude associates him with the hero by sometimes treating the latter as if he were insane. And perhaps the best evidence of his stopping short is precisely his compulsion to leave everyone else behind, his need to be alone in the sanctuary of his private universe. For was not Nietzsche right in saying that one characteristic of the hero is his wanting to have enemies as strong as himself and comrades as ready as he is to encounter what ordinary people avoid?[5] The most tragic kind of psychosis is precisely that which causes one to be deluded by the dream of one's heroism, the dream not only of grandeur but also of suffering and persecution, a dream because the madman never risks leaving the security of his private theater, a tragic dream because he is, in fact, suffering and is perhaps being persecuted. Psychosis is a caricature of the ordinary because it does no more than tragically mimic the heroic.

With regard to that other primal outcast, the doer of violence, we must first note that, when stripped of every vestige of generosity, the will to control, with its disregard for everything other than itself, its obsession with having its own way, is itself violent in its very essence. Our failure to acknowledge this is, of course, essential to the rationalizations we use to justify our ordinary way of living. But this paradox does not justify the claim to heroism made by those who, opposed to an established order of control, will impose on it their own idiosyncratic form of violence. If there is something profoundly violent about the "upright citizen" underneath his disguises, it does not follow that the overtly violent person is heroic simply because his violence is committed openly.[6]

Nevertheless, it should not surprise us, in a world dominated by the will to control, to find human beings made so desperate by it, so enraged by its arbitrary routines, so nauseated by its very ordinariness, that they long for nothing but the purification violence promises. I am thinking here of individuals whose revolt against society is undefiled by practical motive or goal; it is rather a rhetoric of blood, a pure expression of speechless rage. The longing to drown everything in blood is not simply another variation of the will to control; for it does not long for success in the sense of hoping to assume the reins of control once they have been snatched from the fists of the ordinary. Rather, it longs for a final catharsis which will consume the whole universe of the ordinary in an eschatological holocaust.[7] Its motive is not ambition but nihilistic despair, a despair which wills nothing but the purity of its own violences. Instead of espousing an alternative ideology, it wants (though perhaps not consciously) to engulf all the lies disguised as ideologies in universal destruction. But if such a will wills the disappearance of the ordinary and ridicules any compromise with it, if it is courageous enough to carry despair to its logical conclusion, still the very fact that it despairs proves that it has failed to transcend the ordinary completely. For, unable to envision any alternative to the ordinary way of life except violence, the nihilist still makes the mistake of thinking that to be at all is to be ordinary. Despairing of the ordinary, the will also despairs of existence itself. We encounter here, no less than in the case of psychosis, an example of neither the heroic nor the ordinary but the caricature of both. The "heroic" purity of rage, the "heroic" purity of despair, are, at the same time, the paroxysm of a will too pathetically weak to be able to suffer without seeking in violence both a purified form of suffering and a final antidote for its wounds.

These brief observations about psychosis and nihilism have moved us toward appreciating in a deeper way what the heroic mode of being entails. For it is not just that the hero is willing to encounter what the rest of us ordinarily avoid. What makes him heroic is that he does so without armor, without illusion, without madness, without violence. The hero moves without halt into the dark grip of realities over which he has no control and before which he is defenseless. Dread differs from the despair that is at work in madness and psychosis precisely because it remains open to further horror. The dread-filled heart, unlike the despairing one, is still willing to be struck with amazement by the unexpected, the unanticipated, the utterly strange. Despair stands on the edge of an abyss and prejudges it; dread is too respectful of the abyss to draw quick conclusions. Dread demonstrates that real patience is not simply the power to endure agony but the power to remain open-minded inside anguish, the power to postpone indefinitely a judgment about where one is headed, even if one is headed into an abyss.

We can see this more clearly if we consider the implications of the fact that, when I despair, I am implicitly claiming to be able to comprehend my life as a whole insofar as I have already decided that it is unredeemable. I know the betrayal that lies in wait at the end of all the promising possibilities my life offers, without having to waste my life believing in them. Despair prides itself on being able to fix its omniscient gaze on all the horrors from which hope turns away. The black hood worn by the executioner does not cover his eyes: despair, like the executioner, is willing to face the realities which the rest of us, like the victim to be executed, wear blindfolds to avoid facing. Despair claims to be the only blade sharp enough to cut through our deepest avoidances. What else confronts us with the verdict about our lives we most dread to hear? Despair prides itself on its honesty; hope, it tells us, is the attempt to silence its brutal sentence. Despair's willingness to think the worst makes it lay claim to heroic stature.

But that is despair's version of hope and we have reasons for distrusting it. It is the executioner, after all, who blindfolds his victim and executes him. If everything which happens is *bound* to be a betrayal, no event can possibly betray my expectations. The foreknowledge of despair gives me exactly the kind of total control over my existence which despair pretends it has ceased to hope for. Despair, which sees absurdity everywhere, prides itself on its certainty. Like cynicism, its first cousin, it doubts and ridicules everything—except itself. But its certainty that no future will disprove it shows that despair is really motivated by the need to be infallible, and that it is terrified of exposing itself to any hope that might cast suspicion on the verdict it has already made. It must continuously insulate itself against any unexpected possibility which beckons it. Despair lightens itself of dread by smothering the future in its own certain darkness.

But this means that real hope and real anguish are inseparable from each other in the heart of the authentic hero. Hope without anguish is precisely that hollow optimism which despair rightly derides. But anguish without hope is closed off to the future, and therefore both numb to any new horror and insulated from any deepening or intensifying insight: what is such "anguish" if not a new way of making oneself invulnerable? Heroic anguish, on the other hand, continues to be anguish precisely because it does not close itself off by turning inward and feasting upon itself; heroic anguish keeps opening itself to the potentially devastating strangeness of reality. Such anguish keeps on allowing reality to rupture the attempts despair makes to impose a final verdict on it. In the same way, hope acquires heroic stature to the degree that it submits to the merciless tutelage of an anguish that robs us of all the things we ordinarily long to have. Only anguish makes the hero's hope austere and thus different from optimism.[8] Only hope gives the hero's anguish its openness to surprise and thus distinguishes it from despair.

3. The Heroic Ideal of Embracing Crisis

But what, it might be asked, does the hero hope for or hope in when he is faithful to the anguish of crisis? Must not hope have an object toward which it directs its longing, or a power in whose redemptive efficacy it trusts? The hero answers "no" to both these suggestions, as long as they are phrased in this way. For hope has not yet acquired heroic stature as long as it still fixes on some specific outcome or event, or continues to believe it will be rescued by some salvific agency. Someone who uses such a hope to carry him through crisis is still refusing to allow crisis to undermine his ordinary mode of being. It is not simply hope for the wrong thing but the wrong kind of hope. Radically and definitively to give up ordinary existence requires precisely that one despair of it. The hero ceases to hope that he can avoid the radical disruption of his life by dreadful powers over which he has no control; were he not heroic, such a loss of hope would indeed lead to a paralyzing hopelessness. But in addition to giving up his ordinary world, the heroic person opens himself to the radically uprooting experience of crisis itself. He approaches openly, and in that sense with hope, the very ordeal which causes the ordinary person to despair. He sees the crisis as giving him an opportunity to achieve a kind of greatness that is not accessible in any other way. In the heroic mind the outcome of the ordeal is not what matters; greatness is its own reward. The heroic individual hopes for nothing else except the greatness that comes from being devastated. He wants nothing but to receive from the awful powers with which he contends and by which he may well be destroyed, a salute in recognition of having opened himself up to them. In his eyes nothing matters except how he acquits himself in the heroic ordeal, and whether even in his dying he acts in such a way as to deserve the respect of the powers from which most of us spend our lives trying to escape.

So it is on account of this hope, and with disdain for any other, that the heroic individual moves without let or hindrance into the dark obscurity of an abyss. He is not, or is not any longer, so attached to his illusions that he despairs when they are being torn away from him; but, at the same time, he lets go of them with dread and trembling because he knows that, without them, he has no protection against the unpredictable demands of crisis itself. What is heroic about the hero, if not his daring to plunge with hope instead of despair into the very abyss we ordinarily devote our hopes to escaping? But he enters that abyss not just without regret, without self-pity, without looking backward, but with a sense of having hungered all his life for precisely this radical kind of suffering. That is why the heroic individual sometimes seems to us to belong to a different species: the hero seeks out, with the eagerness of a born warrior, exactly those crises which we avoid at all costs.

Here a contrast between the heroic will to greatness and the cool will to control might be illuminating. The "cool" person wants to impose his will on his life so as to deprive it of its power to upset him; he tries to control things so as to secure himself against the threat of their Otherness. Thus, his coolness is only a mask for his terror. At the basis of his whole life is an unconscious dread of every Other in its very Otherness. The heroic individual, on the other hand, is drawn to the very realities which evoke in him the feelings of dread and horror. He knows that these feelings are themselves the evidence of his readiness to open himself to these realities. What he is most afraid of is not the devastating ordeal itself but the temptation he might have to recoil from it. He cannot bear the thought that at the decisive moment of his life, when the crisis has reached its most critical turning point, he might be too weak to suffer it. The heroic individual embraces upsetting experiences for exactly the same reason that prompts us to avoid them: because they are the gravest of burdens and make the most anguishing demands. What makes a hero heroic is not his undergoing any particular experience of suffering, but the fact that he finds in such ordeals the only experience worth living for.[9] The more radically an experience upsets him, the more seriously it calls into question his whole mode of being, the more it exceeds in severity the ordeals he has already been through, the more the heroic individual is drawn toward it, as toward the treasure he has all along been searching for. Indeed, we might go so far as to say that the heroic individual determines the worth of an experience, its deserving to be embraced, precisely by weighing the gravity of the burden it would give him the privilege of suffering.[10] It is difficult for us not to imagine him bent over and crippled by such burdens. But the hero carries himself with a dignity that is somehow exactly commensurate with the ordeals he has the greatness to assume. In fact, the more upsetting the experiences he embraces, the more his manner becomes like that ascribed to the gods themselves in their best moments—dauntless, disdainful of cautious counsel, eager to be put to any test.

This readiness to take part in the most devastating ordeal is, I think, the primary virtue of the heroic will. We might imagine the hero sensing from within the boundaries of ordinary life, the dark contention, the violence, the terrible power of those invisible realities whose very existence is denied by those around him. It is these very intimations of horror that beckon him not to observe but to participate in the awful drama of which they give him so uncanny a presentiment. To follow where they beckon requires that he die to ordinary existence, that he not just reluctantly yield but wholly surrender himself to the sway of these realities over which he knows he can have no control. In some profound sense he must agree to become, to the degree that this is possible for a human person, the companion of the terrible powers before which he trembles with horror and fascination. From the point of view of the ordinary life which he leaves, this transformation inevitably seems like a fall, a radical loss of identity; from the point of view of the extraordinary life he enters, it is precisely one's *becoming like a god*.

From that new vantage point, everything that is ordinarily considered important no longer possesses any real worth. Indeed, we must say, even if it seems extravagant, that in achieving the heroic point of view, one's basic assumptions about reality itself undergo a revolution. For what is usually most real to us is precisely the smoothness with which our lives are run, the structure of everydayness which is built so securely that it seems like the structure of being itself. The consequence of this is that ordinarily we cannot conceive of *anything* undergoing a crisis; just as we cannot conceive of the structure of our own lives disintegrating, so we cannot conceive of any destructuring of the world as a whole. In short, we cannot conceive of death, if by death is meant precisely the undoing of a being in its very core, its liability to *nothingness*.

But for the heroic individual, it is precisely the possibility of nothingness that has become real—and not just the fact that this thing or that thing is liable to nothingness but the fact that our ordinary world as a whole is liable to nothingness. What the heroic individual realizes that we do not is that the structures which hold our world together and thus make it a world can be shattered.[11] What makes him heroic is precisely the fact that he opens himself to this metaphysical insecurity instead of trying to protect himself from it. He realizes that beings themselves are only a kind of temporary hiatus in the ongoing ordeal of crisis. Things are not as real as their emergence and disappearance, their creation and destruction. The world we ordinarily live in is not as real as the ordeal of birth and death we have tried to avoid confronting.

The heroic individual would be betraying his very heroism if he were to harbor the hope that his recognition of nothingness might exempt him from it. But that he is subject to the sway of powers over which he has no control does not mean he cannot be their compatriot. The authentic hero has no pretensions to immortality. While he knows that his willingness to suffer makes him great, he does not try to believe it makes him invulnerable. His sense of his own mortality prevents him from ever mistaking his condition for that enjoyed by the gods with whom, in so many other ways, he identifies. He is heroic precisely because, knowing himself no god, he dares to emulate their deeds. Unlike the gods in having to anticipate his death, he is yet like them in being negligent of his own safety. What gives him his stature, his magnificence, is his embracing as an occasion for heroic deeds what he himself knows is also the occasion of his death. In his heart of hearts does he suspect, as we must, that even the gods themselves, immune to the dangers he courts and finally suffers, are not his equal in heroism?[12] Are they not in some sense less than he, since they possess without having to be vulnerable the greatness he achieves only by risking and eventually losing everything? Is this not his real secret, that precisely his power to be great in the face of death makes him the object of something very much like divine envy?

4. Images of the Heroic Manner: Warrior, Founder, Artist

It might help us deepen our understanding of heroism if, instead of elaborating any further on its ideal, we reflect on some concrete images of heroic character. If, in the process of doing so, we find ourselves continuing to employ metaphysical language, this is because the heroic experience we are describing always has a metaphysical dimension. For once dislocated from our ordinary world, the heroic individual enters into relationship with realities that are so far removed from the everyday that we are ordinarily not aware of their existence. As we shall now see, the warrior, the founder and the artist all experience these "metaphysical" realities in so intimate and profound a way that they become more real to them than the beings that occupy us in our ordinary world.

The image of the hero as warrior might seem to be the image most accessible to us, given its prominence in both literary and popular imagination. But only epic warriors are heroic in the real sense and such warriors are completely outside the range of our contemporary experience, circumscribed as it is by the utilitarian mode.[13] We know all too well the soldier as technician for whom weapons are simply tools for achieving, with more overt violence, the same stranglehold on reality which the will to control always strives to attain. As conducted by such technicians, warfare is simply another system of routines in the operation of which the specialist who launches missles is not easily distinguishable from any other computer programmer. What distinguishes the epic warrior from his modern counterfeit is not just his literal proximity to death but his belief that only by living in its proximity can he be close to what is ultimately real. The warrior is heroic because, knowing full well that he is not immune to death, he deliberately places himself in a situation where his life is in jeopardy. Living matters less to him than his proving to death that he has the courage to be vulnerable to it.

So if we want an image of the genuinely heroic warrior, we must imagine him as someone who embraces war as if it were, as Heraclitus says, the father of all things. War is not, for such a person, a temporary interruption of a normal peaceful existence; rather, peace is a contrived repression of the conflict, the crisis, that is always at work in the heart of things. Death is not viewed as an intruder unjustly upsetting the balance of our lives; there is no real balance except the harmony that comes out of opposites in conflict. Life itself is less important than the bond that joins life and death together in a battle that is simultaneously an embrace. If the warrior-hero wants to take part in this mortal combat, it is not because he harbors any sentimental illusions about its consequences. He knows how much death enjoys mocking our impregnable defenses; even to him death seems to decide by whim whom it executes and whom it pardons. In spite of this, he is willing to give death its due and acknowledge his indebtedness to it: his greatness derives from the fact that his deeds are done in the face of it. The heroic warrior does not crave security from mortal dangers because proximity to death awakens his passionate enthusiasm for life. We should imagine the hero possessed by the kind of joy that is evoked in us by realities that terrify and fascinate at the same time; his openness to those realities includes as much dread as ecstasy, is ecstatic in its very dreadfulness.[14] The hero regrets nothing—not even the death of his friends, not even the necessity of dying himself; we might even imagine him greeting it with a joyful laughter that expresses both mockery and celebration. That laughter comes from his knowing that by embracing death he transforms it into a heroic deed instead of suffering it as a passive victim.

Perhaps we will be able to appreciate the hero as warrior more fully if we examine, as our second image of the heroic ideal, the mythical figure whom the warrior himself acknowledges as his paradigm, the hero as founder. The founder of the polis, as he is revered in traditional myths, is never merely the first citizen, the first inhabitant, the first defender; rather, he is remembered as possessing a transcendent stature comparable only to that of the gods. Indeed, he is revered as being in some profound sense the author of the world, the creator whose primal deeds gave birth to the cosmo-polis as an ordered and sacred whole.[15] The founder is thought to have brought the city into being out of primeval chaos, a creative deed which succeeding generations must emulate if they intend to be heroic. The founder not only transcends the ordinary but in some sense shares in the status of the gods themselves; his dreadful and fascinating character is evoked during the telling of mythic stories that, however often retold, never lose their compelling quality. Transported by the myth back into the original drama of his heroic deeds, later generations almost feel as if they too have broken through the pettiness of ordinary existence, even if only temporarily. Located outside of, prior to, the profane time which governs ordinary lives, the founder's deeds can only be celebrated appropriately by a festival during which the community recreates the original time of its world. Whenever such festivals occur, irrespective of the specific deeds or heroes they commemorate, man retains some kinship, however faint and tenuous, with the dreadful, heroic founder who lived in the company of the most primordial powers that are active in the universe.

Indeed, what evokes later veneration for him is the fact that the founder was willing to battle chaos, and to be exposed, in doing so, to the most harrowing of ordeals. No warrior, brave as he may have proven himself to be, deserves to be memorialized in legends until he too, at least metaphorically, encounters what the founder confronted: primal chaos itself, grotesque in its formless horror, terrifying in its power to surge up from below and undermine the work of the gods themselves. In the stories told of the hero who overcomes it, chaos is always imagined as a monster opposed to being itself; as the primal origin of evil and deformity; the primordial, irrational fault in the heart of the world.[16] If we can imagine it only as degeneracy, deformity, decomposition, disintegration, that is because "it" is not anything positive at all but the terrible negating power of nothingness itself.

In order to engage in battle with this monstrous opponent, the founder has to be willing to look upon it in all its horror. The hero does not avert his gaze from it. Nor does he slay this monster out of terror, as if subject to a desperate compulsion to get rid of what horrifies him by driving it out of existence. For such a "heroism" would be only a disguised version of our ordinary desire to deal with what upsets us. The heroic founder is not

trying to protect his life at all because survival is not of primary importance to him. No portrait of him, in fact, could be more wrong than that
which attributes to him the kind of utilitarian mentality characteristic of
modernity: as if anything at all heroic could ever emerge from the will to
be in control. Habituated as we are to that mentality, it is difficult for us to
realize that primitive people, although much more vulnerable than we are
to mortal dangers, did not have as their primary purpose the drive to make
their existence secure. For them, as for the heroes they sought to emulate,
human life itself was a dreadful sacral drama in which one could fully participate by encountering death.[17] Heroes and their admirers, contemptuous of utilitarian prudence, seek out great deeds precisely on account of the mortal risks which they inevitably involve: for only one's
embrace of such risks proves one's greatness.

Consequently, when the founder slays the dragon, he does so neither to
protect himself against its threat to his survival nor because he wants to
guarantee that he will never again have to confront its horrifying visage.
He wills its defeat, certainly; but he loves more deeply and fundamentally
than such success the ordeal of battle itself, which alone can give his life
the stature that will make it worthy of being remembered in myth. But
this means that he wants his victory to become the occasion for new ordeals, with new enemies who are more terrible than those already slain;
for his greatness is directly proportional to the terrifying character of his
action. He does not engage his enemies in order to kill them. Rather, killing them happens to be the outcome of a life-and-death engagement in
which he participates for its own sake, because of its intrinsically
sublime character.

The festivals which commemorate such deeds are never simple
memorials in the modern sense; they are experienced as repetitions,
revolutions of the original events, so that these events are not viewed as
one-time occurrences which lie, inert and irretrievable, in the ever more
distant past. Indeed, it is thought that without their periodic reoccurrence,
the cosmos founded by heroic deeds would collapse and give way to the
threat of nothingness which never wholly loses its power to rupture.[18] The
ordinary citizens themselves would prefer, perhaps, the final security of a
cosmos definitively and permanently protected from such eruptions. But
the heroic founder would not. He wills not an eternal cosmos but an eternal repetition of the crisis of creation, an eternal repetition of disintegration and rebirth. And this repetition is no routine but the very opposite:
the repeated rupturing of every routine, the repeated destruction of
boundaries, the repeated necessity of recreating them.[19] More fundamental than either cosmos or chaos, creation or deformity, being or nothing-

ness, is the eternal process of their interplay, which is also strife; their an-
tagonism, which is also a dance.

Neither the heroic warrior nor the heroic founder is close enough to us
in our modernity to serve us as a seminal figure of the heroic mode. The
closest we come to such a figure in our culture is the artist or intellectual
who, like Nietzsche himself, leaves the ordinary world behind in order to
achieve something great by engaging in a life-and-death struggle with
powers that are all the more terrible for being invisible. For such spiritual
heroes too, the worst sin is to rest on one's laurels, as Nietzsche took pains
to make clear.[20] For satisfaction with one's accomplishments suggests that
creativity has not so much spent itself as it has succumbed to the luxury of
self-pity or self-congratulation in order to exempt itself from the up-
heaval of a new beginning. Once he has succumbed to this betrayal of
himself, the creator can produce only self-parodies. The alternative is
never to take praise seriously, especially the praise one offers oneself.
Only then can one create an art that is always ready to move beyond itself
even in its moments of greatest achievement, an art that glories in
repudiating what it has accomplished so that it can begin again, without
weariness in the face of this "again," without complaint about the travail
of every beginning, indeed embracing precisely this eternal repetition of
its demands. For such a creator, a work of art is completed only in the
sense that it finally opens up to the artist demands that are more stringent
than those he has already met. Its birth marks the beginning of another
pregnancy, with its patient nurturing and ascetic self-discipline. Like the
founder, the creator who is true to his art never succumbs to infatuation
with his works because he binds himself in single-hearted obedience to
the creative process itself which the work of art, as a finished product,
congeals and fixates.

Of course, this should not be construed to mean that art, to be faithful
to itself, ought to obey no rules, constrict itself to no focus—as if pure en-
ergy, undirected and unabated, shooting off in every direction at once,
were capable of creating anything. Such a refusal of specific focus may ad-
vertise itself as the courage to live outside the security of all rules and inhibitions. But it could never result in anything but a squandering of
genius. The creator who is true to his art submits himself without reserve
to the narrowing specificity, the inhibiting concreteness, of the unique
work, even as he knows that, as soon as it nears completion, the creative
process will command a repudiation of it. The work of art gives the
creator the discipline of focus he needs if he is to prove his genius; but
genius proves its greatness only when it wills to begin again with a new
repudiation of its last achievement and a new obedience to another dis-

cipline. It will want to create masterpieces in order to make the act of repudiating them that much more difficult.

Let us now try to draw from these concrete images of the hero as warrior, founder, and artist, some more general reflections on the heroic mode that might be added to the observations made earlier. We might explore, first of all, the significance of the fact that the hero is willing to desert his accomplishments on behalf of a new possibility of heroism and its more compelling demands. What is this willingness if not a dreadful embrace of that crisis which seems somehow inseparable from time itself—time as the rupturing of the past by the eruption of something original? To consent to this fully would require that one will nothing less than an eternal repetition of time's original eruption; that one will to be reimmersed again and again in the throes of the primal venture of temporality itself; that one say yes to an eternity of time. But, of course, one cannot will this once and for all: to will this is to will undergoing, again and again, the crisis of willing it. And now we finally seem to have reached the most radical inversion of ordinary existence, or rather its radical conversion into the heroic: while the ordinary person wills above all to avoid crisis, the heroic self wills to undergo eternally the crisis of embracing it.

These last observations finally make plausible the traditional impulse to treat the hero as someone who belongs in the company of the gods. We can say that he belongs at least on their side, if not in their company, insofar as he lives in a transcendent world to which other men do not belong. The hero's deeds always exceed our predictions, not because the predictions forecast inaccurately but because, even when accurate, they do not enable us to anticipate the literally fabulous quality of the heroic manner, the way this manner overshadows the deed itself, however extraordinary it is, so that when we come to tell of it we invent exaggerations and hyperboles to do it justice. Only a poet as heroic as the warrior whose deeds he celebrates can give language itself that quality of the marvelous which enables it to speak of what is epochal. Despite its flights of fancy, ordinary language is finally dumbfounded by this figure whose manner gives to even the small details of his acts a god-like proportion. None of his acts contain all of him because in none of them is he finally and completely present. Even his great deeds, left behind as soon as they are enacted, seem too small for us to use them as the measure of his greatness. The hero is god-like by virtue of the fact that he somehow overshadows his own achievements, and so remains concealed from us even in his most revealing actions. Hence his transcendence, his comradeship with those powers, sovereign, imperial, titanic, whose actions, no matter how revealing, never bring them down to our level. Just as the gods never fascinate us without at the same time evoking dread, the hero's deeds never prompt admiration in us without at the same time striking us dumb. Both gods and heroes, located above, behind, underneath ordinary existence, present an opposing and imposing sovereignty in the presence of which we tremble and from which we ordinarily recoil.

And yet, the hero is himself mortal, and his very heroism consists in acknowledging this. Because he is mortal, the hero is not identical with that power behind and above all beings to whose sovereignty everything, even heroes themselves, must finally submit. Although he acquires a stature, a height, that is comparable to that of the gods, he is, like the gods themselves but much more poignantly than they, subject to the disdainful ordinances of Fate, the plaything of that power which even the gods obey. Men and gods are born, die and perhaps are born again; but the power governing these vicissitudes submits to nothing. Men and gods alike are never more than the reflections or ephemeral manifestations of Fate's transcendent power. The hero is heroic precisely because he is not intimidated from doing great deeds by his knowledge that his very greatness pales in the face of the Fate which governs everything. Sovereign and insignificant, creator and plaything, the hero knows he is both the hero who incarnates Fate and the servant who does its bidding. As warrior, founder, artist, he presides over the interplay of life and death, being and nothingness, order and chaos; as mortal, he is himself subject to this interplay which is Fate itself playing out its awful game.

5. Heroism and Modernity

It is not hard to explain why it is especially difficult for us as moderns to understand this whole heroic mode of being. Modern life is in its very essence antiheroic insofar as it fosters in us a Promethean desire for total control over life so that we will never be required to suffer a devastating ordeal. Given such incongruity between the heroic mode and the modern mentality, it is hardly surprising that, when the modern mind turns to interpreting the heroic, its aim is to debunk, i.e. to puncture the naive illusion that there have been men who were willing to embrace the very realities which our culture specializes in avoiding.[21] The debunker proceeds on the cynical suspicion that some pettiness is to be found underneath all heroic motives: he is eager to convince us that all heroes are covert utilitarians not essentially different from ourselves. One reason such suspicions are plausible to us is that in our ordinary lives, perfected as they have been by modernist techniques, we encounter nothing awe-full enough to make heroism even possible. We think we can not only explain but control those events which, in our view, caused man a fear so fearful that he renamed it awe in his desperate attempt to get a handle on it.

But it is this same modernity that, liberated from beliefs it considers naive, permits the adulation of dictators whose feats grotesquely parody heroic deeds. It almost seems as if man cannot bear to live in a world from which the awe-full has been entirely abolished; when forced to do so, modern man has had to invent a substitute for the gods he has lost. Thus we find ourselves drawn, with a kind of compelling fascination, to anything that is gigantic, to rallies and monuments that have been designed to induce sensations of fright and therapeutic amazement. No matter how artificially they are engineered, such inducements work on us all too often. Having forgotten everything sublime, modernity invents the gargantuan. Gods and heroes once possessed presiding power by virtue of a dignity too profound for self-display; the void left by their absence easily becomes a stage for spectacles of self-importance. Such rites can provide the introit to a cult of sadism, with its shameless cruelty and deliberate violences. The individuals who participate in such cults, different as we might like to think they are from ourselves, are only acting out the logical conclusions that follow from the basic premises of the culture of control. What remains to us in our ordinariness, once we have rid ourselves of everything awe-full, except to idolize ourselves and play out each and every one of our small cruelties? The spirit of pettiness always leads to the worship of the gigantic because the gigantic is nothing but an exaggerated version of itself. The sadist measures his heroism by the number of his innocent and defenseless victims.[22]

So it is almost impossible for us, as moderns, to imagine the heroic except in myths now dead, museum pieces, artifacts of an extinct world, retrievable only as dreams are retrieved, wistfully, romantically, so that, if they fascinate us, it is only because they have lost their power to upset us. Our way of appreciating the mythical and the heroic is, generally, a subtle way of emptying them of the devastating impact they would have if we allowed them to undermine our avoidances. We handle myths like relics, out of a self-conscious respect for their "aesthetic-religious value," not because they evoke in us any sense of fear and trembling.

And yet, in spite of all this, in spite of the success which the culture of control has had in influencing every dimension of human life, does not heroism remain possible? How can the heroic be dependent on a particular age in history when what makes an individual heroic is precisely his willingness to leave behind the ordinary world into which he was born? One can be heroic anywhere, anytime, even and perhaps especially in an age which is determined to suffocate all opportunities for heroism. Even we who only read and write, who engage in no other enterprise except thinking itself, are offered with every sentence the opportunity for participating in a heroic ordeal, as playful as a child's game and as serious as warfare. For the process of thinking itself requires that the one engaged in it follow his line of thought no matter how demanding the ordeal into which it leads; it requires him to call into question those basic assumptions on which his world as a whole depends. The crucible of radical questioning, the travail of dialectic, upsets every thesis, however secure and irrefutable it seems. The thinker as hero would want every one of his thoughts to be consumed by the strife of thinking itself, which both fathers and destroys.

It is only our small-mindedness that makes us think we lack the opportunity for enacting deeds which are worthy of being remembered. Heroes never blame their times. They know it is their own fault if they have failed to do something great. They stand outside, above, their age. There is no such thing as a timely hero; the times will last, will be worth remembering, only if they have been radically ruptured by heroic deeds which are of their very nature untimely. One of the characteristics of modernity is our thinking that no one born into it can escape the modern condition. The first thing heroes always do is escape their times. Modernity is not an age without heroes: it is the age which, more than any other, insists on being oblivious of those who, once in it, stand now outside it, in the presence of those awful realities which modernity has successfully repressed.

6. Tragic Avoidance

What remains unthought in these thoughts on the heroic manner? Having developed this portrait of the heroic mode of being, I would like to ask if the hero, as I have portrayed him, is the paradigm of what it means to be open to crisis. The hero embraces eagerly the very realities we ordinarily avoid; he belittles his own achievements and laughs at his own virtues, lest they tempt him to congratulate himself; he longs for enemies great enough to put him through a devastating ordeal. In such heroism can there possibly be any element of the unheroic?

We would never find the hero cowering behind barriers. He is not afraid of wounds, or of death itself. Indeed, in his eyes the possibility of dying is not a horror to be avoided but an honor to be embraced. Death respects him enough to demand of him not less than everything—everything, that is, except his honor, which dying gives him the opportunity to demonstrate in a definitive way. For it is, in fact, by meeting the threat to his dignity which the ordeal of dying poses that he proves his heroic stature. But death is then, for just that reason, the hero's best and indispensable enemy, the enemy from which one must not recoil in humiliating avoidance. By embracing the ordeal of dying the hero insures in a definitive way that he will not lose the one thing that nothing in the world, not even death itself, can make him let go of: his own heroic character.

So as long as he does not humiliate himself, the hero will die intact, in possession of an untainted integrity. The one thing he must not do is die in a demeaning way. Because he has a body, he cannot help but be subject to the vicissitudes of the flesh, with its inclination to tremble and bleed, its liability to incontinence. But he should not let the painfully embarrassing details of his last disease belittle him. Just as the hero needs no help in finding occasions for his heroism, he is always able to transform his death room, wherever it is, into a battlefield. Infinitely worse than any death is the shame of allowing oneself to be demeaned by it. By maintaining one's honor, one outwits death's sarcasm, its derisive smile, its triumph.

When it comes to dying, demeanor is everything. Only the expression of the death face decides what final manner of man one is. The heroic demeanor of which we have been speaking is not to be confused with the false dignity of those who conceal their fear even from themselves under suave self-control and an aristocratic bearing. Such a person keeps up an exaggerated appearance of imperturbability, perhaps all the way to the moment of death, and this stoic persistence, this fidelity to form, to a highly cultured etiquette of self-respect, might convince us that he possesses a dignity which even dying cannot puncture. But, in fact, this "aristocrat" maintains appearances because appearances are what he desperately needs; his overt obedience to the etiquette of self-respect provides him the only evidence he has of his courage. He needs it to convince not only others but himself of his stature. His eye for all the details of his outward dignity proves he is hiding his weaknesses from himself. This kind of pride disguises an inner lack of character; this kind of imperturbability before death only camouflages a secret terror of it. The dying hero, on the other hand, does not need to follow the rules of anyone else's etiquette; he is too heroic to have to be intent on seeming so: he seems so because he is. His courage, quiet and unpretentious as courage always is in its encounter with the dreadful, outwits death's tendency to belittle him by treating it as a beloved enemy.

But now that we have kept him distinct from those who plagiarize dignity instead of possessing it, we still need to examine more carefully the hero's motive for winning this battle for his honor. Heroism cannot, of course, simply be a synonym for being on the winning side. Winners can be cowards blessed by fortune. But to be a hero on the losing side always requires the refusal to be broken by one's defeat. One is heroic only if one has the power to convert even the most humiliating circumstances into an occasion for heroic action.

Now it is just this heroic refusal to be broken that we have not yet adequately explored. We have seen how the heroic individual who takes such pride in his willingness to embrace crisis, not avoid it, is determined to prove himself equal to even the most demanding ordeal. But what about the ordeal of having to acknowledge one's inferiority? How would the hero we have been describing fare if he were required, for some reason, to be ashamed of himself? This would not be just another crisis whose demands are to be embraced like others in the past; for to embrace this crisis he would have to be willing to give up in some profound sense his heroic stature itself. For were he to open himself to the experience of shame, he would have to allow the very pride with which he has always entered into crisis to be mortified. The ordeal of being mortified is, I would suggest, the one ordeal which the heroic individual cannot bear to suffer, because it undermines the one thing which means more to him than everything and which he has not yet let go of—the stature he has acquired by virtue of being heroic. Confronted by a situation which requires that he be ashamed of himself, the heroic individual must choose between recoiling from this ordeal or undergoing the one form of suffering which up to now he has avoided: the experience of humiliation. If from now on we concentrate on this dilemma, it is because it helps us to see that there is, after all, one place in the heart that even the greatest heroes try to shield, one secret weakness which they try to cover up and keep invulnerable.

We should not be surprised by this dilemma since it only makes explicit suspicions which have threatened to emerge throughout our exegesis of the heroic character. How can a human being devote himself so unreservedly to the heroic ideal without recoiling in horror from any experience of shame? The one thing the person aspiring to greatness cannot bear to suffer is a humiliating realization of his own smallness. We have spoken all along of the pride with which the heroic individual refuses to glory in his past accomplishments and of how different such pride is from the hollow pretensions of ordinary vanity. But perhaps from the point of view of a humility whose depths we have not yet plumbed, pride differs from ordinary vanity only in the sense that it is a tragically ironic version of it.

An example might help us to appreciate the import of such an ironic reversal. We might imagine a commander who, in his eagerness for the heroic ordeal of battle, has eschewed whatever scruples he may have about the real necessity of fighting it; he has come to think of war primarily as an occasion for the exercise of his heroic virtues. But let us say that, after having proved himself equal to the demands of battle, and giving words of ecouragement to his wounded soldiers, this heroic commander feels momentarily aghast at the sight of the tremendous slaughter caused by his heroic venture. Perhaps for one moment in the face of such destruction of human life, he feels an unexpected and inexplicable sense of uneasiness at the thought that perhaps the lives of so many men matter more than the exercise of heroic virtue for its own sake. Let us say that during that brief moment he has a sudden glimpse of the possibility that there might be some enormous evil at work in his life, the existence of which he never before suspected. Although he does his best to dismiss this horrifying intimation, the eyes of the dead do not close; even when he turns away so as to avoid meeting them, they keep staring at him as if they have been charged with conveying to him some terrible, wordless message. He recoils from those stares but is he heroic for doing so—for defending his heroic action from this intimation that there was something morally horrifying about it? The hero can afford to be ashamed of nothing except the experience of shame itself, if he intends to keep his greatness intact. But in repressing the intimations of shame, the heroic individual avoids something instead of facing it. Should he be honored for doing so or is this his one unheroism?

To answer this question, we must try to understand what would happen to the heroic mode of being if the heroic individual were to follow these intimations into the humiliating reversal which shame apparently requires him to undergo. Perhaps we should begin by noting how intimately we connect the feeling of shame with the act of turning away from whatever it is that evokes this feeling in us. It is not just the heroic individual but all of us who feel this almost instinctual compulsion. By what deep motive are we governed in such moments? Exactly toward what and from what does shame make us turn?

It seems to me there is something profoundly self-defensive about this moral recoil, just as there is something defensive and self-protective in the instinctual recoil from physical danger. It is not my literal existence which feels threatened but my moral integrity. The feeling of shame makes me want to disassociate myself completely from the thing that awakens it; it makes me want to cleanse myself, as if the very fact that I have this feeling of shame is itself a proof that I have been infected by a contagious and potentially fatal disease. This disease affects me much more intimately than any biological virus; for even the briefest exposure to it can begin to undermine my sense of self-worth. In pulling back and turning away from what makes me feel ashamed, I am trying to prevent my whole image of myself from being shattered. And what would prompt such a recoil? What I draw away from in the experience of shame is the sense of being implicated in something horrifying, something that makes my stomach turn, something evil. Shame is, put quite simply, the feeling of being a participant in something wrong. The physical gesture of turning away embodies my revulsion from something which has the capacity to devastate my being as a whole. Proximity to evil is unbearable precisely because it makes me realize that I myself will become evil if I embrace it. And if, in turning away from it, the first thing I do is close my eyes, that is because I don't want to see what they reveal to me; I don't want to know the full meaning of my horrifying intimation. The intimation alone is enough.

But if what shame tells us about ourselves is true, we will not be able to get away from evil, no matter how quickly we pull back from it. In the example described above, the stares of the dead only serve to remind the heroic individual of a defiling evil that has already found a haven within himself. It is therefore not enough to say that, in experiencing shame, his inmost self feels compelled to turn away from something repulsive: we also have to say that his inmost self is itself the repulsive thing from which he is recoiling. Shame is precisely this experience of feeling compelled to turn away from one's own repulsiveness. I feel as though I will get sick to my stomach if I do not look away quickly enough.

Now the heroic individual, as we have described him, is willing to leave behind everything we ordinarily hold onto; is willing to embrace the most upsetting ordeals, even to the point of death itself; but what enables him to risk everything is precisely his knowing that in doing so he keeps his heroic integrity intact. No human being has as much to lose from an experience of shame as the heroic individual. And now at last we begin to glimpse the impossible dilemma he faces, and why the experience of shame, no matter how he responds to it, must inevitably lead to a radical undoing of the whole heroic ideal. For either he recoils from the recognition of his own evil which shame has begun to evoke from him, in which case he is avoiding what would be for him, more than for anyone else, an upsetting experience; or he will open himself to the truths that lie in wait for him inside the experience of shame, in which case his heroic image of himself will be shattered. For the truth that is buried, like a deadly poison, at the bottom of his shame is that it would have been better for him never to have been born. What would be left of the heroic individual if he looked that truth in the face and did not turn away from it? What could remain except a desire to commit suicide?

We imagined above a warrior momentarily aghast at the evil brought about by his heroic deeds. History provides us, in the case of Ignatius Loyola,[23] an actual example of a soldier whose heroic self-image was shattered by just such a recognition. One can imagine Ignatius, recovering at Manresa from his wounds, fighting day after day against realizations that are trying to cut their way through his conviction that he has lived heroically. At the culminating moment of this ordeal, he covers his face with his hands, overcome with horror at the thought of what his deeds have wrought. None of the pride he used to take in those deeds is left uninfected by the sense of nausea that the recognition of his own evil now evokes from him. His whole being shudders with an abject, inconsolable sorrow. And implicit in such wordless grief is the confession of a double humiliation: his own unimportance in comparison with the importance of the lives he took in pursuing his heroic ideal, and the evil of his whole way of living insofar as it was based on the presumption of his own heroic importance. Shame melts down all the great deeds of his life and proves that they were made of the basest metals.

Precisely because shame would lead him to such an abject state, the hero ordinarily tries to silence its accusations. Instead of allowing shame to wring from him such a humiliating confession, he does his best to dismiss the experience of shame with disdain. He is too used to thinking that his only obligation is to live by the heroic ideal to give any suspicions he may have about his own character the time they would need to fester. He does not take seriously the possibility that there might be something in him of which he ought to be ashamed. But if the hero finds nothing in himself of which he ought to be ashamed, that is not because he commits none of the shameful deeds that are proscribed by the moral order. It is because, in his heart of hearts, he does not believe there is anything for which he needs to be ashamed as long as he never betrays his own greatness. The only thing from which he would recoil shamefacedly would be the fear of violating the moral rules considered binding by those who lack his sense of greatness. The only "ought" he acknowledges is that he ought to be great; indeed, he would in principle be willing to disobey any "ought" if required to do so by an ordeal that had made a claim on his heroism.[24] The hero's sense of heroic decorum is not offended by the violation of moral prohibitions but by the petty ambivalence of the ordinary person's disobedience, his need to resort to self-deception and rationalization. The hero disdains such tactics and does not need them to silence shame's accusations. For he treats such shame as something that has no right to belittle him.

The hero sees his resistance to shame as a defense of the rights of heroism itself. He condemns it as an assault by the ordinary, an effort on the part of the resentful to pull him down to their own level. He eschews shame because he sees it trying to seduce him into being a coward, into being afraid of great deeds because ordinary men resent some of their consequences. Why, he asks, should he be inhibited by the same scruples as those who are afraid of what he embraces?

But I think we have seen that shame is no coward's refuge. It is cowardly to exercise the will to control because one does so out of an unwillingness to experience any reality which threatens to disrupt one's existence radically. But as we have seen, shame promises precisely such a disruption of the hero's life by confronting him with a reality that will shatter the heroic self-image which matters more to him than life itself. To have one's heroic sense of oneself radically undermined is itself the most radical experience of death which the heroic individual could possibly suffer. But it is precisely this supreme ordeal which his attachment to his own heroic self-image causes him to avoid rather than embrace. In that one act of avoidance, he imitates the cowardice of the ordinary will to control, even though what he seeks to protect is his very heroism. Far from being a characteristic of the small-minded, the willingness to suffer shame requires an openness to humiliation which even the heroic individual is unwilling to risk. Nietzsche, in his defense of the heroic mode of being, made one crucial mistake that Ignatius did not make. When he saw that the experience of shame and humiliation caused one to feel small and insignificant, he concluded that such an experience was incompatible with being heroic. What he did not realize is that the experience of being put in a humiliating position is the one ordeal the hero is desperate to avoid because it upsets his most personal sense of self-importance. This ordeal does not lie behind heroism in the geography of crisis for it is not part of the ordinary life which the heroic individual rightly disdains; rather, it lies in front of the hero, across trackless wastes which he does not yet have the courage to traverse. To be unable to bear insights into one's own diminutive stature, insights which promise to deprive one of the sense of one's own importance, may be the only fault, the only frailty, in the heroic character; but it is the crucial fault by which heroism betrays everything it has achieved. The underside of the hero's courage is his terror in the face of what shame might reveal to him. Indeed, we must conclude that, if the hero were truly great, if he were truly willing to suffer an ordeal even more demanding than those already experienced, he would be willing to suffer a crisis which demands the sacrifice of his very greatness to something greater and more deserving than himself. The experience of shame starts one on the road to that sacrifice. Failing to pursue the disruption it would cause, the hero falls back into the comparative ease of repeating over and over the kind of heroic deeds he has already performed. The heroic individual becomes tragically ordinary when he is unwilling to undergo his own undoing.

So when it is said that even in defeat the hero remains unbroken, this really means that he cannot bear to let shame disrupt his sense of his own heroic stature. His defeat represents a humiliating loss; it suggests weakness, emasculation. It insinuates that the one defeated deserved, from the beginning, to be brought down from his extraordinary position. The will to be heroic can always bear defeat but it is unwilling to be open to the nub of truth contained in such humiliating insinuations. Were defeat's insult to his pride to worm its way into his heart, and finally open his eyes to some deep inadequacy within himself, the heroic individual would become, in the eyes of his former followers and comrades, a shell of his former self; once larger than life, he would seem impotent and dispirited, without ambition or passion, as if something had drained him of all his fierce enthusiasms. The dignity with which he might still carry himself would nevertheless look like a soiled remnant of heroism, not its substance. But it is to this broken figure, strong enough to be vulnerable to the experience of humiliation, that we must turn if we are to find someone undergoing the ordeal which even the hero wills not to suffer. Were the warrior in our example to let shame rob him of his heroic demeanor, he would end up being ridiculed by those who used to try to emulate his heroic example. Our argument is that only by being open to such ridicule can he begin to practice the kind of heroism that is accessible only to those who know what it feels like to be ridiculous. The hero without this humiliation remains, however extraordinary his ordeals, on the ordinary side of the most upsetting kind of crisis.

Without the willingness to undergo that crisis, the very heroism of the heroic will is its tragic flaw; one need not search the hero's character for a more specific, definable fault, as if the hero lacked a particular item or items in the inventory of human virtues. His fault is always his wanting to recoil from the experience of being belittled, and this recoil is no single piece of his character but the hidden side of his heroic character as a whole. The will to be as contemptuous of the ordinary as are the gods, to be infinitely hard on one's self, never to need or use excuses, to have no superior in willpower—all this is also the will to avoid any intimations of humiliating smallness, because smallness is, from the heroic point of view, the only wound that mortifies. The hero's very ascent toward the gods is his flight from mortification. The hubris in hubris is not so much its pride as its refusal of shame. And because it is the underside of the hero's very heroism, there can be no remedy for this fault which does not leave him mortally humiliated and broken, his greatness spent, his ideal of heroism shattered. Is there something ultimately tragic about such a fall? Or is the only real tragedy the one that occurs when such a fall does not happen? Tragedy in the real sense happens when a great man is unwilling to fall down because he finds it too devastating to be in an abject position. What is finally tragic is the heroic mode of being itself as an ideal for human life. We miss the main lesson of its irony unless we realize that the fault which always causes the hero's fall is precisely this being afraid to fall down. He lacks none of the greatness needed to be great: what he lacks is the greatness needed to become small.

We would be mistaken if we thought that the hero who does allow himself to be broken is finally one of us. His fall does not bring him closer to us in our avoidances. His courage to fall enables him to plumb depths whose very existence we suspect only in our most devastating moments. It is toward those depths that we now turn.

CHAPTER FIVE

Vicissitudes of Shame

We began this geography with a map of our everyday routines, as they are practiced inside the boundaries watched over and guarded by the will to control. Ordinarily, we are terrified of intruders. And yet, paradoxically, whatever serenity we have comes from our willingness to suffer, our willingness to risk being generous. Under its impulse, we relax our securities and let in strangers, so that our once empty house comes alive with the noise of hospitality. The generous person cannot imagine himself being unpleasant. And yet there are brooding powers which remain outside in the unexplored territory he can only enter by leaving the ordinary world behind. Even if we decide to remain inside the boundaries of that world, we will always be haunted by those brooding powers, once we have received intimations of their existence. The only alternative is more dangerous than welcoming the worst of strangers: to leave our ordinary world and venture into a realm presided over by powers over which we have no control. But by virtue of our very willingness to confront these realities, we can come to feel at home in this geography of the heroic, with its heights and abysses, its severe and pitiless peaks, its sudden cataracts of dread. This geography is the home of the gods and their companions. Among its underground tunnels is one that leads straight down, through the clogged veins of the earth, to the dark abscess of shame at the heart of the world. One cannot be heroic if one is unwilling to undergo the desolate kind of suffering that a journey in that direction requires. This is no high adventure but a lowly, demeaning trudge, a pilgrimage into humiliation. Here is no new stage in the dialectic of crisis; here is the horror of which all stages are stations of avoidance.

In trying to describe the experience of this horror, I find myself drawn to the image of a fall, of our being pulled down by a weight that is inexorable and too heavy to be borne, not a weight that has been arbitrarily foisted upon us but one that we have unwittingly imposed on ourselves. Attached as we are to being in control, we are desperate to believe we can do something to break that fall; but once it begins, we are powerless to prevent it. For this weight within us, inexorable as gravity, is not literally a physical force. Even if it used all its power, the material world would never be able to break a human being's heroic spirit. The weight which makes us fall so inexorably is the weight of a moral horror whose gravity is beyond all measure. Even a brief intimation of such horror is sufficient to evoke a feeling of nausea and vertigo. What happens to us when we allow such intimations to draw us over the edge instead of recoiling from them?

Shame and the Discovery of Moral Order

The person who is overcome with shame for something he has done has begun to take the moral order and his relationship to it seriously. In taking shame so much to heart, such a person is, in fact, submitting his life as a whole to a moral judgment. Generally, we might say that, in order for shame to get through to a person, it must persuade him to take the worth of something Other than himself so seriously that the wrong of not reverencing it becomes devastating.[1] Whether one's irreverence takes the form of ordinary vanity or heroic violence, one can gain no access to the moral order except through shame's abject grief on behalf of a reality one has violated. In short, shame creates conscience.

At first glance, this claim seems to be an exaggeration. Why is personal humiliation the only way of access to a moral awakening? We seem to be arguing that a human being inevitably does evil before realizing he ought not to do it. Does not logic itself require us to say the converse—that shame presupposes moral sensitivity and is only aroused by its violation? If so, we should have discussed the experience of shame long before now as a crisis which disrupts our ordinary sense of being morally upright. And perhaps then we would also have been led to talk about the even more profound experience of crisis which occurs when we lose our moral bearings, when we have a crisis of faith in the moral order which, until then, guided us through life's vicissitudes.

But these objections make certain assumptions of their own which, from the beginning of this essay, I have been trying to question. Where do we get conscience in the first place? When and how do we get the ordinary moral sensitivity which the feeling of shame supposedly disrupts? The views expressed above presuppose that *being moral is a natural dimension of our ordinary lives* and that a crisis is required to dislodge us from this condition. It would be flattering to think this the case—and that alone should make us suspicious. Indeed, what makes this view doubtful is its very lack of suspicion with regard to our everyday lives, the fact that it takes at face value the compliments we pay ourselves about our moral stature. Ordinarily, we have few doubts about our own integrity.

But a brief reflection on the very nature of the moral order itself should be sufficient to make us suspicious of this self-congratulatory point of view. A moral order is a set of "oughts" or commands one of whose functions is to inhibit behavior, to forbid certain practices. As such, the moral order is always impractical in the sense that it bars us from doing acts which in certain circumstances we might find practically beneficial. To be uninhibited by any such "oughts" means that we would feel entitled to do anything, to act out whatever preference happens to take precedence at the moment. Nothing possessing normative import would then infringe upon the free interplay of the world and our desires. We would do whatever we wanted. But that, I would suggest, is exactly what the will to control naturally prefers—to have no inhibitions disrupting the efficient practice of its wishes. The moral order always confronts me with some Other beyond my self, on behalf of which I must give up getting my own way. For me to be subject to a moral order means that my willing to get what I want is subjected to the *disruptive interference* of certain "oughts." On the other hand, if I am free from the interdicts of any moral order, I am entitled to want my own way without such disruption. All of these facts force us to conclude that the very existence of the moral order as such is a disruption for us insofar as it confronts us with an "ought" other than our own preferences. It is, of course, possible to argue that we do not usually want to get our own way and that therefore there is no need for us to experience "oughts" as disruptive. But one fact makes it difficult to take this last claim seriously: the very fact that we want to avoid crisis because crisis disrupts the way we prefer our lives to be.

But if we are to avoid the upsetting experiences that would be caused by the interruption of our lives by moral order, we must not let shame start to gnaw at us. We do not find it difficult to learn how to protect ourselves from its subtle insinuations, how to dismiss them as the vestiges of childhood, when we were compelled to be inferior to some adult's authority. Adults now ourselves, we feel entitled to be our own authority and so not to be ashamed of anything we do, as long as it is in accord with whatever set of "values" we have adopted for ourselves. "Values" understood in this way are only another way of referring to what we want. In fact, we speak of our wants as values precisely when we are trying to emphasize that, as self-governing agents, we are entitled to determine for ourselves what worth to assign things.

Because we usually operate in this manner, discovering the moral order is itself a crisis experience which ruptures the uninhibited practice of our will to control. We do not become moral except by encountering a reality which deserves to be approached with reverence. But ordinarily, we avoid every such Other, precisely because of the crisis which its interruption of our lives would provoke. Generally, we do not want to have a moral compass for directing our lives since its interdicts would require, at every step, a detour from the way we want to go. Strictly speaking, it makes no sense to say that an individual undergoes a crisis when he loses the moral compass that has been governing him. For far from occasioning a crisis, such a loss would let him return to the practice of going wherever he wanted, as he did before the moral order started to block his way.[2] The "crisis" of losing one's moral compass is, in fact, the refusal to suffer any longer the criticism, the crisis, to which a moral compass always subjects one's will to be in control of one's own life. Moreover, if I ordinarily avoid those realities that are deserving of my reverence, the eventual acknowledgment of such realities must inevitably take the form of being overcome by shame: for it must involve my humiliating contrition for all my previous avoidances. Being moral begins with this first contrition. Shame before the Others I have violated is the real start of my fidelity to the "ought." Contrariwise, I protect myself from such shame because I want to keep free of the "oughts" I would have to begin obeying if I took it seriously.

The feeling of shame, which we have not fully thematized until now, has to some degree made its haunting presence felt throughout all our discussions, ever since we saw the first slight cleft in the will to control. For if I offer an Other the least acknowledgment of its existence, the most grudging politeness, the smallest generosity, have I not already been touched, though I am barely conscious of it, by shame's painful insinuations? We try our best to keep it underground and to pay off its debt in silence. But every time we break through our avoidances, we are drawn closer and closer to the chamber where this secret is kept, until at last all else is silenced except the echo and reecho of its reproaches. The cartography of crisis is also, at every stage, the sonography of shame. If we are to sound its depths, we have to understand how it radically alters our whole understanding of good and evil and thus leads us radically to reassess our whole way of living.

2. Crisis and the Revisioning of Good and Evil

When we operate on the basis of the will to control, we are aware of only one kind of "evil": the failure of existence to conform to the plan we have for it. From this point of view, a being has worth only insofar as it performs some instrumental function for me. I experience a being as evil whenever it stands over against me, insisting on its Otherness. Seen from this point of view, evil occurs in its most radical form when a crisis upsets my whole way of living at the most fundamental level. It is important to notice that when we define good and evil in these terms, we cannot possibly conceive of *ourselves* as evil. For from such a vantage point, evil is, by definition, that which runs counter to our wills. By taking the view that the goodness of a being depends on its measuring up to my criteria of what it ought to be, I put myself in the position of being the one who sets up criteria, not the one who has to measure up to them. That is why, when operating on the basis of the will to control, we are incapable of shame. In fact, we feel offended when existence fails to conform to our expectations. We might think here, for instance, of our impatience in traffic jams, our rage when required to wait in lines, our anger in the face of petty interruptions. Ordinarily we are not just unashamed of but unaware of the self-centeredness at work in such situations. Such self-centeredness does not result from our lacking any awareness of good and evil. It comes from the presumption that makes us feel entitled to define the good in terms of our own conception of how we want our lives to go. The will to control takes its own importance for granted; when I see things in this way, I have no inkling that "good" could possibly mean anything except the yielding of the world to my plan for it. That is why we feel perfectly innocent in having extravagant expectations about our lives: we take it for granted that reality would be in the wrong if it failed to live up to them.

Now, in experiencing a crisis, I sense that I am losing control of my life, that I am falling into a void, from whose darkness and emptiness I can foresee no relief. I experience crisis as horrific insofar as it uproots me from a world where I have control. But if I allow this uprooting to happen, I begin to confront what I ordinarily would avoid; and in so doing, I consent to the demands of crisis and acknowledge for the first time its claim on my being, the fact that I *ought* to undergo it, instead of avoiding it. Thus the crisis experience is precisely the process of my discovering a reality Other than my self that deserves my acknowledgment: it is my will's discovery of a good Other than the good of getting my own way. This is why all crisis, by its very nature, constitutes nothing less than the initiation of a moral relationship with whatever it is that, heretofore avoided, now prompts the crisis by obliging one to acknowledge its claims. It is not just that moral awakening is a crisis experience. A crisis experience is, by its very nature, a moral awakening. It must be experienced as a loss, a fall, a horrific undoing, but that is because it is the revolutionary appropriation of one's will to control by an Other one ought to recognize. The horror of being devastated is also the breakthrough by virtue of which one acknowledges a reality Other than and external to oneself. Usually unaware of our presumptions, we begin to become moral at the very moment we begin to suffer in any way, to any degree. But no suffering is complete, no crisis reaches its culminating depth, until we finally suffer shame, i.e. until we finally experience our guilt for having lived a life of avoidance. The experience of shame and moral awakening is not simply one possible example of crisis into which we might be plunged: it is the experience that brings crisis to its culminating point. For in shame we acknowledge for the first time the violence done by all our avoidances to that Other which even now we would prefer, for our own sake, to keep avoiding. When we really recognize the Other, we bow before it as its penitent. Only so, in this posture, do we reverse the will to control and thus complete the crisis that started when our control was undermined. Shame is not just a version of suffering: suffering becomes most perfectly itself when, at the end of its road, it becomes shame explicitly.

Thus, we begin to recognize how radically misleading are our ordinary diagrams of what might be called the chronology of the moral life. We would like to think that we are generally obedient to moral imperatives and that it is only after the occasional violation of them that we are required to be ashamed. But it is the presumption of the will to control that makes us think ourselves innocent in our ordinariness. In fact, the reason we do not usually experience guilt is because we avoid those realities the acknowledgment of which would evoke it. Only in the crisis precipitated by discovering their existence do we begin to have an inkling of the "oughts" we usually violate. And only when bowed in shame before them do we acquire, for the first time, something like an appropriate moral rapport with them. The experience of shame is no makeshift compromise between ordinary innocence and the occasional act of evil-doing. Shame is the radical exception to our ordinary evil. Shame is something like our becoming innocent.

Only under the impact of such shame is our usual definition of evil radically transformed. Ordinarily, it means what is contrary to my will. Shame punctures precisely this presumption when it confronts me with a reality Other than myself which I have violated with avoidance. It wrings from me the acknowledgment that the locus of evil is I myself. But it is not enough to say I now recognize my evil, as if I simply acknowledge something I had previously denied. Rather, what has happened is that my whole understanding of evil has been radically altered. Shame signifies my discovery of moral evil as such, my realizing that I have been wronging the world all the while that I was accusing it of disappointing me. Evil, I now realize, is not equatable with events which upset me; rather, evil consists in my not allowing such upsetting experiences to happen. The intruding Other is no evil but a reality worthy of reverence; my resentment of its intrusion as if it were evil is the real evil for which I ought to be ashamed. That, briefly put, is the conversion shame persuades one to suffer.

The doing of evil is not itself a crisis experience. The evil will is, by virtue of its very evil, not upset by even its worst deeds. Doing wrong is always painless: for it is the will insisting on its own way and determined not to suffer. On the other hand, where there is suffering, it can only be because the habit of the will to control has been wounded with at least one irritating splinter of generosity. The most radical form of generosity is the kind required if I am to open myself, without any protective devices, to the anguish of shame. The latter is the purifying demand at the heart of crisis. The great paradox of the moral life is that only those who undergo the most profound experience of shame are capable of being profoundly good. The more profound my awareness of evil, the more tormenting my shame, the more piercing is my perception of the moral order.[3] Thus, if we are to continue following the path which crisis opens up in our lives, we must now try to track the unfolding consciousness of shame, the ever deeper, more penetrating awareness of evil which it evokes in us.

3. Our Identity with Evil

If it is true that our moral life really begins with our shameful recognition that we have failed to live it, it must awaken in us a sense that we are already given over to evil, already in some profound sense in fellowship with it. By the time I discover what moral evil is, my bond with it is habitual; we are bound together in the kinship of vice. Everything that has been said previously in this essay suggests that, for all of us, the one vice that underlines and includes all others is the will to control. We are expert practitioners of it long before we are aware of its moral significance; it is so close to us as to seem our very selves. Does this mean that we have not just done evil but that in some radical sense we have *become* it?

Once vice takes possession of us, its demands become as urgent as instinct, and it makes us feel that we have no recourse from its claims. Too deeply ingrained in us to be distinguishable from ourselves, it governs our conscious intentions. We are, in a real sense, the victims, even the slaves, of our own characters, even though character begins as the deposit of individual acts. We get caught in an undertow that we ourselves set in motion. How can we effectively resist the momentum of evil when the willpower we would need to do so has already been undermined by our vices? We don't feel that we have enough strength to hold out against them. We are helplessly subject to the gravity of evil, once it is weighted with all the bad moments of our past.

But, even so, it seems that evil can be no more than our second nature. For no matter how deeply vice has become engraved, it never becomes first nature since it never wholly takes over our subjectivity. That is why we cannot wholly excuse ourselves as victims of our faults. Each of us is, in the final analysis, more a culprit than a victim because we never lose the power to disassociate ourselves from evil. To the same degree that I actively cooperate with my vice, it remains disownable. However often I have chosen evil in the past, I am never wholly transformed into it. Every choice I have to make gives me a new opportunity to break the bonds which my previous choices have forged. All the evil I have done can be undone so far as my commitment to it is concerned; my doing of it cannot cause me to *be* evil.

Plausible as the argument has made it seem, however, this last claim should give us pause. In emphasizing the revisability of choice, we are robbing it of its most personal, most intimate significance. For we have made it seem that our choices are *retractable*, and that they do not make any definitive mark on us. But if that were true, the story of our lives would be not just revisable but erasable; a choice would become weightless at the very moment we finished making it. As soon as it was past, its reality would evaporate. Were we to think of our choices as retractable and weightless, we would not hesitate to do evil, since we would know that we could always disown it at a later date. This point of view needs criticism not because death will at some point make some decision in fact final by cancelling consequent retractions, but because it deprives all our choices, even this last one, of any intrinsic gravity.

Choice does not create character in the sense that the latter follows the former as one of its consequences. Choice *is* character because in the act of choosing, I appropriate what I choose to myself. Once that appropriation is effected, I can do nothing to disassociate it from me. I will always be the person who embraced that act as my own. My having done so has indelibly colored the fabric of my character. Every choice, no matter how ephemeral it seems, leaves this unremovable deposit in us. The choices we have made do not remain within us as mere relics from the part of our lives that is already finished. In fact, by choosing an act and thus irrevocably appropriating it, I make it a part of the self I will bring to every future. For us humans, the past is not something that happened to us once and is now over and done with. For in every choice we made in the past, we appropriated that moment of the past into ourselves forever. Choice is therefore always both irrevocable and unretractable, even though it is in some sense revisable. In every choice I engrave something in my self in a definitive way. We must not stop short of saying that I will never be without this choice. I am bound to it for as long as I exist as myself, even if that happens to be for all eternity; I *am* this choice, from now on. In the future I can choose to revise it but not in the sense of going back to who I was before I made it. I will never be able to be anything more than an act of contrition for the evil I have appropriated into my self. Even though all of my choices would not weigh equally in the scale made to measure their contribution to my whole character, each of them brings to that whole its own specific gravity. Choices are revisable only in the sense that we can be sorry for having made them a permanent part of our selves.

This is why there is something awful about human freedom. This power to make a choice which will never cease to reverberate, this power to impose on myself the perhaps eternal weight of each decision, is enough to make me swoon as soon as I have an inkling of its implications.[4] The depth to which it penetrates into my self and the indelibility of what it engraves there as character are sufficient to make human freedom terrifying. But ordinarily, we don't become conscious of its import until we suffer the devastating import of deeds we chose with no awareness of the horrifying momentum we were thereby setting in motion. Only those schooled by the suffering their deeds cause begin to feel the mysterious gravity of choice in all its incomprehensibility. To undergo such suffering, to realize with horror the full import of even one act of choosing, is in itself a profound moral accomplishment which is ordinarily achievable only by those who have chosen wrongly.

Someone who has become sensitive to the enormous weight of each choice needs to remember only one wrong from his past, one instance of his complicity in evil, to feel deeply and permanently contaminated by it.[5] And if one evil choice endures, unerasable, no matter how one tries to annul it, how are we to estimate the intransigent evil of vice, of actions not just multiplied but united in organic compact so as to create, instead of an indelible mark, a whole indelible language whose grammar governs one's life? Initially, I am only my individual acts of evil; eventually, I become my addictions. My self is not divided into single evil deeds but united into a single character by its vices. If some suspicion of their evil is awakened, I disarm it with the promise to change tomorrow. If our addictions allow us to make such promises, it is because they know we have become too weak to keep them. Vice has already brought tomorrow under the sway of its obsession. The promises it lets us make are really no more than excuses. It is not that it is impossible for the will to break the sovereignty of its vices: but, they constitute a permanent warp in my very subjectivity so that I know I will never get beyond being a convalescent. There is no such possibility as innocence regained in its original purity, before even the first thought of falling.

The desire to distinguish sharply what we are from what we do, first nature from second nature, our selves from the character we acquire through our acts, originates perhaps in the desire to believe we can disown the evil which we have appropriated so intimately into ourselves. We would like to think we are not affected by the gravity of our wrong choices. But each of them burdens us with a permanent weight which we are powerless to eliminate or diminish. The heavier that weight becomes, the more we regret having bound ouselves to it. The more profound that regret, the more we wonder what gave evil its power in the first place. The whole history of our lives seems to have been mysteriously determined by our original fascination with it. Were we somehow fated from the beginning to yield to its invitations? Is there some underlying kinship that exists between evil and ourselves even before our decision to commit it?

4. The Dark Side of the Self

I think we sense even now, underlying our acquired habits and specific addictions, not just a susceptibility to evil but a fascination that awakens an impulse actively to explore it. The person who thinks he has succeeded in eliminating his vices and severing his addictions still feels welling up within him an interest in doing the very things he struggled so hard to quit. Something in us does not ever want to learn the moral lessons we try to teach ourselves.

Insofar as we are determined to be moral, we do our best to disassociate ourselves from this part of us that refuses to be docile. This inevitably leads us to think of this "dark side" as a separate entity whose inclinations and impulses we are not responsible for. How can I be blamed for desires that well up from this dark cellar when I do my best to keep the door leading to it shut?

And yet it is precisely the closed door that makes what is behind it fascinating to us. And even if the impulses and inclinations we find morally objectionable are first bred and nurtured in the cellar of the unconscious, it is some part of our conscious self that stands by the door, intent on detecting what is on the other side of it. Our protestations to the contrary, we *wonder* about what is hidden down there and wonder always awakens a desire to explore. This inclination to explore constitutes a willingness to be engaged with evil that is rooted in the heart prior to any of our choices. In the small child, still innocent of deliberate intentions, we see in its undisguised state this fascination with the very things that are forbidden, this desire to open the very doors that have been closed to keep one out. Even as adults determined to disassociate ourselves from evil, we never get rid of this original fascination with it, this feeling that draws us to the very acts we are most ashamed of doing. My eyes keep waiting for me to relax my guard for a moment so that they can steal a brief, excited look down the cellar steps into the unconscious. When I do give in to evil, I succumb not to some outside seducer but to the curiosity about it that is already operative in me.

But even when we acknowledge our deep-set curiosity about the dark side of ourselves, we still presume that it is legitimate to treat the dark side itself as a separate entity. The ego has a natural tendency to think of the unconscious as an alien presence that has taken up residence within the psyche. Fascinated as we may be by the images bred in the unconscious, we nevertheless like to think of ourselves as essentially independent of it. But can my unconscious be called *mine* in any sense of the word if I disassociate myself from it in this way?

The more one reflects on the relationship between the self and the unconscious, the more it opens up the even more fundamental question of our relationship with our own bodies. This issue becomes most personal and painful when what surges up from the unconscious, from my body itself in its foreignness to me, is something I find utterly horrifying. It might be helpful in this regard to think not of the father from our previous example, but of the son whose anguished discovery of his homosexuality led to suicide; or we might think of a person who is subject to an addictive urge which he is impotent to curb, or of a person who finds it almost impossible to restrain impulses to violence. What makes such examples germane here is that they reveal in an excruciating and often poignant way the deep ambivalences that characterize our relationship to our bodies. For the real reason why we recoil from such feelings with horror is precisely because we do not want to realize that they belong, in all their foreignness, to us. What makes them so horribly strange is precisely the fact that we have to acknowledge them as our own. They originate, in their Otherness, in the part of our selves that we wish did not exist.

The first thing to be said, as we try to understand this anguished ambivalence, is that it shows how wrong we are in thinking that the body is an instrument at our disposal, something we can put to use in whatever way we see fit. As Gabriel Marcel has explained,[6] we cannot use instruments except through the body, by virtue of the body; the body cannot itself be an instrument since it is the condition for the possibility of using any tool. It belongs to us too intimately and too immediately to be "at our disposal." An essential dimension in our experience of our bodies is precisely how intractable they are in pressing upon us desires which we would be willing to do anything in the world not to have. We try our best to disassociate ourselves from our addictions as soon as we begin to realize we have them. We would like to think that they could not possibly be ours. Or we would like to be incapable of having such feelings, even if it meant not having a body at all. But the very fact that we would like to sever ourselves from our addictions reveals that in our heart of hearts we have a horrifying sense of their belonging to us. We would not experience such a need for disassociation if our bodies were as extrinsic to us as the word "instrument" implies. Precisely because we have these addictions, we are desperate to deny our synonymy with them. The humiliation we feel on account of them is not due to an anticipation of being discovered by Others but to our realizing we are not, after all, pure selves related to our bodies in a merely instrumental way.

We have all undergone innocuous versions of this humiliating experience of being our bodies. In any circumstance in which our bodies embarrass us, we feel bound to them as to something shameful, and for that very reason try to sever this bond. Blushing reveals this struggle, and at the same time our defeat: it shows on my face how unseverable I am from my body. Blushing itself, like the bodily behavior that causes it, is not an act we intend to perform or freely choose. Indeed, the more we try to prevent it, the more inevitable it becomes; our very act of trying to betray our bodies is what sets their revenge in motion. That we blush against our will is thus an essential element in it, but this does not mean that it happens to us like an accident, as if we were simply its victim and had no part in it: blushing is precisely my body's revelation of the fact that it belongs to me as my own. The subject of which blushing is the predicate is neither my body nor my self. The "I" that blushes is not my self as distinct from my body since what is excruciating about blushing is precisely its physical overtness, the fact that there is physically displayed something from which, were it not for my blushing, I could have disassociated myself; nor is it my body in its separateness from my self that blushes, for that would make blushing indistinguishable from a mere physiological process like breathing or swallowing. The I who blushes is precisely my subjectivity as inescapably bound to my body, my body as the very embodiment of my subjectivity. Blushing is the body's revenge for my wanting to separate my subjectivity from it. It is the body proving to me that I cannot ever escape *being* its embodiment of me.

But most of the time we try to avoid realizing the truths that reveal themselves in our blushes. Even as the blood rushes to my face, as if it cannot wait to betray me, I try to disappear under the rug, no longer in the hope of escaping my body, but to escape existence itself; to cease being this subject embodied in its shame, this body that is so evidently revealed as mine by my blushing. If only I could be a bodiless spirit, capable of disappearing into thin air! And it is not just the presence of Others I flee from, but their knowing about me what I prefer to hide even from myself. What they see before them is not *a* body but *my* body in its very mineness. For even breaking wind is no mere physiological process but the publication of a smell idiosyncratically one's own. I want to free my self from my body because it implicates me personally in its offensiveness.

Given the fact that we react in this way even to the innocuous, everyday humiliations to which being a body subjects us, it is difficult to describe the depth of shame we feel about the forbidden desires and addictions which we cannot bear to acknowledge and yet are impotent to repress. What we find unbearable is not our selves or our bodies but precisely the intimate bond that requires our acknowledging the body as our own. We cannot pretend to be completely innocent of what the body does, as if we were simply its victim; instead, we have to accept as ours compulsions we never wanted to have, compulsions which originate in an unconscious that seems to have a deeper hold on us than we have on ourselves. It is not surprising that, at the moment when we are in the throes of our addictions, we resent having been born, resent existence as a whole which requires us not just to associate with our bodies but to identify with them.

Foreign as we may like to think such an experience is to us, it is all too similar to the sense of horror we are likely to feel when our bodies exact, as they will from all of us, the ultimate humiliation involved in the process of dying itself. If we often say "I could have died," or speak of how "mortifying" it was to be in a certain situation, it is because, even in our ordinary world, we recognize death as the analogue of all our embarrassments. What makes dying seem so mortifying is not the extinction it perhaps causes but the humiliating, dehumanizing details to which it subjects us. One is required to lose all control over one's bodily functions and thus to become the plaything of their vicissitudes. The hero is willing to be the loser in heroic combats and will embrace the very gods who slay him; but even the hero resents having to become a hapless participant in the grotesque last act of the body's comedy. Even more so than others, he is likely to be mortified when the drama of his life culminates in this humiliating joke which his body has been waiting to play on him. In that terminal situation we will have to succumb to its excretions, repulsive and unpredictable; we will have to lie there impotent, incapable of doing anything that will save us from *being* this body whose original appetites are in the end replaced by the carnality of decay. Our most horrifying images are the images of dying—the gaunt, vacant eyes of disease, the bloated ganglia, the pools of vomit and diarrhea, the skull itself with its hollowed orifices: all these images are suggestive of the final indignity to which the body brings us and which we try to avoid by treating the body as an appendage instead of experiencing it as ourselves.

For it is I who die, not "merely" my body. That is precisely why we find it so mortifying. Usually, we do our best to avoid or minimize the mortifying character of death. The belief in immortality is often used as a therapeutic technique to assist us in this avoidance. I do not mean to dismiss the possibility of afterlife simply because of the fact that it is often employed for such a therapeutic purpose. But if there is an afterlife, we cannot reach it except by dying and we cannot enter into the experience of death except by the mortifying acceptance of the body that suffers it as our self. There is no part of me which is exempt from having to participate in that act of acceptance. The "who" who undergoes dying is the whole me.

Having said all this, we may be better prepared to appreciate the despair we experience in the worst moments of our addictions, when our bodies subject us to an undertow which we find more horrifying than death itself—so much so that death is preferable to it. In such moments we experience the body not just as a symbol or outward sign but as the very embodiment of a moral curse. The body's addictions assail us against our wills, as if a different law reigned in their members from the one we would like them to follow. A stranger seems to have usurped the role we deserve to have, the role of being in control of this body that was designed to serve us. What horrifies us is precisely our having to acknowledge this body and its desires, neither of which we choose to have, as fully and irremediably ours. This is the one doom which no action of our will enables us to outrun or undo because, while we can always remove ourselves from our situation, we cannot cease being the body which situates us in the one place we do not want to be: in the inescapable undertow of its compulsions. When those compulsions are morally horrifying, we feel helplessly and permanently bound to an evil we did not choose and which we must nevertheless acknowledge as our own. My body is like a stone hung around my neck, one that weighs so much that nothing I can do will prevent it from plunging me into the very evil I find most repugnant.

5. Heroic Self-hatred

I have been describing how we try to disassociate ourselves from moral evil, once we have an upsetting realization of its horror, and why such attempts at disassociation are bound to fail because evil is an inseparable part of our selves. There can be no more profound illustration of these themes than the experience of shame suffered by the heroic individual when he realizes the evil he has been doing. An examination of that ordeal will enable us to bring this stage in the geography of crisis to its completion.

Precisely because the hero's whole way of life depends on his resisting shame's ordeal, no experience of shame is more excruciating than the one it is his privilege to suffer. He has the most to lose and for that reason the most to gain from having his self-image shattered. He can bring to the experience of shame the same readiness to suffer, the same fervor for undergoing the most upsetting ordeals, which he brought to all his other heroic enterprises. The very passion of will which gave his deeds their heroic character can now be concentrated on his experience of humiliation. This can give a momentous weight to his recognition of his evil. Once he is exposed to this recognition, his heroic character will prevent him from trying to break his fall into the abyss it opens up before him. He can give a final proof of his heroism by bringing to the consciousness of its monstrosity the same radicality of will, the same contempt for avoidance, he brought to all the crises he embraced before with joy. But the dues shame exacts are infinitely worse than any of his old deaths because it requires him to sink helplessly into the void of humiliation. If he is to open himself fully to that experience, he must not just surrender to humiliation but actively embrace it.

Once the heroic individual chooses to acknowledge his evil, instead of repressing it, his very heroism will make him want to get all the way down to the very bottom of it. He must pour into that effort all the passion and discipline he once devoted to his original heroic enterprises. He wants to leave no facet of evil unturned, no vice unfingered, that he might yet achieve, by the very passion with which he prosecutes himself, at least a tragic kind of greatness. Heroism is never half-hearted. It would rather give itself over wholly to the very swoon of shame and the self-disgust it awakens, than settle for quiet mediocrity. Perverse as this attitude of self-hatred might seem to us, it is, in fact, simply heroic greatness turned in upon itself. We do not, ordinarily, think highly enough of ourselves to be able to hate ourselves in this heroic way for our failures.

Sophocles provides us the paradigmatic example of such self-hatred in his portrait of Oedipus, at the very moment when he gouges out his eyes in recognition of the fact that the evil he has sought to locate and expel from the city is none other than himself. In the excruciating violence of that single gesture he brings all the grandeur of his heroic passion to bear on that part of his body that we immediately recognize as a synecdoche of his deepest self. These eyes that outstared the Sphinx, this mind that pried open the best kept secrets, led him unblinking down the very road of his undoing. Oedipus is too heroic simply to recoil helplessly from the horror of what he has done, and collapse in a pathetic heap. Instead, the horror summons up in him the same outrage he has always felt in the presence of evil, and the proof of Oedipus's greatness is that now he does not hesitate to focus that outrage on himself. His act of self-mutilation has a definitive, unretractable character that makes it comparable to suicide; but unlike the literal version of that act, it does not provide Oedipus with an escape from his suffering. In fact, the purpose of the self-mutilation is precisely to make the horror he has seen unforgettable, to fixate himself eternally, as the gods fixated Prometheus, at his moment of supreme pain and self-hatred. He has put himself in a position where he will be able to reenact over and over again, day after day, the same horrific realization and the same heroic rage. The act of self-mutilation is the exemplary enactment of a ritual that he means to repeat for the rest of his life. He will always be an outcast but it will always be he, Oedipus himself, who casts himself out of the city. That casting out is his heroic attempt at a kind of meta-physical annihilation.[7]

Others might, perhaps, be able to convince themselves that some future good they do will be able to make up for the evil of the past. But this rationalization works only if one is first able to convince oneself that the evil one has done is finite. But just as there is something infinite about the greatness to which the hero aspired, so he realizes that there is an infinite weight to the stone around his neck. Oedipus's discovery of the fact that he has killed his father and married his mother undermines his heroic life as a whole only because these crimes possess the same titanic character, the same sublime, inhuman stature, as his heroic acts themselves. Just as the height to which he aspired was god-like, so the evil which brings him down from that height is recognized as demonic. Only because its weight is beyond all measure is it able to crush him. He is like someone whose efforts to become pure spirit have led through a tragic reversal, to his being forever bound to the heaviest of bodies. What can such a "soul" do except be sick of itself day in, day out, and vomit itself up?[8]

If a person consumed by such self-loathing does not commit suicide, it is because that seems to be too facile and too superficial a way out of its suffering. Self-loathing of the type we have been discussing is very different from self-pity, which keeps looking at its wounds in order to feel sorry for itself for having had to suffer them. The distinguishing mark of self-hatred is its insatiable desire to inflict suffering on itself. Determined to suffer without remission, the person who hates himself eschews suicide because that form of self-punishment ends too quickly and definitively. His anger, far from seeking to spend itself wholly in a single catharsis, does not ever want to be satisfied. That is why self-hatred is always starting over again from the beginning and never tires of the cycle of self-accusation and punishment.

But if the person filled with self-loathing does not commit suicide, the acts he does, like Oedipus's, are metaphors of it; as poetic versions of suicide, they have the advantage of being indefinitely repeatable. One can keep on killing one's self if one does not do it literally. But this is not the only benefit of such metaphors. Literal suicide always involves some paraphernalia and requires some technical skill, however minimal; in fact, the act itself is utilitarian in character, and the person who commits it has death in view as the goal to be reached. Suicide is an act one does in order to reap some benefit for oneself; for someone who wants to punish himself, it is too much an attempt to do away with the suffering involved in having to be oneself. It is too much like an escape motivated by self-pity and too little like an execution motivated by self-hatred.

Self-pity blames existence for not measuring up to my expectations. Oedipus, on the other hand, blames himself to the point of thinking it would have been better for him never to have been born. The only kind of act which corresponds to that conviction is one which expresses a willingness to commit not physical but metaphysical suicide; Oedipus would like to be able to annihilate his whole self in order to execute the judgment he has made that he should never have been created in the first place. Far from its being the last tactic in a strategy of self-pity, such desire to cast oneself into nothingness is the only heroically virtuous act one can do, once one has recognized oneself as evil. Someone drawn toward suicide by self-pity still takes for granted not just that he deserves to exist but that he deserves to be free of the suffering to which existence in the world is subjecting him. But the person who is resolved to commit metaphysical suicide has the exactly opposite attitude: he is responding with moral outrage to the realization that his very existence is morally horrifying.

Sophocles' play ends without his giving us a very clear picture of exactly what Oedipus does out there on those trackless wastes to which he exiles himself. But the kind of heroic self-hatred Oedipus has already exemplified suggests the direction he will choose to take if he decides to carry it to its logical conclusion. Are we not familiar with a certain kind of religious asceticism that flourishes in such desert-like places, that has a very definite heroic appeal to it, and that proves itself congenial to those headstrong, uncompromising spirits who are tormented by their own failures?[9]

Is it surprising that a person filled with self-hatred should fasten on the rites of abstinence and abnegation, the literal discipline of renunciation and scourging, that this kind of asceticism fosters? Its advocates would have us think of such practices as the synecdoche for a religious purification that allows one to get one's revenge on the desires which have subjected one for so long to their demands. In the context of such asceticism, the annihilation of one's appetites becomes a kind of sacramental violence that serves a deeper purpose than the denial of the body. It is a preparation for the will's annihilation of itself.[10]

In order to fulfill that darker purpose, the ascetic will must bring its purifying flame to bear on its most recondite faults. But the self is a torturous labyrinth, and those who enter it for the purpose of rooting out its deepest flaws are easily misled into blind passageways by their heroic enthusiasms. It does not take many false turns for the way to sainthood to become the way to delusion. The person filled with self-hatred is led by it to think that he can reach the highest level of sanctity by working toward his own extinction. Would it be surprising if such a person went so far as to pursue the mystical life in the belief that its ecstasies would be the culminating experience of that self-annihilation he tries to practice? He thinks that in such ecstasies one's ego finally ceases to be and that through this self-extinction one can achieve what even literal death does not deliver: the experience of becoming God. The pursuit of this kind of mysticism unites the extremes of self-debasement and deification in one delirious enthusiasm. By ceasing to be one's self, one is rid of a defiling excrescence and thus saved from being evil. But this self-annihilation is motivated by nothing less than a fervor for perfection which remains unabated even though it has despaired of itself. The person filled with self-hatred has not given up the dream of being perfect. In fact, it is precisely because perfection remains the single object of his longing that he feels compelled to annihilate himself; for only by being rid of himself can he achieve what he seeks. The desire to be perfect and the feeling of self-hatred are simply two sides of the same delirium.

Moreover, the introspection which the ascetic practices to uncover the subtleties of his own evil does not just teach him about his own idiosyncratic faults. Such introspection enables him to seize on truths about his life which are simultaneously verdicts on human existence as such. When Oedipus puts out his eyes, he does so, as he has done everything else, on behalf of all of us. He knows what none of us is heroic enough to acknowledge, that it would be better if none of us had ever been born. He knows now the dark side of everyone's life, and that each of us harbors within himself the evil we project onto others. Nothing is more universal than the desire to keep one's shame so secret that, even in one's most private moments, one remains convinced of one's own self-worth. Once one pries open that secret as Oedipus did, it leads one to see the whole world in a new light: the world should never have existed in the first place.[11] At the moment when he puts out his eyes, Oedipus stands at the heart of the world as the self-consciousness of its evil and the embodiment of its self-hatred.

But such self-hatred differs from the easier despair of nihilism because it is rooted in love of the Good. Evil, in all its vicissitudes, is horrific only to the degree that one is aware of the demands of a moral absolute, the demands of perfection itself. If the person filled with self-hatred were to give up his love of perfection, he would lose the very thing that makes him morally sublime. His self-hatred, and the hatred of the universe into which it metastasizes, offer him the one and only chance he has left to fulfill his moral ideal for himself. Once one has recognized one's evil, what other route can one take to perfection? The last dream of the tragic hero is to become perfect through self-annihilation.

We are beginning to glimpse here the dialectical nature of self-hatred, the fact that it is really an inverted version of its opposite. The ascetic mysticism to which it can lead gives free play to these dialectical antinomies. For what is at work in such mysticism is not simply self-love, monomaniacal and Promethean, nor the cynical kind of self-hatred which results from simple nihilism. It is self-hatred and self-love bound to each other in an inextricable unity. One annihilates oneself because one cannot stand to be evil; but the reason one cannot stand to be evil is because one is still in love with the dream of one's own perfection. In fact, one hopes to fulfill that dream through the very act of self-debasement. Oedipus's act of putting out his eyes looks like the most bitter expression of nihilistic despair—until one realizes that only a god could punish himself so cruelly. He hopes to achieve through the very act of inflicting punishment on himself the moral perfection that he knows he cannot attain now in any other way. Has Oedipus broken through the circle of tragic irony by embracing that hope? Or is there a tragic irony in his refusal to give it up?

6. The Tragic Irony of Self-Hatred

If up to now I have not called self-hatred of the type exemplified by Oedipus tragic, that is because it is itself an attempt to respond to tragedy and transcend it. That it fails to do so, that it instead repeats the very same tragic failure that it seeks to overcome, puts the person who practices it in a doubly humiliating position. For no one should have to be taught tragedy's lesson twice. But those who suffer it once usually bring it on themselves again and again, with every succeeding attempt to pick themselves up from their prior humiliation. The unfortunate and discouraging truth that emerges from these reflections is that, ordinarily, there is no counting our repetitions of tragedy. We set our own downfall in motion over and over again, in our very labor to rise above our last failure. But such unintentional repetitions of the same fault no longer evoke the same dread and sorrow as a tragic fall. The person who never learns, no matter how often he has the same fault pointed out to him, loses the tragic stature he once had. We gradually begin to see that there is something ridiculous about him. What are we to think, for instance, of someone who gouges out his *eyes* in order to punish himself for his *blindness*? For all its heroic grandeur and horror, is there not something almost ridiculous about such an act?

When one is first confronted with its violence, it is tempting to believe that self-hatred errs by going too far, that its mistake lies in imposing *too much* suffering on itself. It might be suggested that the evil which evokes such self-hatred is made too much of, that its magnitude is exaggerated, its unretractability overemphasized. Perhaps no fault deserves so severe a punishment as Oedipus tries to make himself suffer. The person we have discussed is, it seems, too hard on himself, and thus unjust. He is so contemptuous of pity that he forces himself to undergo unnecessary torments just to root out of himself any unconscious desire he may have to avoid suffering. Self-hatred seems to result, in this case, from an excessive moral sensitivity that takes its own evil too seriously. At last, it seems, we have come upon someone who suffers too much and who, if he is to be blamed at all, should be blamed for putting himself through an unnecessary crisis.

But what if this suffering, with all its torments and excesses, is objectionable not because it is undeserved but because it enables the person filled with self-hatred to avoid an even more upsetting experience, an even more radical form of mortification? The fault in self-hatred would then be precisely its unwillingness to go far enough, its desperate hanging back, its fear of suffering a wound that is deeper and more intimate than any of those it inflicts on itself. We get an inkling of how painful that deeper wound would be when we see what excruciating pains we are willing to suffer instead of undergoing it.

I do not mean to doubt that self-hatred is real hatred or to call into question the authenticity of the suffering it causes. I mean to draw attention to the duplicity that is unconsciously but inevitably at work in it. For when I hate my self, I take upon my self both the activism of the agent who hates and the passivity of the target of the hatred. This duality of status also occurs in the trial and judgment which precede the verdict of self-hatred. I am prosecutor as well as defendant, jury as well as accused, judge as well as judged. Each of these roles enables me to step back and disassociate myself from the self that is being tried. But they suggest more than the distinction of mere distance. The I who steps back from my self does so in order to examine it from a position of *superiority* which enables me to look down upon the self to be examined. I am the criminal guilty and worthy of punishment; but I am also the judge and I am ready to become the executioner.[12] If I experience in my role as criminal all the humiliation of being debased, I experience in my role as judge all the self-righteousness and moral outrage which crime arouses in the virtuous. Perhaps I am so intent on looking down on my self as criminal, that I have only a kind of subliminal awareness of my superior upright position. But I bring to the act of punishing myself those feelings of horror and rage that are characteristic of someone whose sense of moral purity has been violated. Self-hatred is possible only by virtue of the utter separation of oneself into two personae. I am utterly evil and deserve extinction; but the "I" who proclaims this verdict is separated by its height, its transcendence, from the "I" that is being condemned. Were I to realize, in my role as judge, that I am contaminated with the very evil I detect in myself in my role as criminal, I would be overcome with shame and deprived of the superior position which enables me to pass judgment on myself. In order to hate oneself, one has to be able to believe in one's own purity, one's own innocence. Otherwise, one would not be able to summon up the righteousness necessary for being a judge. Thus, self-hatred's victory is shame's defeat. Shame always seems so frail, so unmanly, so quiet; its embarrassed voice is silenced by the rhetoric of self-hatred which is always inflated with self-importance. Why does self-hatred speak with such bombast, if not to drown out shame's shy but mortifying cry? I must silence shame because the only alternative is to die of it.

The fact that self-hatred requires two personae explains why, although it need not be psychotic itself, its rhetoric is much the same as that used by madness where the duality of the self as executioner and criminal takes the form of autonomous personae which can no longer be consciously integrated into a single identity.[13] If this does not occur in the person filled with self-hatred, it is because ordinarily his role as judge takes priority over his role as accused and provides him with an axis of coherence for his world. He *acts* as judge; the accused is only the passive sufferer of his violences. The evil he sees in his self is subordinate to his act of condemning it. This is why self-hatred always harbors within it a profound arrogance that goes undetected because what the person sees is the debasement he inflicts on himself, not the pride which enables him to do so.

Thus self-hatred easily deludes one into thinking it can succeed where all one's virtues failed. For in hating my self, do I not finally own up to my evil and its inextricability from my self? Without such an acknowledgment, hatred would not be turned inward in the first place. Does not shame achieve its purpose by wringing from me an admission of my repulsiveness? I cannot any longer stand apart from evil, above it, exempt from it. Self-hatred represents a profound internalization of evil, my owning up to the horror of its owning me. But in this act of internalizing evil, I still will to remove it, to expel it; it is simply that, given the fact that it is inextricable from my self, this now requires my own annihilation. When one thinks according to the logic of self-hatred, one internalizes evil, and yet at the same time one manages to retain a superior position where one is exempt from it. Self-hatred, which cannot exist unless I discover my own evil, is nevertheless my continuing refusal to be anything less than perfect. We might say that it is the ideal of perfection in me trying to get rid of the evil in me. Its violent excess, the severity of its vengeance, its refusal to take pity—all these signs of how seriously the self takes its own evil, really only reveal the lengths to which it will go in order to avoid humbling itself. No one is so self-righteous as the person who hates himself enough to will his own self-annihilation. It would be hard to find an example of pride which is more demonic.

So when such a person suffers as a result of the punishment he inflicts on himself, we must not object that he is being too hard on himself but that at the deepest level he is being too lenient. Indeed, the very fact that he insists that his punishment be self-inflicted is the proof of this; the more painful he makes the punishment, the more certain he can be of his own purity for being willing to inflict it. I am never happier, never more assured of my innocence and humility, as when I feel repulsed by my own worthlessness. Beneath all its psychic contortions, all its involuted strategies, beneath its mystical contradictions and tortured ecstasies, self-hatred is as simple as all other faults: I hate myself in order to avoid having to be myself in my imperfection. And we know that, whatever the sufferings we may bring upon ourselves through our avoidances, we endure them only because we are unwilling to suffer a more poignant wound. Self-hatred is the heroic struggle to avoid the crisis I would have to undergo if I were to accept fully the self I am ashamed of being. What makes the person who hates himself a prey to ridicule is the fact that he prides himself on having recovered from the exact fault which this pride proves he is still repeating: the evil of wanting to be perfectly good. He prides himself on fulfilling to the letter exactly what he continues to avoid: the real demands of guilt. How can the person who hates himself be less presumptuous, less aggrandizing, than the tragic hero when he brings to the demands of shame the same will to be perfect, the same contempt for fallibility, which the hero brings to the demands of honor? It is as if a man who once claimed omniscience were to put out his eyes upon discovering his fallibility, in order to fix them forever on the absolute truth he has now recognized with infallible certitude. There is something ridiculous about the fact that such a person continues to believe in his infallibility at the very moment he realizes the mistake of doing so. It is a mistake ever to be convinced that one has perfectly acknowledged one's imperfections. Only a fool thinks he has learned all there is to know about his ignorance. It belongs to the very essence of our fallibility that a true recognition of it does not enable us to transcend it. It brings us down to the bottom of our shame, instead of helping us rise above it as we would like.

Generally, we are not strong enough to put ourselves down into that position of inferiority. We rob shame of its mortifying power by turning it into self-hatred. Lost in the labyrinth of self-torture, we suffer so safely that it ceases to reach us. What realizations do we take such pains to avoid? What wound is the suffering we inflict on ourselves designed to prevent? What mortifying depth are we always trying to rise above? These questions lead us to the next and final chapter in this geography.

CHAPTER SIX

Prostration

The weary reader might well ask if these detours will ever end. The geography of crisis would, indeed, be a great deal simpler were it not required to follow the track of avoidance as it delays and misleads and even waits in ambush for the fallible pathfinder. Any one of the virtues we have praised, from the first risk of generosity to the last and shyest whisper of shame, could have led us straight ahead, without pause or hindrance, to the heart of crisis, if only we had given it rein. But we prefer any sidetrack, even trackless wastes, to the hard relentless road of any one of our vulnerabilities. We would rather die of thirst than get to where they lead.

Were we to have our first preference, we would never leave the tight, airless room of our egocentricity. We become generous enough to welcome strangers into our homes, but we will not tolerate them for long if they do not cease to be strangers: we make our generosity stingy, and unconsciously self-righteous. Nothing ruptures our satisfied consciences until we discover, in a moment of horror, that our very hospitality, however ingenuous, is itself an ironic avoidance of the Other as Other. With one such breach, we are no longer safe inside the boundaries of ordinary generosity; we have begun to open ourselves to strange things, in all their strangeness, the most upsetting of which have the capacity to undermine our whole world.

The person whose world is shattered will finally find himself homeless, bereft of his belongings and deserted by his acquaintances, at the mercy of powers which are beyond his comprehension and control. He can regain control over the very experience of losing it through madness or depression or despair, each of which immunizes him against further suffering by cutting him off from the future. Should he eschew these modes of avoidance, he will discover that the shattering of his ordinary world provides him access to the heroic dimensions of the universe. Dread before the awful is then no longer seen as a danger to be avoided but as a demand to be embraced. Inspired by such dread, instead of being terrified by it, he can seek out death and work to make himself worthy of the ordeals it promises. But the will to be heroic, eager as it is to embrace demanding ordeals, is usually only the surface of a deeper cowardice; the person animated by it shies away from any reality which threatens to require a humiliating acknowledgment of his inferiority. Even the hero cannot bear to become as small as shame demands. He runs from one heroic enterprise to another to keep from owning up to the things he finds humiliating. All such heights he reaches are just evasions that keep him from exploring the fault that lies inside the heart, where shame keeps vigil like a forlorn and homely lover. To embrace her is the opposite of ecstasy. So it should be no surprise that the heroic individual, close enough to shame to feel its breath on his cheek, punishes himself mercilessly for the offenses which have cost him the humiliation of such proximity. But in spite of its unrestrained violence, the heart thus turned upon itself is still motivated by avoidance. It is making another attempt to retain its high stature and avoid shame's belittlement. But it achieves nothing except to betray shame by lying with its prostitute, self-hatred.

It is as if each virtue redeems its predecessor, only to succumb later to the same enemy. Each advance the heart makes toward what, for brief moments, it senses to be its true and dreadful destiny, is compromised when it recoils from that destiny in terror. Still, it would not be true to say that every gain is lost. For even with all its starts and stops, its hesitations, its excuses, its desperate procrastinations, the heart has nonetheless moved gradually closer and closer to that crisis which from the first both beckoned and terrified it. Crisis keeps on trying to undo our avoidances; it is patient, watchful, quick to take advantage of the least opening; it gives no respite to the heart intent on silencing its demands. The heart keeps transforming its ruptures into interruptions, but each interruption cuts into it more deeply, as if preparing it for an eventually mortal wound.

We have reached the point where the heart has run out of new avoidances. If none of its other strategies were as extreme as self-hatred, that is because the latter is the will's last (and for that reason its most desperate) evasion. Either we remain safe inside its demonic antinomies or, for the last time, we stop avoiding crisis: this either/or leaves no room for maneuvering. We have nowhere to go, if we want to move at all, except straight ahead into that crisis which, from the beginning, has been our destination.

1. The Dignified Acceptance of Nothingness

I would like to approach this destination by focusing on a topic which I have frequently mentioned but not yet directly addressed—the topic of death. I spoke of death in discussing the hero who acquires his heroic stature precisely by virtue of his acting in the face of death with full knowledge of his vulnerability. But I have argued that the hero is generally afraid of anything which threatens to *dwarf* him, that he wants there to be no reality in comparison with which his own claim to greatness would be proven vain. But this means precisely that the hero resents his finitude, if by finitude we mean the smallness of stature that results from being bounded on all sides by a reality over which one has no real power. Ordinarily, heroic resentment takes the form of defiance: one either defies finitude by acting as if not even death were one's equal; or one turns upon one's finitude in an act of heroically defiant self hatred. If humility would require the hero to accept his finitude, not resent it, would it not be more heroic then any defiance? And what dwarfs us, makes us finite, requires our humility, if not death itself?

If I have spoken of death frequently before now, that is because every crisis, even when it only *interrupts* and definitely when it *ruptures* one's established mode of being, exposes one to some kind of death, i.e., a loss of the whole world one has been living in. This is why we are tempted to say that all crises, however radical, only approximate and anticipate the crisis of death itself. If this is true, then all the ruptures I have considered up to now are only metaphorical versions of the literal rupture I am now thematizing. This view certainly possesses a certain prima facie plausibility since all metaphors seem to pale in the face of death's literality. Death, it would seem, is *the* crisis of which all of us are horrified, usually in the mode of avoidance. It is this suggestion that I would now like to test.

It is misleading to speak of death's literality, if this is taken to imply that I am equating death with its "objective data," as if we were closest to death, and therefore to crisis, when we exactly understand the biological facts as reported by the attending physician or pathologist. We know that such a reduction, precisely because it makes death comparable to all other events which happen, deprives it of its distinctive character.[1] Nevertheless, it is not just possible but even typical for us to view death in this way, even when we are ourselves the ones whom death threatens. Insofar as I can continue to view my own death as an event that is definable in scientific terms, like any other event, it is not able to rupture my ordinary way of experiencing and looking at the world. And this requires us to say that death, viewed literally in the sense just described, is no crisis at all; physically painful as it might be, it entails no suffering as we have been using that word. Not even death is strong enough to make us suffer against our will. Thus, while it is, of course, true that everyone must die, it is equally true that no one need suffer his death. Drugs enable me to die painlessly; avoidance enables me to die without losing control over my situation. Even my dying would then be ordinary and not a crisis.

If such an approach to death is objectionable, it is because it does not do death justice. Death is only comparable to other events in the world for those who are not dying; for the one who is dying, it is not an event *in* the world but the end of his world in its totality. Death ought to upset one in a radical way, infinitely more so than any rupture in one's mode of being in the world. For it undermines the condition on which every possible way of being in the world is based.[2] That is why it seems appropriate to call it *the* radical crisis of which all others are metaphors: does any other crisis disrupt the very be-ing of my being, my very existence itself? Even if something happens to me which shatters the meaning which I want my life to have, I am capable of transforming that crisis into something positive by becoming heroic, i.e., by adopting a new way of existing. My very be-ing has not been undermined. A human being can be the creator of all sorts of worlds, but only on the condition and in the context of his already being in the world. It would seem that this underlying context can be disturbed only by death, and that the "worlds" ruptured by all other crises are only metaphors for the world ruptured by this terminal ordeal: the world which made it possible for me to be at all. Since death calls my very existence into question, it is, apparently, the paradigm of all identity crises.

The difficulty we face in trying to think through this claim is the paradox that death, while apparently the paradigm of crisis, is precisely the crisis about which we inevitably know the least. And we are not rescued from this difficulty by the suggestion that we can learn about it by studying its analogues. For if death is the paradigm of crisis, it would be a mistake to think it is like all other ruptures. That would precisely deprive if of its exemplary stature. Rather, we would have to admit that all other ruptures only imitate and approximate the crisis death involves: but the latter is precisely the crisis which is least available to us.

Death would not be paradigmatic if it did not confront us with this difficulty. Essential to the claim that it is the most radical of crises is its inaccessibility, the impossibility of our bringing it, as such, to the surface, without thereby superficializing it. For death raises the possibility of my not be-ing, my ceasing to exist at all, insofar as it pulls the world as a whole out from under me. It may, in fact, be a transition to a radically different mode of being; yet even this "may" faintly intimates, with its quiet but fertile uncertainty, that death may be my utter extinction.[3] Death insinuates the *possibility* of my own nothingness—and avoidance typically tries to silence precisely this insinuation. Why is it felt to be so unbearable? Because, as Heidegger tells us, nothingness is the utterly Other, the absolutely incommensurable; it is not even similar enough to a being to be called its opposite. We can understand it only by acknowledging its unfathomability, the fact that it eludes all the efforts we make to handle it. Nothingness, by virtue of its not being a thing we can manage in any way, leaves us utterly incapacitated.

Perhaps there is no more expeditious way to emphasize the plausibility of this claim than by juxtaposing it to the peculiarly modern ambition of bringing death into the open, to which I referred obliquely in previous pages. It is assumed by contemporary thanatologists that previous generations were afraid of death and ignorant of both its psychology and physiology.[4] Fear, supposedly, led to repression; repression to further ignorance and phobia; phobia to our present incapacity for dealing with death and dying. In this view, death has been the innocent victim of a conspiracy of silence. To liberate culture from its phobia, we must liberate death from the closet in which we tried, out of ignorance and cowardice, to keep it hidden. If we start talking about death openly and honestly, dying will cease being the upsetting experience our dread of it causes it to become.

This claim of the modern therapeutic consciousness is true but in a sense it does not intend and fails to comprehend. When brought out of darkness into the light of the ordinary, dragged out of hiding and put on display, its silence broken by the talk of clients and therapists, death does, in a sense, lose its capacity to devastate us. But what is thus brought into the open, spoken out loud and exposed to full view, is not at all the possibility of nothingness but merely another event that fits into our world instead of shattering it. We are never more unaware of what death really entails than when we speak of it without reserve. Because it fails to recognize that death's power to shatter our world cannot be accommodated within it, the new ethic of therapeutic openness avoids death just as effectively as the most heartlessly scientific observation.

The profoundly right reason for not speaking of death is its unspeakability. Death raises the possibility of nothingness, and nothingness inevitably eludes all our attempts to render it transparent. Speaking of it in the therapeutic manner is like bringing darkness into the light of the noonday sun and then claiming that one has seen through its opacity. Bringing nothingness "into the open," where it can be treated with the same directness as everything else, insures better than any other strategy that nothingness will never be encountered in its radical strangeness. The experience of nothingness is falsified whenever one tries to diminish that strangeness by speaking about it. Only by recognizing the impropriety of such speech does one begin to give nothingness the quiet deference which is its due.

We can contrast such deference with the inappropriate frankness of the therapeutic approach. When one defers, one yields to an Other. One does so because one recognizes that this Other deserves one's respect; one steps back from and gives way to the Other not so much out of generosity but in order to render to it the recognition which it deserves because of its stature and importance. Now death seems to deserve just such deference by virtue of the fact that its opacity and unspeakability prove the poverty of all human sight and speech. Instead of demanding their way and insisting on their rights, our tongues ought to fall silent and our eyes ought to be covered so that at least when we are in its proximity we allow death to hold us in the sway of its upsetting darkness. The very least we can do, the barest justice, is to refrain, for one moment at least, from doing and saying anything. What is wrong about our therapies is that they do not see the rationale behind such politeness.

But when we are mindful enough to show death such deference, we must, in fact, have already sensed, however dimly, that it would exact a more upsetting kind of surrender if we gave it its full due. We ought to be in dread of it. Dread differs, I have suggested, from fear's self-preservative recoil; when afraid, my egocentricity is intensified because I am more conscious of my vulnerability, and more eager to find a safe spot for myself. Self-serving as it is, such fear of death rightly estimates the danger; the urgent desire to escape reveals a much more profound respect for death than the therapeutic attitude which does not get close enough to the possibility of nothingness to recoil from it. But, unlike fear, dread beckons me to move close enough to nothingness for its shattering impact to hit me. It would not have me resign myself to nothingness but defenselessly open myself to it so that I can realize that nothing I do will prevent it from swallowing me. This realization evokes an incapacitating sense of horror, since it shows me how helpless I am in the face of this Other. But it also creates an uncanny sense of peace precisely because it renders all action futile.[5] Only in the speechless calm which dread brings does one genuinely acknowledge one's inability to control nothingness in any way.

As precise as I might try to make this description of dread, it lends itself to misinterpretations which I will try to put right.

First of all, the experience of yielding to the upsetting impact of nothingness, as dread requires, differs radically from that willingness to annihilate oneself that we have seen to be characteristic of self-hatred. The person filled with self-hatred tries to get rid of the part of himself that he would find it humiliating to acknowledge; but dread is dreadful precisely because it leaves one exposed in humiliating defenselessness. It is upsetting because it requires me to accept myself in my impotence before nothingness instead of trying to get rid of that impotence. The person who hates himself finds annihilation appealing precisely because it promises to free him from having to be this impotent, vulnerable being that is helplessly exposed to nothingness. Death can be alluring but only because it enables us to escape the dreadful ordeal of dying. On the other hand, our existence becomes dreadful when we realize that we are always on the verge of not being.

But this last expression threatens to create another confusion. I have emphasized that nothingness is radically Other and as such incongruous with all we know and say, and that we are uprooted and displaced by a real encounter with it. I have suggested that dread makes us realize that the tiny island of one's self, one's being, is completely encircled by an abyss. But this image will mislead us if we take it to mean that I am, and that nothingness threatens me like an alien intruder, coming toward me from the outside. Were this the case, I would be justified in considering myself a victim of death's injustice. I would think of it as infringing on my inalienable right to exist. This way of thinking presupposes that I am, in and of myself, radically disassociated from nothingness. But if death can threaten me, it can do so only because I am *able to die*. And what can this mean except that intrinsic to me is a corruptibility, a liability to not be, an innate inclination toward nothingness. My very being includes within it an openness to the possibility of not being.[6] I *am* this being who is able to not be. Nothingness does not, therefore, invade from the outside: it would be much more accurate to say that deeply within my self I am already turned outward toward it; already, I belong to it. Nothingness is, indeed, radically Other, too incongruent to be encountered without dread. But part of the dreadfulness of its incongruity is the fact that I am in my very being already given over to its sway. There is a fissure, as it were, in my very existence, a metaphysical fault in the heart of what I wrongly think of as my substance. Given this intimate kinship with the very nothingness which is its utter Other, my being is not a substance characterized by firmness and solidity, but something slight and fragile, like the body of a hemophiliac.

Now, ordinarily, we cannot bear to acknowledge this hemophiliac status, not just because it compels us to face death's obdurate silence, but because we find it humiliating, even dehumanizing, to have this impotence in our being exposed. Were death an alien trespassing against me, I could adopt an attitude of indignation or resentment toward it. But the fact that my liability to nothingness is a fault intrinsic to me undermines my justification for those feelings.

Inseparable from dread in the face of nothingness is the humble acknowledgment of how unfounded were one's former conceits, especially the pretension to perfection that is at work in one's resentment of death. That I am, in the very heart of my being, liable to nothingness, proves that, contrary to what I have always presumed, I am no exception to the rule of contingency and finitude. I *am*, but can *not be*—it is not necessary that I exist. Up until the time when dread wins from me a humble consent to this truth, the fact that I exist has the status of an obvious and unquestionable truth that I do not think to doubt or even notice; my existence seems to be something I can take for granted as a normal fact. But dread ruptures just this unblushing self-certainty, this assurance which has been so secure that I never stopped to examine it. Now I feel the cold whip of the wind, and find myself shivering uncontrollably; I realize that someday I will be trapped out here in the frozen wasteland, alone in the deep drifts of some winter storm—and at that point nothing I do will make the shivering stop. This uncontrollable shivering is like the spasm of my vulnerability. I wrongly thought my clothes would always protect me. In some such terms as these, death teaches us our name is frailty. When I once shudder like this, when even the heart shivers in cold, uncontrollable horror, I can never again be sure of my existence.

Only such shuddering does death justice. It gathers together in a single ashen gesture both my horror when facing death's silent obscurity and the mortification of having to own up to the fact that I am not exempt from its sway. We know from the attitudes we have already studied how many ways there are to avoid such shuddering: the somnambulism of depression, nihilism, mindless hedonism, madness—all forms of despair and of the unwillingness to suffer. The heroic individual does not employ such avoidances; his heroic courage differs from brashness, his pride from conceit, his wisdom from vain pretension, precisely because he acknowledges his vulnerability. Real courage is not possible until death has made one shudder with horror. Heroic pride is too proud, its wisdom too wise, to cower from the truth like conceit. But while willing to be vulnerable, the hero is not willing to be mortified; he will not let death prove him small in stature or otherwise rob him of his heroic grandeur and worth. Even he, with his heroic virtue, turns away from the humiliation which the often obscene details of dying involve, and tries to find some way to defy his finitude. He hates himself for being subject to such a mortifying ordeal and ends up cooperating with death in order to punish himself for being vulnerable to it.

Opposed to all these attitudes is the humility which is already implicit in dread itself. In consenting to one's mortality without reservation or resentment, one finally agrees to be the vulnerable person one is, instead of avoiding it. Easy as it might sound at first, one can achieve this modesty only if one acknowledges that one is smaller than either ordinary vanity or heroic pride lead one to believe. All the attitudes I have described attempt to justify the claim to the superior stature which this humility requires one to renounce. To break through all these defenses is no mean achievement for so frail a virtue. But, paradoxically, the experience of accepting one's mortality does not turn out to be the debasing ordeal of which both vanity and pride are so afraid. For one will find one's mortality degrading only if one still believes one deserves the suprahuman stature which immunity from death implies. To give up that stature without recourse to numb resignation is the delicate feat of a genuinely self-accepting human modesty. From the point of view of such modesty what is humiliating is not one's liability to nothingness but the fact that one has pretended all along to be exempt from it. When my acceptance of my vulnerability to nothingness frees me of such pretensions, it awakens me by that very fact to my specifically human dignity. Because for the first time I am not ashamed to be mortal, I can be proud of my strictly human eminence, without needing the false inflation of any vain or heroic vaunt. Simply to be this frail finite self is an honor.

What do I mean by our "specifically human dignity"? We think of human dignity as something which everyone naturally possesses; and yet at the same time we think of it as something we must work to attain and deserve. If I have some sense of my dignity as a person, I am convinced that I deserve to be recognized, to be taken seriously. Convinced of this, I have a duty to take myself seriously. Such self-respect insists only on one's intrinsic worth as a person, and pretends to no greater stature. But even to say it "insists" on its rights is misleading. For, unless circumstances back him into a corner, the person aware of his human dignity refrains from "insisting" on his rights, since ordinarily this would involve a kind of self-aggrandizement which is itself beneath his dignity because it involves pretending to a priority in the universe he does not presume to claim. It takes conceit or insecurity, not self-respect, to think that nothing in the world is more serious than my being taken seriously. Real dignity is above making loud demands on its own behalf; it rests securely on the conviction that, simply because of one's stature as a person, one deserves to receive, without having to demand it, neither more nor less than the respect that is rightly one's due. One should not have to plead for such respect; one's very being as a person ought to command it. Now this human dignity is innate in the sense that one is worthy of respect simply because of one's natural stature as a person. But knowing this to be so, one's awareness of his intrinsic dignity—this is an accomplishment of soul-searching and self-discovery which, as we have seen, even the hero does not achieve in the right way. Genuine self-respect exists only as the fruit of my coming to acknowledge the intrinsic worth I possess not by virtue of any heroic accomplishments but simply by virtue of my modest stature as a person.

Now it is crucial for us to realize that nothingness itself cannot diminish in any way this sense of dignity, this pride which is too proud of being simply human to demean itself with any vanity. Our liability to nothingness has the power to humble our pretensions to a more than human stature. But it is powerless to humble me if I claim no more than the modest but real honor of being my finite self. The power of nothingness goes no further than this; it cannot take away from me the human dignity that makes me superior to it.

I have no intention of denying what I have said about the upsetting character of death. In opening me up to the possibility of my own nothingness, it exposes me to an Other over which I have no control whatsoever. Before nothingness, I am not just defenseless but overcome, to the point of being speechless with horror. It ruptures my pretensions. It leaves me emptied, hollowed out. But how does it accomplish this? How does nothingness provoke me out of my vanities? It mortifies me when I allow it finally to prove to me how intimately akin we are, how familial it is to me, despite my always pretending the contrary. But if my kinship with nothingness can mortify me, if it can confront me with a fact about my self incongruent with the more-than-finite stature I have always claimed, this necessarily means that this nothingness to which mortality makes me liable is itself the opposite of positive value or worth. Only because nothingness itself has no worth, no stature, can my being akin to it be humbling. It is the very negativity of nothingness, its being the opposite of the heights I have wanted to occupy, which gives it the power to humble me, once I realize I am intimately bound to it as to one of my own possibilities. But this means precisely that it cannot be greater than I; were it so, my kinship with it would elevate, not diminish me. Nothingness proves me less than what I pretend to be. But it is not itself a reality in comparison with which I realize my smallness. It is by virtue of my association with it in its negativity that I am proven to have a less positive stature than my vanity and pride pretend. Nothingness cannot awe me in the sense of making me feel insignificant in the face of its sublime stature. For to be humbled by a reality which I experience as profoundly superior to me in stature, I must feel my dissimilarity and distance from it. But in the case of nothingness, what humbles me is precisely my bond with it, the fact that it is included within my very being as one of my own possibilities. And the same line of reasoning requires us to conclude that its opacity and unspeakability are not the portents of a positive grandeur too rich for my merely human thought and speech. For if my experience of it as opaque were due to my inability to comprehend the overwhelmingly positive meaning of this nothingness to which I am liable, my very kinship with it would be no liability at all, but uplifting evidence of a greatness that would be mine by virtue of my participating in it. Its opacity can rupture the univocally positive meaning I ordinarily want my life to have only by virtue of its unintelligibility. If nothingness humbles me, it is because I am caught in the sway of its *nullity*, its utter lack of being and worth.

Indeed, only when one admits its utter negativity, its complete lack of meaning, does one cease romanticizing this nothingness to which we are liable. Perhaps in saying that nothingness deserves the courtesy of our horror-filled silence, I made the mistake of implying that it merits some honor by virtue of its own positive and noble stature. In fact, we owe nothingness nothing. We would demean not it but ourselves and our capacity to face the truth if we did not humbly acknowledge its power. It is our unwillingness to be horrified by our participation in it that is at work in our failure to realize its radically negative character.

In trying to deromanticize nothingness, it may seem that I have made it more triumphant, since I have been emphasizing that we are bound to it in its very nullity and lack of worth. But it is the very negativity of nothingness which diminishes its power. For insofar as I am infected by nothingness in my very being, and horrified by my helplessness in the face of it, I am certainly humbled *by* it. But this differs radically from being humble *before* it. It cannot demand that I lie prostrate before it as before something greater than myself. For I *am*, and I am a person. And my very being, with its irremediable frailty which I now acknowledge, is nevertheless *superior to* and possesses *a positive* stature in comparison to the nothingness which admittedly infects it. I stand, as it were, on the verge of nothingness, looking down into its abyss; but even so, I still occupy the higher position.

Nothingness has no proper claim on my heart except for this humbling admission of our familiarity. The very speechlessness of my horror, the vertigo of dread itself, these signs of my being humbled by nothingness nevertheless can be, at the same time, the first tokens of my resolve to resist death with a modest, unpretentious dignity, without pretending in the least that it is not inevitable or that I deserve to be exempt from it. Real acceptance of my liability to nothingness does not forbid a long, hard struggle against its success. Indeed, only if I unpretentiously resist it do I prove that I accept it in all its negativity without wrongly honoring it. Dreadful acknowledgment of my vulnerability to its humbling mortifications, indomitable resistance to its actual encroachment: if I can adopt this paradoxical attitude, I will have accepted death in its radical negativity, without in any way bowing to it.

We know there is a wrong kind of defiance, exemplified by the hero when he refuses what he thinks would be the humiliation of losing his stature: the dignity he is ashamed to lose is a dignity subtly but tragically confused with conceit. When he does, in fact, lose his stature, he ordinarily hates being what that loss reduces him to: utterly finite and human. He hates himself for losing the god-like dignity which alone still matters to him: his more-than-human stature. On the other hand, the self possessed of *authentic* dignity has not only ceased to pretend himself exempt from death and its mortifications. He has ceased pretending that he deserves such exemption. He will not object to or resent nothingness since being human means being liable to its humbling absurdities. But, at the same time, he never makes the admission which death, in fact, is always wrong to ask for—an admission of his inferiority before it. I am of greater worth than the nothingness to which I am already given over. Death has, so to speak, the right to rupture our pretensions; but it does not deserve our reverential awe. This is why an authentic acceptance of death requires that one still battle it as an enemy which deserves no easy victory, even as one admits that nothing entitles one to be exempt from its mortifications. Here at last is a heroism without pretensions which can nevertheless raise up, against nothingness, a protest that testifies to humbly human greatness.[7] The point is not to be exempt from nothingness, nor untouched by its mortification, but to affirm, even in the face of its impenetrable horror, not just our indestructible dignity but the inimitable glory of our strictly human be-ing. Indeed, no one is as genuinely dignified as the person who, liable to nothingness, neither avoids it nor turns in fear from it but suffers all of death's indignities without resentment and without losing his quiet decorum. Nothing so proves the authenticity of my dignity as my preserving it in the face of this nothingness which could so easily arouse my resentment or convince me that I am worthless. And the final proof of my superiority to it is the fact that I imprint on my death whatever indelible character I choose it to have. By one's very manner of dying one decides the meaning of one's death.[8]

We can now draw the unexpected conclusion toward which these reflections have been leading us. If I have accurately described the encounter with nothingness, it cannot, in fact, be the paradigm of all crisis experience. For nothingness, in spite of the literal disruption with which it threatens us, nevertheless leaves our modest dignity intact. Precisely because I am humbled by my kinship with nothingness, I cannot be dwarfed by it. Convinced by it that I lack the stature which conceit makes me seek, I am yet right to resist it on behalf of the real though finite stature I possess simply because I *am*. Nothingness cannot be the Other by which I am most radically disrupted because it leaves intact some sense of my own importance. With regard to the radicality of the crisis which it requires me to suffer, death, it turns out, can be surpassed; it is not my most radical possibility.[9]

This long excursus on nothingness has not been for naught. It points us past death toward a reality we ordinarily want even more desperately to avoid because it threatens to disrupt precisely that sense of our own innate dignity which nothingness itself leaves intact. If we stop at death, we have still not gone far enough in the sonography of humility or the geography of crisis. Death itself must be, in spite of its literality, only the metaphor for a deeper rupture, one which does not leave the self erect but shatters it in its very stature as a self. That kind of rupture, we must now try to see, is indeed a death, one more personal and more devastating than that prompted by one's encounter with nothingness. We ought to know already where to look: in the direction of the experience of shame which alone makes us bow down under the mortifying weight of our failures. For shame entails my abject grief on behalf of some reality which my acts have wronged. As such, it implicitly includes my acknowledgment that the reality so wronged deserves my reverence. Shame, as my bowing down under the weight of guilt, is already my bowing down before something Other than my self, in acknowledgment of its being superior in stature to myself. In that sense and for that reason, it constitutes a kind of contrite obedience to what one experiences as sacred. Shame is the prefiguration of worship. When, instead of remaining implicit as it is in shame, it becomes fully explicit, this obedience requires of the heart a complete prostration. If we are to complete this pilgrimage in search of radical crisis, we must try to describe the religious experience which such prostration embodies. For dying lets us look down toward the abyss of nothingness from the height we still occupy, even as we die. But more radical is the possibility of looking up at a reality before which we realize that we are nothing. It is toward this crisis, than which none greater can be conceived, that we must now move.

2. Authentic Shame and the Beginning of Humility

I have suggested that the experience of shame foreshadows an explicit encounter with the Sacred. To explore this suggestion we will try to understand where shame leads when one does not deflect it into self-hatred but follows it all the way to the sorrowful end of its pedagogy.

Let us first recall the closed dialectic in which self-hatred imprisons one. The person filled with self-hatred does not look for scapegoats whom he can blame for his evil. But if he is determined to acknowledge his own evil, he is equally determined to detest himself for committing it. The act of condemning himself actually enables him to stand above and look down upon his evil from a superior position. Whatever indignities he makes himself suffer, the fact that he inflicts them on himself raises him to the stature of judge and executioner.

This has led us to the conclusion that, far from being its opposite, self-hatred is the final version of desire to be perfect. The person consumed by self-hatred is on the verge of a real reversal, and for that very reason he desperately holds onto the one thing which all along has meant more to him than everything—his ability to rise above whatever happened to him. Height is the position we always seek, in the geography of the heart. We always want to be able to *look down*, even if the Other we look down on is in the end our very selves. Intimately associated with this location is the privilege of being contemptuous, and the power to humiliate. When it is dragged down from the height it has always assumed to be its rightful place, the heart inevitably experiences its fall as a humiliation. What an observer not subject to the same delusions would describe as our being brought "down to earth," we ourselves always experience as a debasement. For the desire to be perfect makes one incapable of conceiving of the least loss of height as anything but a degradation.

Now what must occur for this desire and the vicious circle of self-hatred to be broken? In hating my self, I stand above my own evil so that, in the very act of owning it as mine, I distance my self from it. Paradoxically, it is exactly this therapy of detesting oneself which enables me to avoid the genuinely mortifying experience of shame. If I am really to acknowledge my evil, if I am to realize how thoroughly mine it is, I must cease willing not to be the radically flawed self which I am. I must consent to the existence of my self, with all its unretractable evil. The moment one begins to feel shame, one is confronted with a choice which we might express this way: I can either look away from my self (under the impulse of shame) and refuse to accept what I have seen except as a reality to be annihilated; or I can bury my face in my hands and consent to keep on being this self I now realize through shame to be horrifying. The latter gesture alone signifies real acceptance of shame's teaching. In burying my face in my hands, I stop trying to free my self from its accusations. I cease pretending to be anyone except this self, stained with evil, which I am. I give up in a radical way the will to transcend my self, to the degree that this involves trying to disown my character. Instead of rising up self-righteously against my own evil, I finally identify my self with the culprit from whom, up until now, I have tried to disassociate myself. What does it mean to "identify" with this self? It means I agree to *be* the culprit; I finally accept the fact of my evil without denying any of its horror.

This last phase adds the crucial qualification and accentuates the paradox at the heart of the self-effacing attitude I am trying to describe. As we have seen, part of the very evil of evil is precisely the fact that doing it causes us to be unaware of its horror. In exercising the will to control, we do not ordinarily feel any inhibiting sense of shame. The banality of evil, the nonchalance with which it is done, follows from its very essence. The heart of its darkness is precisely the fact that one does horrifying things without being upset by them. Becoming aware of that horror is, as we have seen, the beginning of conscience; and that horror is so upsetting when it is glimpsed for the first time that our instinctive response is to disassociate ourselves from it. That recoil leads to the vicious circle of self-hatred by which one recognizes the evil in oneself and rejects it at the same time. The only route that leads beyond its antinomies without circling back to the will to control is the one that leads straight into the fault in the heart: the dark road of shame itself. Nothing compares to the quiet, mortifying sorrow the heart experiences when one finally agrees to be shame's pupil, and to accept its truths. The great paradox of the moral life is that one begins to live it only when the horror of what one has done is allowed to have its shattering effect.

Mortifying sorrow is as exact an expression as I can find to suggest the particular kind of suffering which the heart undergoes here. Avoidance has so long required the heart to keep its rationalizations straight, to muffle nervously all upsetting intimations of truth and horror, to squelch the suspicions and anxieties that have occasionally assailed it, that this decisive wound, precisely because it wounds so deeply, creates a sense of excruciating catharsis because the heart is finally free to express the cry which it has struggled so long to keep suppressed. The heart knows that now, at last, it has reached the place it has spent its life avoiding. One is finally there, inside the fault which splits open the hard ground of one's heart. When the heart at last surrenders, when it not only ceases resisting, but yields to shame's mortifying truths instead of recoiling from them, that surrender fills it with a pain that is strangely peaceful because it could not possibly be more complete. This excruciating serenity cannot be ruptured by horror because it is itself the complete letting-be of what horrifies. His own evil does horrify—even to the point of nausea—the self who severs his deepest avoidances. When the mortified person buries his face in his hands, it is because only by looking there, into that solitary darkness, can he keep on seeing who he is. He has ceased hating himself not because he no longer sees himself as evil but because he has ceased pretending he can achieve that distance from his evil which such hate still tries to attain. He ceases hating himself because that is too proud a way of acknowledging that he ought to be mortified through and through.

The mortified person realizes how profoundly *just* such mortification is, and that his experience of it is no temporary emotional episode. Indeed, he must accept it as the permanent condition of his existence. He must go on being himself but utterly deprived of all stature. He must shrink to the size of the dwarf he had always tried not to be. We might recall the fact that, even when suffering a small embarrassment, we say "I wish I could disappear into the woodwork"; that is, I wish I could become so small as to be unnoticeable—so that others would be unable to see me. But why do I want to avoid their look? Because of how small it makes me feel—because it confronts me with my inadequacy and lack of worth. If we gave up all our different ways of looking away from it, shame would reveal that we are exactly as small and as inadequate as the look of the Other sometimes suggests.

When the heart finally owns up to its diminutive stature, it moves, in a sense, past shame to humility. The genuinely humble person sees himself so shot through with inadequacy that he recognizes the pride that hides beneath the desire to be his own punisher. Indeed, he knows that none of his acts deserves to be completely exempt from ridicule. But if such a person knows that trying to stand above and look down on oneself is only another one of pride's follies, does not that knowledge and the humility which accompanies it *elevate* him above all those occupying any of the positions previously described in this geography of crisis?

This is a question which pentrates deeply into the paradox at the heart of humility. For it seems that either one is aware of one's humility and of the fact that it raises one's moral stature, in which case one acquires through humility exactly that superior position which it requires one to surrender; or one does one's best to remain ignorant of one's humility because this virtue is incompatible with self-consciousness and requires a child-like naiveté. Now I think we find ourselves on the horns of this dilemma because we have not yet taken seriously the insights which the mortified person has about himself. Placing him as we have at the deepest position in the geography of crisis, we find it hard to believe his protestations of inadequacy. We think we know him better than his humility permits him to know himself because we recognize how extraordinary he is, how set apart he is from Others by virtue of his willingness to be mortified. If the argument of this whole book is correct, our judgment of him is accurate. But our way of making this judgment only proves how difficult it is for us to think in terms of the paradoxes which govern the thinking of the humble person himself.

For, in the first place, humility is always a destination, never a position one can claim to have reached; one's awareness of one's inadequacies is itself always in some way inadequate. The person who, as shame's docile pupil, knows how little he measures up to all the virtues, knows more about himself than those of us who praise him. For he has a much clearer inkling than we do of how far he has yet to go; we only think he has arrived because, having stopped at the verge of it, we are not in a position to realize that the abyss he is exploring is bottomless. His reasons for deflecting our praise of him are more profound than our reasons for offering it. His knowledge of his inadequacy is a deeper truth than our knowledge of his excellence. He already knows that he will learn shortly how superficially he has understood his insignificance.

Nevertheless, it is true that such a person, precisely because he is headed into the abyss of humility, precisely because he knows he cannot ever get to the bottom of it, has reached a depth of existence compared to which all other modes of living are superficial. The person who reaches that depth cannot help but be aware of having done so. If he allows us to adopt him as our model, it is on the condition that we recognize him not as an *achiever* who, happy, successful, raised up on the height of his deeds, breathes the heady air of his own greatness, but as a *failure* who is plunged, by a vertigo he ceases to resist, into a crisis he can neither understand nor control but only suffer. If he does not take our praise seriously, it is not because he is naively unaware of his exceptional character or of the extraordinary depth at which he lives. Rather, it is because he appreciates, as we do not, that humility is not a virtue one practices like any other. For one possesses it not by virtue of an accomplishment but by virtue of a fall. He smiles a knowing, ironic smile at our words of praise because he knows that, far from humility being his achievement, he did his best to prevent the mortification that has brought him to it.

Does not the whole reasoning of this essay make his disclaimer plausible? For what, after all, is an accomplishment? Is it not something we achieve through our own efforts? Is it not always brought about by our raising ourselves up by our bootstraps to some level of being that is higher than the one from which we started? But being mortified is not something we achieve; it is something we suffer. It is not brought about by our own efforts; it occurs only when we make no effort to interfere with shame's unique capacity to upset and horrify. And instead of raising us to new heights, the experience of being mortified pulls the ground out from under us. Far from being an accomplishment we can claim credit for, it is precisely the experience of failure which we devote our lifetime to preventing.

3. The Geography of Crisis as a Dialectic of Descent

If, as moderns, we find being a failure especially upsetting, that is because our moral imaginations are almost irresistibly drawn in the opposite direction. We work to make our lives a spiral of transcendence, to rise above our finite selves not just by doing something good but by becoming something higher, by actualizing our selves *vertically*. This height we seek is no heaven or mystical after-world, but a this-wordly stature we imagine to be achievable through self-discipline and self-transformation. In every such transformation, the will, refusing to rest on its laurels, cleaves to a new and higher resolve, giving up its secured achievement for a more demanding task and a higher perfection. We like to think that the dialectic of human life drives upward.

One apparent proof of our power to practice such vertical transcendence is the dialectic of self-consciousness.[10] For if I am conscious of my self and can therefore discover some truth about my self, that very act, that very achievement, alters who I am. The power of reflexivity, and the fact that I can step back and examine myself, proves I can transcend myself. And even if I fail to put into practice what I learn through self-criticism, the latter is itself already a transcendence, a standing above the person I was before. The power to actualize one's self vertically is inseparable from this power to be reflectively self-critical, the power to take up a position of *superiority* toward one's actual self. The human person is always already ascendent. He is his own transcendent. Insofar as I become conscious of my limits (inadequacies, faults), I am already beyond them.[11]

I certainly have no intention of denying that human life can and ought to take the form of a dialectic, or that the motive and momentum which powers that dialectic is self-criticism. But to take such self-criticism seriously, we need to identify rightly its nature and the conditions which make it possible. I have been trying to suggest throughout this essay that the dialectical path of self-criticism ought to be imagined as a vertical *descent*, as our tumbling off one pretension after another until we begin to plumb our smallness. Our lives call for a geography of crisis, not an astronomy of ascension, because, as Heidegger realized, to get to the highest truths one has to take the path that leads down to our nothingness. In this dialectic of descent, we reach no terminal point but only a critical turning point: not our becoming infinite but our finally acknowledging as ours the small and mortified selves which we use our pretensions of vertical transcendence to avoid.

If this claim has merit, it should enable us to develop a different and more adequate reading of what occurs in the act of becoming self-conscious and self-critical. Let us begin with the latter. First of all, it is impossible for me to be radically critical of my self *on behalf of my self*. If I accused myself of not living up to "oughts" which I myself invented, I would be criticizing my self without calling into question my underlying assumption that there is nothing superior to me.[12] Such criticism would leave my own superior position intact. If there is nothing higher than myself in relationship to which I judge myself, I cannot take the criticisms I make against myself seriously. My self-criticism can pull the ground out from under me only if I make it not on behalf of myself but on behalf of a reality which reveals my smallness and unimportance. For only such a reality would require my calling into question even the sense of superiority which one enjoys when one prosecutes and judges oneself. Self-hatred of the type we have dissected is only one example of the sense of self-importance which is operative in every kind of self-criticism whose purpose is to raise the self to a higher level. The only alternative to such self-importance is prostration before an Other in the presence of which one acknowledges one's insignificance. Genuine self-criticism does not leave one's own self-importance intact; that is why it is made possible only by one's taking up an attitude of inferiority before an Other that is more worthy of one's devotion than one's own will. The self-improvement, the so-called transcendence, which follows from self-criticism is precisely *a consenting to one's relative inferiority*, an agreeing to give up all the efforts one has been making to transcend one's nothingness. What one criticizes in genuine self-criticism are precisely one's old claims to transcendence.

Nevertheless, it might be argued with some plausibility that such a conversion surely presupposes and entails a *heightening* of consciousness so that, in achieving it, one transcends one's ignorance of the Other and reaches a new knowledge of one's self. But this way of describing the conversion about which we are speaking fails again to take seriously the disruptive paradox that is operative in humility. For what occurs when I discover a radical new truth about my self? If radical, it ruptures my previous "self-knowledge," revealing the unsuspected delusions on which it was based. But if my new insight purports to provide me exhaustive knowledge of myself, it has left undisturbed the presumption underlying my previous way of understanding myself.[13] It would have failed to shatter me into realizing that the desire to have complete knowledge of oneself is itself an aspect of one's will to control. The only kind of self-criticism that radically disrupts us is one that leads us to realize that we are always unknowable to ourselves. For then we have to surrender to the radical insecurity which such a lack of knowledge entails. Since its inception, philosophy has encouraged us to know ourselves. But the highest form of this knowledge is the wisdom of knowing that we do not know. Because we look upon them as definitive, we turn the truths we do reach into delusions. Each time I think I finally see with perfect clarity how blind I used to be, I am letting that new clarity blind me to the fact that I am repeating the same folly. That *exhaustive* self-knowledge is unachievable follows from the very reflexivity which makes our partial self-knowledge possible. That to know my self I must step back from my self proves that I am not immediately present, immediately available, to my own thinking. We never fully catch up with ourselves. Far from proving my power to stand above my self, the stepping back I do to become conscious of my self always carries me forward into a new world I have never before explored. The changes that will be wrought in me by my deepening self-knowledge are themselves shrouded in obscurity. The only real breakthrough, the only real rupture, with regard to self-knowledge, would be my beginning to realize the impossibility of ever exhaustively attaining it. This is indeed a new truth which as such possesses the power to disrupt me radically, and it does so precisely because it confronts me with the fact that I must always fail to secure the kind of finality I have always hoped to achieve.

That failure is, as Socrates tried to explain at the end of his life, the only true kind of success. He saw that the whole point of knowing is not to transcend ignorance but to plumb it. We never come to the end of it.

The journey toward self-knowledge is no ascent toward a definitive truth; it leads us downward, toward a more and more profound insight into unfathomable depths. The dialectic proper to self-consciousness is this descent into an always deepening darkness, this step-by-step stripping away of pretensions, so that consciousness becomes more and more destitute.[14] The person undergoing this descent discovers his limits time and time again, but this discovery does not liberate him from them; the one real liberation is from the delusion that one can transcend them. In making that breakthrough one understands one's limits not in the sense of mastering them, but in the sense of becoming consciously *subject to* them so that one is aware of being enveloped by an inescapable mystery that never ceases to unfold in unforeseeable ways. Finitude is asymtotic. But if it is impossible to exhaust the depths of my ignorance, it is not impossible for me to surrender to this very inexhaustibility. And the breakthrough to this surrender is part of the last turning point in that descent I have called crisis.

So we return, here at the heart of our inquiry, to the image with which we began: the image of boundaries. If, ordinarily, I will to impose them on the whole wide expanse of being, I do so because I want my control of it to be absolute. I myself do not want to be *bound* by anything. The will to control is, we now see, the will to absolute transcendence, the will to stand above everything, the will to have everything beneath me. The route we have followed is the dialectic of its reversal, and the consummate moment of that reversal can only be my consent to the fact that I am bound in on all sides by a reality which dwarfs me and on whose account I must be ashamed. What makes crisis upsetting is that it requires my embracing this dwarf-like stature, without defiance or resentment. The stiff neck of pride breaks only when the head bows. This act of consent, wrung from one in a moment of uncontrollable anguish, is the small, barely audible "yes" of one's self to an Other before which one is aware of one's nothingness.

4. Worship as the Experience of Nothingness

I have intimated that we can realize our smallness only when we find ourselves in the shadow of a reality which dwarfs us. There is no such thing as a solipsistic humility, for humility requires bowing down before an Other. Nor can there be a humble solipsism, for by remaining closed up within himself the solipsist makes it impossible for his life to be disrupted by a reality that would require an acknowledgment of his inferiority. Were I the only reality in existence, I would not have to be humble. Conversely, all humility takes place not just *before, in the face of,* an Other, but *because, on account of,* an Other which radically awes us. But even that is not enough. We must say that humility is also *on behalf of* this Other. For, as the humble person experiences it, this Other evokes from him—rather, its very reality requires of him—an act of oblation, an offering, even though in making this offering he does not presume to be giving it something it needs.

We cannot deepen our understanding of this humility except by thematizing the experience of the Other which evokes it. This experience is of its very nature an experience of the sacred, if by "the sacred" is meant an Other over which one has no control and in relationship to which one is aware of one's insignificance. As such, the sacred is, I suggest, what death cannot be: that Other in relationship to which the self suffers a crisis than which none greater can be conceived. More of a dying than death itself is the surrender of the will to what it experiences as holy. We must now try to discern the distinguishing characteristics of such an experience, and the nature of the act of prostration by which one surrenders one's whole self to it in an unsurpassable way. Just because of the radicality of that surrender, our account of it must include, in constant interplay, not just ethical but also epistemological and ontological motifs: for a prostration of one's *whole* self radically undermines not just one's stature as a chooser but one's stature as a knower and even one's stature as a being.

Now if we are to examine the experience of the sacred with a view toward understanding the radically disruptive effect it must have, we ought to concentrate on it in its purest form, where its distinguishing features stand out in all their unrelenting radicality. Humility before the Other can take the form of reverence or the form of worship. When I acknowledge an Other to be more important than my own preferences, I reverence it as sacred in some sense and to some degree; but when I acknowledge an Other to be more important than anything else, including my own preferences, I worship it as ultimately Sacred. Reverence is, as it were, the limited obedience one owes anything which one acknowledges as participating in the Sacred; worship, on the other hand, is the unconditional surrender which, according to the religious person, must be reserved for the Ultimately Sacred itself, for that Other which, in our culture, is called God. But this means that the demands of reverence are, in fact, included within the more fundamental demands of worship because what deserves reverence deserves it because and insofar as it participates in the Sacred. Consequently, we will not be inappropriately restricting our focus if we concentrate on worship's unreserved surrender to the ultimately Sacred.

Now the worship of the Sacred entails, I suggest, a much more radical experience of one's own nothingness than occurs in an encounter with death. For standing before the nothingness to which death makes me liable, I can still affirm that I *am* and am not nothing. But, standing before what I experience as ultimately Sacred, I am compelled to acknowledge that *in and of my self I am precisely nothing*. Before the Sacred, I feel, in and of myself, utterly insignificant, utterly without substance. I cannot take myself seriously. It will help here to recall the distinction between dread and terror. Terror, which is itself fear rendered acute and panicky by an imminent danger, has, of course, always been recognized as an appropriate response to the Sacred. We can be so stricken by its Otherness, by its radical incongruity with our lives, by the radical threat it poses to our selves, that we pull back and flee from it even though we might sense that all flight is futile because it has the power to find us, no matter where we hide. To be stricken with such religious terror, one must have ventured close enough to the Sacred to realize how awful it is.

But the person who is terrified of the Sacred has not yet broken through the will to control. For the awe he feels before the Sacred is effaced by his compulsion to survive his encounter with it. Dread, on the other hand, is serene and quietly bowed. If dread before the Sacred does not motivate us to flee, it is not because it makes us think we can stand up to the Sacred, nor because it makes us stoically resigned to the fact that its power renders all flight futile. What dread makes one realize is precisely the radical insignificance of oneself.[15] One does not flee in terror to save one's being because the purpose of such flight would be to keep the Sacred from casting one into nothingness; and what dread makes one realize is precisely that, in and of oneself, one is already nothing in relation to it. The person overcome by dread has already surrendered to the abyss which terror is trying to flee.

It is important to understand how such an acceptance of one's nothingness differs from the desire to annihilate oneself which we associated with self-hatred. What fills us with self-hatred is precisely some recognition of our lacks and inadequacies, some realization of our nothingness. But in a dreadful experience of the Sacred, it is the pretension underlying such self-hatred that is taken away from us. Humility requires us to give up the desire to be perfect that underlies our resentment of our nothingness. Unlike self-hatred, which makes us want to get rid of our inadequacies, humility requires us to keep on being just this nothingness, even as we realize that it deprives us of the kind of importance we have always wanted to have.

I will now try to explore the ramifications of this sense of poverty which humility tries to awaken in every dimension of our lives.

5. Being and Nothingness from the Perspective of Prostration

If, in trying to describe the nature of worship, I have focused on the sense of nothingness it entails, that is not because of any desire to import a particular metaphysical theory into religious experience. Such words, laden as they are with metaphysical implications, arise from the experience itself. When the religious person prostrates himself before what he experiences as radically Other, he cannot speak of that Otherness or articulate the import of his prostration before it, without employing terms that suggest its radical nature. He must find words to express the fact that the discrepancy between himself and that Other cannot be more extreme than it is. All the terms used by the religious worshipper are synonyms for his radical inferiority before the Sacred or its radical superiority to him. If, by metaphysical thinking, one means the effort to break through common-sense assumptions to the fundamental underlying truths about our being, then religious utterances are always at least implicitly metaphysical for, in the eyes of the religious person, the act of worship gives us the privileged position for finding such truths: the position of prostration.

That for whose sake such prostration occurs is always experienced as absolute being, even if such being manifests itself in a mountain or tree. I do not mean the phrase "absolute being" as I use it here to be identified with any particular philosophical theory. Rather, I use the phrase as religious man himself uses it, to express the perfect plenitude, the unconditional fullness that makes the Sacred worthy not just of his reverence but of his worship. What worship always says of the Sacred is simply that nothing can be beyond it, superior to it, that it is, as it were, the absolute beyond, beyond which there is no beyond. The religious person must speak of this reality as absolute being, unmixed with negativity.[16] For if he were to attribute any negativity to it, he would be implying that it shares in the nothingness with which he identifies himself. The terms "being" and "nothingness" both acquire their meaning from the same single act of prostration by which the self bows down to its radical Other. When looked at from that prostrate point of view, our very being itself is nothing in comparison to the richness of the Sacred. It is not appropriate, therefore, for one to use the words "being," "positivity," "existence," etc. to describe oneself; strictly speaking, they should be reserved for the

Sacred.[17] We are accustomed, of course, to the opposite assumption—that these terms, if they can be applied to the Sacred at all, must be borrowed for that purpose from the context where they naturally belong, our descriptions of ourselves and our world. But it is precisely this common-sense point of view that the act of prostration literally turns on its head. The religious person leads the whole universe in a confession of its poverty. In the experience of worship, all things other than the utimately Sacred evaporate into their own inner hollowness. In the presence of the Sacred, each being suddenly sinks inwardly into its own insignificance; the long-kept secret of its nothingness is finally exposed. The whole universe falls to its knees—not to plead, or flatter, but to undo the pretense of its deserving to stand upright and sovereign. Only the Sacred requires our ceasing to treat ourselves as the paradigm of being. Facing it, we cannot commit the blasphemy of even claiming *to be* at all, since the Sacred *is* in so transcendent a sense. Its is-ing is so utterly unlike ours that it requires us to say that it alone is being, and all else nothing.

But the religious person knows that such a statement, precisely because it leaves the two terms of prostration so separate and unrelated, does not adequately convey our dependence on the Sacred. Compelled to identify himself with nothingness, the religious person knows that, nevertheless, he exists. Condensed in this paradox is, indeed, what might be called the humbling metaphysical reversal which occurs in every authentic religious experience and, if our argument has been correct, in every crisis, if one sees it through to its end. If I did not exist, I would be released from what my pride experiences as the humiliation of being just my small self in all its poverty. On the other hand, if I were still able to believe in my own importance, I would still feel justified in resenting the profound kinship that ties me to nothingness. I am nothing—and yet I am. I stand apart from, distinct from, the Sacred—but that is impossible because to be utterly distanced from it would mean being separated from being itself. In consenting to the Sacred as the paradigm of being, I have to acknowledge that my be-ing is utterly derivative in nature. I can only be said to be in a radically secondary sense of the term; in the primary sense of the term, being belongs only to the Sacred.[18] That I am, in any sense of the term, that there is such a derivative sense to the term "being", is the radical privilege that is not just unearned and undeserved but incongruous with what must be called my intrinsic nullity. It is not just that there is no necessity for me to be. My self, considered apart from what it is by virtue of its being derivative of the Sacred, my self considered in complete independence and autonomy from the Sacred, is exactly nothing. On my own, I am not at all. I exist only as a pale reflection of the Sacred itself. All that I am, I am as an derivative version of that ultimate reality.

This way of putting it describes only my stature, not yet my origin as it is revealed in an encounter with the Sacred. For we have described the experience of the Sacred as paradigm, but not yet the experience of the Sacred as power. But one inevitably implies the Other. For the Sacred would not be the paradigm of being if it were not itself the agency which presides over every exercise of power, especially the creation of its derivatives. If the religious person is to speak properly of his nothingness before the Sacred, he must say not only that he is nothing except its pale reflection, but also that the Sacred itself *casts* this reflection. All that I am, according to such a person, is vouchsafed me by the Sacred. The religious person sees the whole of himself as the gift he is given to be. Moreover, the religious person feels required to say this not just about himself but about everything that is not the Sacred itself. Everything which is owes its being to the Power of the radically Other. It can claim nothing as strictly its own accomplishment. It is the recipient of its very self. This is the confession I want least of all to utter since it entails giving up, in a finally decisive way, my fundamentally being in control of my self and my life. Having to embrace such primal gratitude, having to be unworthy of everything and yet helplessly dependent, having to be this metaphysical beggar, this nullity: it is the posture expressive of just this inferiority and engiftment which the person animated by some residual pride still refuses to adopt: the posture of prostration, the very body of worship. We recoil from such an indentured stature, and from its gesture of indebtedness, as from nothingness itself.

Essential to the metaphysical irony at the heart of the religious experience is the fact that we are, after all, autonomous beings. We are independent of the Sacred in the sense that we stand over against the Sacred as a reality distinct from it. My being is mine alone, not its. But this very independence, my very distinctness from the Sacred, is itself a gift it gives to me. The Sacred stands me over against itself and gives me my very otherness from it. If, like Prometheus, I revolt against the Sacred, it is not because I am trying to become autonomous; I am already autonomous— and what fills me with such resentment is precisely the fact that I have to be thankful even for what is most intrinsic to me. In the act of worship, on the contrary, one agrees to be dependent on the Other for one's very independence from him.

6. The Prostration of the Mind: Socratic Humility

But how, it might be objected, can such worship occur if the Sacred which the religious person claims to experience, transcends, as he claims, everything that derives from it? If the Sacred is transcendent, must it not be outside the reach of our experience? On the other hand, if we can experience and know it, how can it be transcendent? Both alternatives seem to prove the impossibility of the religious experience as we have been trying to describe it.[19] Moreover, if we look inside the logic of this objection we will find that it calls into question the very possibility of our being able to experience a radical crisis. For the latter requires that I encounter a reality which fundamentally disrupts my existence: but either this reality, as radically *Other*, is totally inaccessible to me, in which case an encounter with it is impossible, or this reality *is* accessible to me, in which case it belongs to my world and is not disruptive of it. Both alternatives seem to prove the impossibility of our undergoing a crisis that is as radical and uprooting as the one I have been trying to describe. In putting us on the horns of this dilemma, is logic trying to show us that we have made the rupture of crisis too severe?

Before trying to answer this question, let us first reflect on any one of those small but exemplary experiences which suggest the complexities of our knowing and unknowing. Most obvious is the very fact of my asking questions, something I only do when I am aware of being puzzled, baffled, lost, mystified. But there is also the experience of being caught up in a work of art which so surpasses my comprehension that I cannot even find the insight needed to ask questions about it: a sense of being not just puzzled but dumbfounded and overwhelmed.

It is important to distinguish such an experience from one where we are confronted with something completely irrational. In the latter case, I am in the presence of something which I find incomprehensible not because of my limited capacity but because of its innate lack of rational coherence; I view it as *inferior* to me because it does not measure up to my minimal standards of meaning. But when a work of art gradually draws me into its complex web of meaning until I realize I am "in over my head," I feel pulled beyond my limits into a universe that surpasses my comprehension. My inability to understand this universe may be due to a deficiency in me that is in principle correctable, or it may be due to natural limits of the human mind and therefore be incorrectable. In the latter case, I am confronted with a universe of meaning which I know I cannot possibly enter, so incommensurable is it with my world. But precisely at this point, the issue at stake emerges clearly. For how can I *know* that something possesses a richness of meaning that surpasses my comprehension—if it surpasses my comprehension?

And in fact we ordinarily judge something irrational and inferior to us if we cannot understand it. If the richness of a work of art is not evident on its surface, I usually consider it a failure; what it has failed to do is to make itself fully accessible to me. Generally speaking, the intelligibility of things is judged by the degree to which they yield to our ability to understand them. We tend to identify the meaningful with what is meaningful to us. And from that perspective, an inaccessible meaning is simply a contradiction in terms; the meaningful is what does not hide but presents its face to the inquiring intellect. But it is not difficult to see that what underlies such a perspective is the will to control making, here in the realm of the intellect, its same self-serving demands. It convinces the intellect to exercise its autonomy and to set itself up as the standard of rationality. But this is simply the intellect's refusal to consider even the possibility that there might be a reality that is capable of dumbfounding it. Every rationalism is a version of this secularizing refusal.

Now, if we pause to reflect on the path which this text has taken in charting the experience of crisis, we will see that it has involved a series of upsetting realizations, each of which requires acknowledging a truth that undermines one's whole world. These horrifying recognitions are the most painful form of knowing, for, as we have seen, they shatter one's whole way of understanding one's life. They wring from us the admission that the whole web of meaning we have used to make sense of our lives has really been based on a desire to avoid facing certain realities we were too terrified to acknowledge. Are not these moments of horror our truest moments? And are they not horrifying because they make us see that our lives do not have the meaning we thought they had? The human mind is closest to the deepest truths precisely at those moments when all knowledge it thought it possessed is undermined by dreadful realities about which it knows nothing except that it is ignorant of them. The experience of crisis thus confirms the Socratic paradox which philosophy throughout its long history has tried to escape: the deepest wisdom attainable in this mortal life is the knowledge of one's ignorance. The path of crisis, with its series of upsetting realizations, confirms as well the Socratic claim that this wisdom can only be attained by the person who dies not once but over and over again. The person who wants to become wise does not try to avoid those deaths, but embraces them, not, like the tragic hero, because he hopes they will transform him into something god-like, but, like Socrates, because he hopes they will humble him. If Socrates couples wisdom with the humility of acknowledging one's ignorance and the pursuit of wisdom with the practice of dying, he is intimating that the *mind* can become wise only by undergoing again and again the death it suffers when it acknowledges that reality always undermines its desire to control it by knowing it.

It is surprising that Socrates speaks about God in the same apology that

he uses to explain why human wisdom consists in knowing we are ignorant. We wonder how he can justify talking about the ultimately Sacred
as if he knows that it is real when he is telling us at the same time that all
he knows is that he knows nothing. But knowing that the ultimately Sacred is real, far from diminishing Socrates' sense of being ignorant, is precisely what makes him so certain he cannot possibly transcend his ignorant
condition. God is that which we cannot ever fathom; but only in realizing
that God is real does the mind come up against a reality that can wring
from it a confession of its poverty. Only by acknowledging that reality
does the mind undergo the upsetting experience which its determination
to know has made it avoid.

But in coming up against the unfathomable reality of God, in undergoing this reversal that turns all its knowledge into ignorance, the mind is
only suffering a more radical, more dreadful version of the upsetting experience it has every time it is seized by wonder and driven to question.
That we can be aware of a reality which nevertheless surpasses our comprehension only seems impossible if we forget what it is like to be caught
up in the throes of our first amazement, when we found ourselves standing dumbstruck before a reality that overwhelmed us. Perhaps the fact
that wonder in its very essence is a crisis experience, that it uproots our
thought from its assumptions and common-sense routines, becomes clear
to us only when wonder takes the form of horror, and fills us with a terrible foreboding of something that is totally foreign to our world because
it is the very end of it. In such moments we suddenly become aware of the
awful realities we cannot know. But even though we know nothing of them
except that they exist, the avoidances that have always kept us oblivious
of them have failed to do their work. From the beginning of this essay we
have observed the crucial role those avoidances play in preventing crisis.
Now we see that the opposite of avoidance is not knowledge as we ordinarily conceive of it, for such knowledge itself provides us a way to
avoid the upsetting ordeal of dread. The opposite of avoidance is the Socratic wisdom that consists in surrendering one's mind to the throes of a
horror that undermines everything we thought we knew. The dialectic of
knowledge takes the form of a downward trajectory. And if Socrates was
right, we never get all the way down to the bottom of it.

And yet if we cannot get to the bottom of ignorance, it is only because
we are continually confirmed in it by looking up to a reality which our
finitude prevents us from knowing. The God Socrates believed in can be
known, but only in that knowing ignorance which he called wisdom and
which I have called dread. It is only through dread that we experience the
very transcendence of the transcendent. The Ultimately Sacred is that

which cannot be experienced except in our knowing our ignorance of it. It compels the mind to become aware of its destitution.[20] But anyone who delves this deeply into the crisis of being human prizes his ignorance of the Sacred infinitely more than all the knowledge that can be attained about everything else. To deepen one's awareness of this ignorance, to plumb its depths and, in so doing, to die over and over again, is the only way for the mind to mine its richest ore. It is not true that for one enrolled in this tutorial, no advancement is possible. One can get closer and closer to the Sacred as one realizes, with every discovery of one's ignorance, how utterly Other it is. Real closeness between the Sacred and the human self is the opposite of geographical proximity. We get closer to it as we look further and further up from a position further and further down in the abyss of our ignorance.

And now I think we are finally at a point where we can understand the ramifications of the distinction made earlier between an encounter with nothingness and an encounter with the Ultimately Sacred. For nothingness is not able to make the mind aware of its poverty. It is true that nothingness, like the Sacred, has a forbidding aspect and that it undermines every attempt I make to define it. It is true that it renders my whole repertoire of predicates useless. The mind must finally confess its ignorance in the face of the insurmountable impasse that nothingness puts in its way. But how would the mind express the fact that nothingness surpasses its comprehension except by saying, without exaggeration, that all its insights regarding it amount to *nothing*? Whenever we want to speak of our inferiority, our insignificance, our lack, our poverty, we compare ourselves to nothing because we know that nothingness itself is the ultimate inferior, the ultimate poverty. Every upsetting and humbling experience, whatever its source or occasion, including the intellectual humbling about which we have been speaking, prompts us to identify with nothingness. There can be no such event as our being humble *before* nothingness because nothingness is what we are required to identify *with* whenever we encounter a reality that humbles us. We cannot revere nothingness as if it were superior to us because what deserves reverence reveals our kinship with nothingness by depriving us of the stature we claimed to have.

If we flounder whenever we try to describe or explain this nothingness, that is because it is always *less* than any thought or image suggests. Our thought always tends to give it a positive character it does not possess. But it is wrong humbly to confess our nothingness in comparison with it because it is the very nothingness to which we relegate ourselves when we need to confess our destitution. What makes us flounder in describing it is not its plenitude but its negativity, not the fact that it is superior to our minds but inferior to them insofar as it lacks any positive meaning or coherence.[21] We are unable to comprehend nothingness not because of our ineptitude but because of its lack of intelligibility. Confronting nothingness cannot be the exemplar of all crisis precisely because we are justified in insisting on our superiority to it. It is only when we encounter something infinitely greater than ourselves that we are required to give up this superior position and identify with the very nothingness which up till then we had looked down on. If we are right to object to those types of science and therapy which try to tame nothingness, it is not because it is sacred but because such attempts to tame it help us forget how radically diminished the authentically religious person feels when the Sacred proves his kinship with it.

On the other hand, the person who does not get close enough to the Sacred to realize his identity with nothingness will still feel superior to the latter. It does not take the mind long to figure out that our inability to understand nothingness is due to its lack of intelligible meaning. The existentialist who confronts nothingness is likely to feel that our liability to it renders our lives absurd. But this sense of being caught in the throes of an absurdity, far from humbling the mind, makes it feel the victim of a horrifying injustice that calls forth the passion of heroic revolt.[22] If our liability to nothingness renders our lives absurd, it also leaves the point of our lives up to us. We are free to make them mean whatever we want. To stand on the edge of the abyss and look down can be an upsetting, even nauseating, experience.[23] But, after all, if one only has to *look down* at something inferior to one, one's superior position has not been undermined; in fact, it has been confirmed by the very act of looking down. From that existential point of view, the absurdity that nothingness introduces into our lives also leaves it up to us alone to decide the meaning of the universe. If life in itself is a tale told by an idiot, we all have the freedom to make up our own story.

But, for all his dignity and courage, the person who emerges from such an encounter with absurdity is wrong to think he has suffered the most upsetting of all ordeals. For it is more upsetting to fall into the abyss of nothingness than to stand on its edge, and even more upsetting than falling into it is the experience of looking *up from it* toward a reality that confirms not just one's liability to nothingness but one's identity with it. Nothing the existentialist says is more misleading than his musing about how comforting his life would be if it were saturated with meaning by the Sacred.[24] He knows not what he says. The very absurdity he experiences protects him from the experience of an Other infinitely more discomforting than nothingness itself. The person who thinks existence is absurd occupies the highest, most privileged position of all that exists in his universe. He is triumphant in his very anguish. He has not begun to suffer the reality of anything higher than himself.

7. Worship and the Experience of Unworthiness

I have been trying to suggest that, standing before the Sacred, the religious person experiences himself as being metaphysically and intellectually destitute. But there is a third motif already implicit in and coloring the account of this destitute state. For the mind can learn how ignorant it is of that Sacred reality before which it experiences its nothingness only if the heart finally surrenders its desire to be in control and consents to its own radical insignificance. Our present task is to appreciate this surrender, which strips the heart of its last disguising garments and leaves it naked and shuddering, like a helpless child.

What does this loss of one's sense of importance entail? In encountering the Sacred, the religious person realizes for the first time that all along he has viewed the world as if he were its center. Given the fact that in and of himself he is nothing, he must now acknowledge his lack of any *innate* worth. To his realization that his existence is derivative is added the deeper and more embarrassing truth that his existence is undeserved. From the religious point of view, the fact that we exist is due exclusively to the generosity of the Sacred. That existence is itself sacred follows from the fact that existing in any sense engenders a real, if distant, similarity between oneself and the Ultimately Sacred. But in and of ourselves we are unworthy to be this gift we are given. Genuflection and prostration are the expressions of this unworthiness, but the religious person feels unworthy of making these gestures because one must put oneself in God's presence to do so. This sense of unworthiness would remain even if the religious person did not take into account his particular history of sin; it comes from his sense of being *ontologically undeserving*. He knows he has no claim to existence which requires the Sacred to give it to him; nor does he think he can gradually merit existence by his actions because the very powers he would use to do so are themselves gifts to begin with. Unworthiness is the embarrassed heart of finitude. From the religious point of view, our very being is to be genuflectors. If we were deprived of what is vouchsafed us as unearned gift, we would simply be the nothingness we already are, in and of ourselves. We *are* our indebtedness. Inadequate as the gestures must inevitably be, we genuflect because it is the only way to give over the whole of our undeserving and undeserved selves to the Sa cred Other which deserves everything, even if it cannot gain from our giving since all giving only returns to it its original gift.

What evokes from the religious person so deep a sense of unworthiness? He prostrates his will because of what he experiences as the awe-full Goodness of the Sacred, its transcendent excellence, its infinite superiority in the moral order, the fact that it is the Good itself. But such phrases are misleading insofar as they imply that the religious person thinks of the Sacred in abstract terms. What must be emphasized is that the heart experiences the Sacred as the ground of all the goods it has ever embraced and the animating source of its deepest longings.[25] The Sacred is that which, having been encountered, must be loved. Its perfection makes it irresistible. The heart cannot do anything sensible, under its impact, except freely surrender itself.

It is important to distinguish the heart's free surrender of itself to God from an attitude with which it is often confused—the subservience of the terrified to the tyrant who threatens him. In the first place, when a person is overcome by terror he tends to act out of panic-stricken concern for his own survival. Forgetting everything but that, he can be reduced to doing the most degrading acts. But this means that, far from evoking a recognition of his goodness, the tyrant has only succeeded in making the terrified person so afraid of him that he will do anything to preserve his life. He sees in the tyrant a power which is not inhibited by any oughts, and is therefore capable of anything. Before such a power the terrified person feels helpless and impotent; he loses his sense of being in control of his life. But he has no sense that the tyrant deserves to be acknowledged as intrinsically more important than himself. Indeed, the very fact that the tyrant coerces him into assuming a servile position proves that he is not worthy of reverence.

Now if authentic worship is profoundly different from such terrified subservience, it is because the Other that evokes it is not experienced as tyrannical. Uninhibited power evokes terror and makes one ready to do anything to protect oneself; the sacred evokes awe and wrings from the heart a confession of its insignificance. The fact that the latter, not the former, entails the more radical self-effacement is proven by the fact that whereas terror causes one to focus on one's own survival, awe leads one to realize one's nothingness. Terror intensifies to an extreme degree one's ordinary desire to be in control of one's existence; but awe shatters the assumption of one's importance which underlies the will to control itself.

Finally and most importantly, terrorized subservience is prompted by coercion, whereas worship, if it is genuine, is given freely. In fact, what is misleading about this way of putting it is that it treats freedom as if it were only an adverb attached as a modifier to the act of worship. But if worship requires of the heart an admission of its own unimportance, if it is an acknowledgment by the person, in his very character as moral agent, of a superior reality, then the very essence of the act is the freedom with which it is done. Someone overcome by terror ceases to act like a human person because his terror temporarily suspends his very power to act as a moral agent, his ability to act from the intimate center of his self. But the ironic consequence of this fact is that terror is incapable of evoking any profound change in our deepest attitudes; it merely incapacitates us. Awe, unlike terror, is not awakened by something that threatens my survival; it is awakened by a reality that threatens my ordinary sense of being important. And that means that it affects my way of conceiving of my personal worth. Awe reaches all the way into my most intimate sense of myself.

But because the Ultimately Sacred deserves not just reverence but worship, the radical nature of religious surrender might make it superficially resemble the kind of servitude with which we have been contrasting it. For that reason, it is especially helpful to ask what effect the experience of awe before the Sacred has on the religious person's sense of human dignity. For awe cannot be as different from terror as I have been arguing if the person humbled by it has as little self-worth as a slave. Can the religious person have a sense of human dignity and yet at the same time have a profound sense of his own nothingness?

The conviction that my existence should be taken seriously, that I possess, simply because of my nature as a person, a just claim to be treated as an end in myself, not as a mere means, this sense that it is profoundly worthwhile that I exist, is more than an abstract philosophical postulate. It expresses our most intimate and fundamental sense of our dignity as selves.[26] No one recognizes me unless he realizes that I deserve to be reverenced for my intrinsic worth. I have argued, on the other hand, that a person who encounters the Sacred is convinced by that experience that, in and of himself, he has no worth. But there is no need to construe this as meaning that his existence is devoid of value. In fact, his existence has an intrinsic value; indeed, the religious person must go so far as to affirm that he is himself sacred insofar as his existence is a participation in the Sacred itself. But all the value he has by virtue of being the person he is, is due to the Sacred in which he has the privilege of participating. And that means that even one's innate dignity is not, strictly speaking, something one can claim as one's own.[27] For one cannot claim as one's own what one must acknowledge as an undeserved gift. The Sacred gives us the very stature which justifies our standing erect and protesting against indignities. If I had not been given this dignity, I would not be able to be ashamed of myself, even for committing the worst atrocities. Only my possessing this dignity makes it wrong for me to murder or to be murdered. Without it, there would be nothing in me or others demanding my respect, or anyone's.

It is because he feels appropriated by these truths that the religious self falls on his knees in genuflection. We are now better prepared to appreciate the strangely dignified self-effacement expressed in this gesture. To think it signifies slavish flattery or debasing humiliation is to mistake it for its counterfeits. The person who is out to flatter may get down on his knees, but only long enough to get what he wants. The person who never gets down on them because it would be too belittling to do so does not realize that he did nothing to earn the dignity he takes such pains to protest. Neither slavish nor debasing, genuflection is dignity itself bent in gratitude. The person who spends his life in that posture of meekness develops without even intending to do so an unprepossessing nobility and a heavenly bearing. This is the only kind of nobility that is free of pretension, because it is the only kind that makes no claims for itself. The modesty, the self-effacing shyness, which worship of the Sacred requires, engenders in the person who practices it a quiet realization of how awful it is to have been given the gift of being oneself. Far from inducing a sense of worthlessness, real humility includes an astonished gratitude toward the Sacred for its giving one a sublime stature.

If the religious person's view of the self is correct, such astonished modesty is called for by our very nature; we ought to be diffident before the Sacred simply because we are. But in addition to that ontological motive, there is another whole dimension to religious shyness which our earlier discussion of shame has prepared us to appreciate. For besides our nothingness in and of ourselves, there is the fact of sin. Besides the poverty of our natures, there is the evil of our histories. We are not just blemished by occasional wrongs but permanently disfigured by faults that are lodged much deeper in our hearts than we can bear to admit. That is why, if we get close to the site of worship, it is usually only after frequent delays and evasions, and only after having tried all the paths leading in other directions. If we get there at all, it is against the better judgment of our long reluctance and deep refusal. Worship must be, for this reason, not just *adoration* but *apology*. We underestimate the reversal which apologizing requires us to undergo unless we realize that it is itself the process by which we become conscious of our sinfulness as such for the first time. For as we have seen, our unwillingness to recognize evil for what it is is an essential part of our commission of it. Only in the very act of encountering the Sacred do we realize what our avoidances have been avoidances of, and so acknowledge our life as a long betrayal of it. For the Sacred is experienced as that to which everything is owed, and that on which everything should be spent. The idea of half-hearted or occasional worship is a contradiction in terms. If the Sacred is worthy of the kind of radical self-effacement I have been trying to describe, then it cannot be right for us to resume our ordinary lives after we have encountered it. If we acknowledge it at all, we must acknowledge that it deserves to become the center of our world.

This is why a holy day, a day reserved for addressing the Sacred, is never meant to be simply another day, after and before others, in a succession of repeatable nows; nor is it outside ordinary time as a momentary interruption. It is intended to represent time itself.[28] All of time is supposed to be modelled after and generated by it. The holy day tries neither to suspend ordinary time nor continue it, but to convert it. And an encounter with the Sacred must include precisely our realizing this—that the whole of our time is the only thanksgiving which our astonished gratitude will accept as a metaphor for what the Sacred deserves of us. If we have long refused to acknowledge the reality of the Sacred, it is precisely because we have known in our heart of hearts that its claim on us would be total. That our act of worship has a beginning is itself the proof that we have been unfaithful. That is why it can only begin properly with an apology.

I suggested earlier that the generating impulse behind worship is the religious person's experience of his nothingness before the Sacred. I am now suggesting that a truth more horrifying and more mortifying than even that first crestfallen insight prompts one to begin worship with an apology: the fact that one's life as a whole has been something like a blasphemy. It is possible in principle for a person to realize his nothingness before the Sacred from the very beginning of his life, in which case he could genuflect before it innocently, without having to bury his face in his hands. But the fact that we are not now before the Sacred is itself proof that we are all fallen. To approach the Sacred from the world we ordinarily live in, we have to bring forward not just our intrinsic unworthiness but our deserving to be expelled from its presence. If the religious person does not on his own exclude himself from the site of worship, that is only because he realizes that running away would be another sin. He realizes how profoundly *reticent* he ought to be, how unworthy he is to *come forward* toward the Sacred under any circumstance, but especially under the circumstance of sinfulness. He must come forward with his fault because he can confess to the magnitude of his blasphemy in no other way but by revealing himself to the Sacred in all his nakedness. He must be willing to let the Sacred *see* him, down to the last shameful details of his most embarrassing offenses. We know all too well that we find the meanness, the sordid triviality, of these details most mortifying. Were it not for these details, the religious person could worship the Sacred in silence; instead, he has to speak the particularities of his shame. It is knowing that the Sacred deserves adoration that accounts for guilt's stammering eloquence.

But we should beware of one last temptation—a counterfeiting of guilt itself. However weighed down we are by its gravity, it is not our having to bear this weight which ought to concern us most. We should be able to recognize by now the ironic egoism at work when a person is chronically depressed by the knowledge of his evil and cannot stop thinking about its defiling effect on him. A person consumed by the thought of his evil takes his guilt more seriously than the offense of which he is guilty. Even when he goes so far as to hate himself because of his evil, he has not ceased to be in love with the dream of his own perfection—it has only become an unrequited and despairing love. So when we speak of the religious person advancing toward the Sacred apologetically, this should be taken to mean that the Sacred matters infinitely more to him than his own perfection—means more to him, even, than being forgiven. Forgiveness is, indeed, a gift for which one cannot dare to ask because one well knows that one deserves the opposite. Real apology is not offered as a means for releasing one's self from a burden of guilt. Indeed, to apologize for this reason would not just compound but exceed the original fault precisely because one's principal concern would not be apologizing for the wrong done but getting rid of the suffering which the experience of being guilty entails. On the contrary, real apology must emanate from my willingness to do whatever I can to release the one wronged from the wrong I have done him. It expresses my owning up to my guilt, not my trying to wash myself free of it. If forgiveness were forthcoming from the Sacred, its effect would be not to diminish the religious person's sense of nothingness, but to *double* it. For forgiveness which cannot be earned would add a new dimension of unworthiness to his original, already destitute, condition.

Finally, if the religious person brings himself forward in order that the mortifying minutiae of his shame be exposed before the Sacred, he does so because he is already claimed by it, feels that he is already seen by it, wherever he hides. Incapable of knowing it, he is known by it. And, indeed, the Sacred cannot encompass all, dwarf all, in all possible ways, unless it can know all, down to the smallest particularities; unless it knows all possible hiding places ahead of time, before one thinks of them. The Sacred is not, the religious person tells us, really present to us; we are present to it.

The Sacred is that by whose dreadful wisdom we are seized, enveloped. These verbs are not meant to suggest that the Sacred is intent on judging and condemming us. Rather, it means that the religious person encounters it as the power which dwarfs him by virtue of its having always known him more intimately and more profoundly than he has ever known himself. In attributing such knowledge to the Sacred, he does not diminish its difference from him: it is the fullness of divine knowing which confirms the fact that our knowledge is only ignorance. Our lives are journeys whose real significance could only be known if we had the divine map and knew the science of a divine cartography. All we can draw is the map of our insignificance.

8. The Route to the Sacred

Now that I have tried to describe from a variety of angles the sense of nothingness that I think is characteristic of the religious life, the primary question that remains to be addressed is the hardest one that faces us in this mortal life: how does one get to the place where the Sacred is found? The Sacred, I have said, can be known only as unknowable; but even this negative knowing is made possible by a positive experience, a real encounter with the Sacred; and the question regarding how it is to be achieved deserves more of an answer than the aphorism that all conversion is received, not achieved at all. I do not want to suggest here, near the end of this text, what I denied at the beginning—that there is some method for reaching what we seek, as one achieves a goal by using the right tactics. Conversion cannot be planned, it cannot be brought about through any technique or therapy. But it does not occur unless one puts oneself in a position where it can happen. Where must human beings place themselves for the Sacred to become real to them?

The only answer I can give to that question is this text as a whole. My purpose from the beginning has been to follow the footsteps of a pilgrimage toward the heart of crisis. If we have been led to think that at the heart of crisis is an encounter with the Sacred, that means, conversely, that the only way to find what is Ultimately Sacred is to take the road that leads past all the way-stations of crisis to its dreadful center. If a human being is to find the Sacred, his will to control must give way to generosity, his generosity to heroism, his heroism to shame, his experience of shame to worship of that reality which he was avoiding all along because it requires identifying with nothingness. If the encounter with the Sacred is the consummate anguish of all crisis, it is also true that the anguish of radical crisis is the unknown but inevitable destination of a person intent on encountering the Sacred. Just as all horrors only approximate the experience of one's nothingness before the Sacred, all religious worship is authentic only to the degree that it participates in what we have called suffering. I would like to offer a few final reflections on this double truth.

I have already had occasion to speak of ordinary religion, i.e., of the way we use the Sacred for future benefits or immediate ecstasies, welcoming its aid or embrace but, in either case, employing it for therapeutic purposes. The most dramatic religious experiences of this therapeutic type are those which save us from what we sense to be a radical crisis. But this means that, ordinarily, religion helps us avoid any realities that are radically at odds with our mode of being—a mode of being whose basis is our will to be in control of it. But if it is this will to control that underlies our unwillingness to experience our nothingness before the Sacred, the first thing to be done if we are to find the Sacred is to give up religion as therapy. And to do that means to let crisis occur, instead of trying to prevent it from radically disrupting our whole existence.

What follows upon this initial change of heart? If our reflection has not been mistaken, when the boundaries of ordinary existence collapse, they leave us exposed, in sudden dereliction, to powers over which we have no control: awful realities which seem to bear down on us from above and surge up from below, ready to overwhelm us like the gods of old. By letting go of the ordinary, and allowing these realities to have their devastating effect, we open life for the first time to the things that matter ultimately. In breaking with ordinary existence, we discover that the awful realities which rupture our life possess by virtue of that very fact a sublime, terrible stature. All things then seem to be full of the gods. It was only our will to control reality that levelled the whole of it down to the superficiality of its surface. Giving up that desire for control is a terrible ordeal, but one which for that very reason initiates us into the religion of the heroic, where the Sacred is identified with whatever causes us to be overwhelmed. From this point of view, death is as sacred as life, evil as sacred as good, because both inspire terror in the ordinary heart and fascination in the heroic. In such a religion, the only distinction that matters is that between the sublime and the pedestrian. The hero is proud to possess his own heights and depths, in the steep terrain of his own interiority. He longs to explore his own dark recesses and unspeakable abysses. Death, life, gods, heroes, great virtues, great vices—all belong together in this view by virtue of the titanic stature they have in common.

But if the hero is really looking for the most demanding ordeal, he will find it only by going beyond his own greatness toward the experience of radical self-effacement which worship alone requires. The humility involved in adoration is more upsetting than any ordeal he might imagine. The reality that evokes such adoration is not a god whose deeds the hero can try to emulate; one can only genuflect before it in quiet humility. But between the hubris of emulation and the humility of worship lies the mortifying ordeal of shame. Only by crossing its trackless wastes can the hero aproach the sacred precincts of a reality that can teach him about his nothingness. Prostrate before the Sacred, he surrenders that conviction of his own importance to which even heroes cling, when they praise their gods by imitating them. Worship is not truly itself until it exacts from one the acute reversal of this total surrender. Its insistence on so radical a surrender is exactly what distinguishes worship from even the highest form of admiration. Ordinary religion is blasphemous just because it is the opposite of this self-effacement. And one can move from the blasphemy of ordinary religion to the self-effacement of worship only by opening oneself to crisis, and suffering the full impact of its dreadful rupture.

But this suggests that the religious dimension of human life is not merely one dimension to be juxtaposed to and compared with others. For the Sacred, it turns out, is not something we simply happen to find at the heart of crisis, as if it had been accidentally left there and we stumble on it by chance. If the Sacred is found at the heart of crisis, that is only because it is what we all along have lived to avoid. The blasphemy which we noted to be one among many elements of ordinary life is, in fact, essential to its very essence. The reason it is so difficult for us to find the Sacred is that our lives are ordinarily a flight from it. The Sacred is the Other which every avoidance avoids, although part of what makes avoidance work is that we unaware of this. Far from religion helping to lighten our anguish, or to comfort us when we face something horrifying, it evokes the deepest anguish and stirs the worst horror, when it does not betray the inner logic of worship itself. All relief is relief from the excruciating ordeal of prostration; real worship does not give us something to hold onto when we are losing control of our life. It takes everything away and leaves us with our nothingness. Worship is the paradigm of crisis. But it would be wrong to conclude from this that it is simply the most acute example of the many crises which can befall us. For all other crises are crises only to the degree that they suggest or broach the crisis of worshipping. The former get their power to disrupt from their participation in the latter and are understandable only in relationship to it. Indeed, only its proximity to the crisis of worshipping or its distance from it enables us to locate the meaning of any experience in the geography of human life.

Even now, this might sound like an exaggeration, as if I am melo-dramatically heightening the import of one particular event. But if we are to prevent crisis from disrupting our lives, we must try to keep out of them that Other whose radical Otherness poses the most serious threat to our being in control. This Other is the Sacred, because only before the Sacred do I realize that, in and of myself, I am nothing. No disruption can conceivably be more radical than this demotion of myself to nothingness. My whole life is governed by my underlying, unconscious terror of the Other on account of which such a demotion can occur. Only because and to the degree that it awakens this underlying terror does *any* disruption of my life possess disruptive power. Nothing threatens me unless it tem-porarily seems to be as strange as this Ultimate Other from which I am unconsciously always in flight. On the other hand, were there not this un-derlying terror for it to tap into, nothing would threaten me. In trying to control our lives, we do not simply try to avert particular crises as they come along; we try to prevent crisis in principle, crisis as distinguished from interruption, crisis as radical rupture, and only an Other radically different from all other Others can prompt crisis in this sense of the term. The Sacred never has to compete for our heart: it always holds sway over us. It is the always absent Other that hides at the bottom of all our thoughts and choices, and secretes an unspeakable dread. Ordinarily, we spend our whole lives trying not to heed it. However we live, we are always haunted by it, and no matter what direction we take, our lives are always the twisting irony of this obedience.[29]

But this means that there can be no such thing as our beginning to have a relationship with the Sacred, as if, prior to a certain point, we had been unconcerned about it. The Sacred, in its Otherness and its transcendence, is not something with which I have to create a spiritual relationship if the latter is to exist between us. I am always already bound to it, before even my first decisions. This is why the Sacred does not have to be found, and why no one needs a map to lead him to its location. The Sacred is already here, with us, at the bottom of our evasions. To find it, we need only to cease avoiding it. We need only to let be that before which we know our-selves as nothing. The Sacred is, as it were, always waiting, has been wait-ing from the very beginning, in the most recessed sanctuary of the self. If I repress it to the depths of my unconscious, that is because I am and have always been terrified of its holiness and what it would require of me. But my repressing it in the first place is my refusing the claim it makes on me when I experience it as the reality that made me from nothingness. I *am* the claim it makes on me. That is why, to prevent an encounter with it, I have to find a way to avoid being myself.

But this means that, in a real sense, nothing is easier to achieve or more readily available than an encounter with the Sacred in its very inaccessibility. Nothing is simpler than to live in the dreadful tension of this transcendent mystery, nothing more straightforward than the practice of genuflecting before it. But our lives are ordinarily our running away from this horrifying proximity. Our distance from the Sacred is always much too close for comfort. We would rather not experience it. To get our wish, we have to create one evasion after another so as to become ignorant of that original truth graven in the very heart of consciousness: its nothingness before the Sacred.

9. A Death-like Birth

Perhaps what seems most objectionable about the way I have been describing religion is precisely my insistence on its upsetting character and my failure to take into account the joy that seems to characterize religious lives, especially the lives of those most universally recognized as saints. It might be suggested, in fact, that I have done religion a disservice by suggesting that it deepens and accentuates the very dread which religions have always promised to relieve. In short, I have made religious experience part of crisis, indeed its essence, instead of considering its claim to be the cure. At the beginning of this inquiry, I distinguished between the crisis experience itself and the visionary insights which purport to resolve it by answering the questions it raises. Does not every religion offer such an answer to a heart in crisis?[30] And if so, how is this to be reconciled with the argument developed here that the experience of worship is itself the deepest of all crises and not a resolution of them?

I would not want to respond to these questions in a way that tried to prevent them from undermining the starting point of the essay itself. The crisis of thinking requires that one follow the ramifications of thought even when they coil back on one's initial presumptions. So we must consider the possibility that our original way of asking about crisis has brought us insights which require a rupturing of that original method. Given the point we have reached in our reflections, what are we now to make of the whole idea that there is an answer to crisis? What would a "resolution" of crisis be like?

Customarily, crisis is viewed as an apocalyptic event in one's personal life, a radical uprooting, a death. Structures fall apart; the center does not hold; one's life as a whole collapses. Nothing remains of one's old self except its scattered shards. But such a disintegration, destructive in the extreme, opens up new possibilities which would have remained forever closed off, were it not for the very destructiveness of the crisis. The death of one mode of life makes possible the birth of radically different alternatives. Life as a whole collapses; but thus a new whole, with a new center, becomes possible.[31] Apocalypse presages a genesis; crisis prepares the way for resurrection. In that sense, crisis seems to be part of a cycle of metamorphosis; in the long run, the death it brings serves life. Taking crisis seriously does not, in this view, preclude subordinating it to a larger scheme. Far from underestimating crisis, this view seems to emphasize its importance: its destructiveness is understood to be essential for the emergence of a new life.

But we must ask if this view does, in fact, take crisis as seriously as it claims or whether it has, in fact, missed the point entirely. It claims to offer us a way of interpreting change of the most radical sort, the metamorphosis of one's life as a whole from one whole to another. It envisions a fundamental redirecting of one's self as a self. But, however radically the new structure which I give to my life differs from the structure which has collapsed, it is essentially the same insofar as it is precisely, like its predecessor, a structure, a way for me to organize existence. That is why this way of viewing crisis as part of a metamorphic process finally reduces crisis to the status of a radical interruption. Crisis changes the structure of my life but not, in this view, the fact that I structure it.

This view fails to appreciate the fact that when it ruptures my whole mode of living, a crisis ruptures all my ordinary assumptions about crisis itself and about the idea of giving structure to my life. We must recall some of the crucial insights that have emerged from our reflections. A crisis can occur only when some Other undermines the structure which I want my life to have. I experience the Other as a threat only because I cherish my way of life and want it to be permanent. But this means that what is of ultimate importance to me is not the particular structure I try to impose on my life, but my power to structure it as I see fit. Thus, a crisis, to be radically disruptive, must rupture not just the structure I want my life to have but the underlying attitude of the will, its demand that life conform to it. All real crisis is a calling into question of the heart's desire to have its own way. We have discovered that this calling into question can always be avoided. No matter what happens to us, we can treat it as a problem to be solved by some technique or therapy. And this means that the heart can suffer a crisis only to the degree that it allows its will to control to be questioned—and this very act of consenting to its loss of control is itself the critical event of all crisis. To give up one's stature as the director of one's own existence: this is, for us, the ultimate death, the crisis that undermines our being in the most radical way.

Now if, consequent to such dying, I were to resume control of my life by developing new structures for life to obey, I would hardly be venturing into virgin landscape: I would be returning to familiar terrain. The new structures would be structures in the old sense, and the heart would be resuming its original intention of being in control. The crisis now past would have been no more than a brief hiatus, resurrection only a deceiving name for a reversion to the normal way of being. Indeed, we must now conclude that any new structure, any set of beliefs or framework of meaning one might adopt to put an end to crisis are just so many versions of its betrayal. All answers which promise a new security to the mind and will in crisis are for that very reason seductive falsehoods. In order truly to surrender to crisis, one must not seek a way to resolve it, an Answer that enables one to resume an unquestioning way of life. I suggested at the beginning of this inquiry a criterion to be used in evaluating any answer offered to the heart in crisis: no such Answer, I said, can be true if it is incompatible with what we can know of human life as a result of studying the crisis which such Answers purport to resolve. Now I add: all Answers, precisely insofar as they offer the heart a way to restructure its life, are by that very fact unacceptable to a heart which has had its desire to structure life undermined by crisis. Religions which offer to be Answers in the above sense are for that very reason not religions but therapies.

The heart, in consenting to its own nothingness, gives up having its own way; in so doing, it gives up its very will to structure. The word descriptive of such surrender is *abandonment*.[32] With reckless abandon, the heart abandons itself to the Sacred. It gives itself over to the Sacred without reservations or conditions. The authentically religious person relinquishes every plan—but also every spontaneity. He gives up his will to structure—but not in order to do whatever he wants. In abandoning himself to the Sacred, his will surrenders to the radical Other. Radical crisis never occurs except in the first awkward moment of such effacement. It will not do to say of that person who has abandoned himself in this way that he has given a new direction to his life. *It would be more accurate to say that, from the ordinary point of view, he has permanently lost his way.* His life now follows whatever path the Sacred carves out for it in the geography of crisis. Religion is not his new way of organizing his life; it is his way of abandoning himself to a crisis that is never resolved but always deepening. According to the authentically religious person, we should never stop offering our self to that ordeal. The rupturing of the heart is to

be no one time or sometime thing; the whole of one's life is to be a rending, a fissure. There ought to be no structure to our lives except the structure of crisis itself. We should alter our posture of genuflection only to
make this gesture more prostrate. The reversal which crisis effects is not
complete unless one ceases to look for a way to suture that splitting open
of one's heart which is crisis itself.

But that splitting open is itself a healing. It constitutes the only genuine
redemption, not consequent to crisis but identical with it. The person who
has been broken by the realization of his nothingness is not sustained by
the hope of somehow becoming whole at a later date. His clinging to such
a hope would only mean he was not yet wholly willing to be nothing.
Rather, he knows he will *never* be anything in his own right. But this
recognition of his poverty is inseparable from his recognizing the richness
of the Sacred. And this requires us to say that no joy compares to the joy
which is inseparable from his radical anguish. In saying this, I seem
perhaps to contradict everything I have argued heretofore—as if all along
I was holding in reserve this redeeming ecstasy, so that I could reveal it
now in order to make desirable an experience which would otherwise be
horrifying. But the difference between this joy and all others is proven
precisely by its inseparability from anguish. What kind of joy is this which
hides inside the recesses of suffering, so opposite to all our pleasures and
all our hopes for ecstasy?

The self convinced of his own nothingness cannot, in the first place,
take seriously either his own happiness or the lack of it. Before the Sacred,
he ceases to be in earnest about anything having to do with himself. So
nothing seems more ridiculous to him than the seriousness he used to
bring to his desires. Here again, we must return to the theme of self-abandonment. What is reckless about abandoning one's self to the Sacred is
precisely the foolhardy disregard of one's own wants which such abandonment entails. This disregard is not mere indifference; the will, having
given up its desires, could still avoid suffering by withdrawing into an
inner vacuum. The person who practices such indifference thinks that
there is nothing to take seriously once one gives up one's wants. But the
religious person, instead of withdrawing from his wants into such acedia,
is inspired to give up his old desires by a new extravagance: his desire to
be nothing in as radical a way as possible. The heart engaged in worship
gives in to a sacred impetuosity that makes it surrender all its accomplishments and demands, literally, even its clothes and food, so that, destitute
and unprotected, ceasing to provide for itself, it can be what it knows itself to be, wholly dependent on divine generosity. Humility is, finally, the
willingness to receive everything as undeserved gift.

This very eagerness to surrender its own accomplishments and possessions, this reckless improvidence, this impetuous renunciation of its old longings—these are nothing but the blushing gestures of joy itself. What is characteristic of the religious heart is not that it renounces its self-centeredness, but precisely its doing so not just without melancholy or regret but with unrestrained ardor. The religious heart no longer takes its desires seriously enough to mourn their loss. For this reason, real worship is always celebrative; indeed, there must always be in it something frankly uninhibited. The Sacred deserves nothing less than our being boundlessly happy before it. And indeed, no happiness can be as deep, as certain, as animating as the religious person's joy over the very existence of the Sacred. The Sacred cannot be encountered without ecstasy. One who really worships cannot restrain himself, nor does he wish to do so. He holds back nothing. He spends himself lavishly, laughing at what it costs him. The worst sin against the Sacred is to be frugal in celebrating it: all sins are only versions of this utilitarian prudence which refuses to waste its wealth on the foolish business of worship. The religious heart, on the other hand, saves everything just so as to waste it on this profligate liturgy.

Uninhibited in its giving up of its own desires, profligate in spending itself on the Sacred: here, if only we could appreciate it, we come up against the animating paradox of the religious person. He is happy, indeed elated, to want nothing for himself. In lavish and ecstatic extravagance he abandons himself to the Sacred. So it seems, at first glance, that having renounced ecstasy, we are destined to receive it in the end as grace; joy, it seems, will finally arrive when we stop seeking it as a reward for our anguish. But this is, in fact, a misleading way of describing the consummation of the religious life. For this way of putting it suggests that the religious person experiences an ecstasy of the same sort as those he has given up along the way. And this would mean that the radical consent to one's own nothingness only proves to be a subtle way of attaining the very thing one has purportedly renounced. If this were true, the religious self would reach the happiness we all seek, only he would do so by going down a path of anguish and dispossession. How much we would then envy his elation, and regret our unwillingness to suffer enough to get it ourselves, in spite of our desire for it!

But, unwilling to undergo the religious person's suffering, how can we help but misunderstand his joy? If we understood it, we would flee from it with the same terror which prompts us to flee from his anguish. The religious person does, indeed, experience ecstasy but, far from it being the same ecstasy he gave up, it is exactly its opposite.

If an example would help to make this plausible, we might think of the story told about Francis of Assisi,[33] who, shortly after his conversion, asked God to send him some sign of what he was now to do with his life. In response to that prayer, God told him to embrace the next person he saw coming down the road. No sooner had he received this answer than he heard a sound which had awakened in him, from the earliest days of his childhood, the most horrible sense of repugnance—the sound made by the bell that lepers were required to wear to warn the healthy of their proximity. Only when he embraced that leper, only when he kissed the very ulcers and stumps he had always found so abhorrent, did he experience for the first time that joy which does not come from this world and which he would later identify with the joy of crucifixion itself. How are we to account for the fact that the very reality from which he had always recoiled with horror gave him his first taste of that ecstasy which the mystics say is impossible to describe? How else except by the paradox that, for all of us, the only road that leads to God is the one that leads in exactly the opposite direction from the one we want to take. If Francis felt drawn to the leper instead of compelled to recoil from him, it was because he saw embedded in the wounds of this outcast the priceless gem of his own nothingness. The joy which has often been recognized as characteristic of the saints, and for which Francis himself is so celebrated, springs right from that wound as from its original source. For inseparable from the experience of nothingness is, if we are to trust their testimony, the discovery of that reality whose love cannot be felt except by those who allow themselves to be put in a position of radical destitution. The very thing that we call crisis the saints call grace. It is not as hard to find as we are accustomed to think: it is there in the cancer patient, the AIDS victim, the rape victim and the rapist, in all the strangers who awaken a feeling of repulsion. What we avoid when we turn away from them is the original wound we have buried as deeply as we can inside ourselves. The joy of the saints comes from reopening it.

Still, this suggests one last and finally right objection to the long argument of this essay. No crisis, I have claimed, exacts a higher price than an encounter with the Sacred, for only the Sacred requires us to confess our nothingness. It is not possible for an act to be more exactly contrary to our desire to be in control. But the person in the throes of worship does not count the cost, even though what he is doing costs not less than everything. His very consent to his own nothingness would not be unreserved if he gave it with reluctance or regret. The person truly prostrate in worship is happy to be nothing. In that sense, not just his consciousness of it but his suffering itself is transformed. Because he no longer holds onto his own preferences, the painful act of giving them up has become part of the extravagance of love. To the degree that the will gives up its preferences, worship becomes festival, the self an eager maiden, longing to be ravished, able to concentrate on nothing except the beloved. The person fully engaged in worship is, in fact, transported out of himself and unaware of himself; for as long as such worship lasts, all his faculties are gathered together by one eager flame which melts them into love. Such worship is like the elation of fire itself.[34]

At that point, the religious person does not suffer. Indeed, no boundaries can contain this joy, which asks the whole universe to join in its prostration. So it is that the geography of crisis and suffering prepares the way for the topology of ecstasy. But we must set down this, set down this, severe as it might sound, in the heart of whatever hope we have of reaching such intensity. Suffering ends because the harsh blaze of love consumes it. Suffering ends not because the heart ceases to die its death, in its most intimate depths: it ends because finally the heart agrees to its death so graciously, so quietly, with such perfect self-effacement. We, if we experienced it, would find in this joy only the most excruciating suffering because our wills cannot bear to be ravished, only to control. Between the active voice of the verb "control" and the passive voice of the verb "ravish" lies the whole geography of crisis which it is the purpose of this life to traverse. One who begins to worship begins to cease suffering because he begins to let go of the self-centeredness which makes it so hard to prostrate one's self. The geography of suffering comes to an end here because what makes for all suffering is the will's resistance to the Sacred and its insistence on having its own way. Without selfishness, the will would not have to suffer its reversal: it would be, so to speak, already reversed, turned away from itself toward the Other. In short, we begin to realize only now, near the end of this essay, that all along we have only been following that one fault in the geography of the heart which makes us experience as suffering our being nothing on our own account. So radical is that fault, it makes us desperate to avoid the one real joy.

But if this text had been written from the perspective of the person who has become a worshipper, everything I have said would have been explained in a different way. For such a person understands the doom he has suffered as providence, the gods as holy messengers, shame as a special unearned gift, the fall into the abyss of crisis as the encounter with what is Sacred. He would ask me to rewrite everything I have said so as to make it clear that what I have been charting, without fully realizing it, is not the geography of crisis or the sonography of shame, but the astronomy of grace. And that wound of nothingness at the heart of the universe which he undergoes and which he is—what would he call it if not the happy proof of his dependence on divine charity?

EPILOGUE

The End of All Arriving

We shall not cease from exploration
And the end of all our exploring
Will be to arrive where we started
And know the place for the first time.
T.S. Eliot, "Little Gidding"

It is precisely when it is over that crisis springs on us its last surprise. Even as it sinks into the past, its drama completed, it claims us again, in a wholly unexpected way.

To realize that this is the case, we might begin by reflecting on exactly the dramatic quality of a crisis experience. It ruptures, I have argued, those routines which make existence orderly and ordinary, the skein of anonymous and repetitive nows which succeed each other so un-eventfully. One remembers nothing from one day to the next because nothing which happens is significant enough to claim the attention of memory. Crisis cuts through this ordinary time like a blade; it does not just interrupt my life but disrupts it radically. I find myself caught up in the sway of a drama which seems to revolutionize time itself. Unlike the ordinary time of everyday life, the extraordinary time of crisis is taut, tensed, no longer a string of nows but a kind of unpredictable undertow which holds me fast and makes me feel that the very continuation of time itself has become suddenly uncertain. What makes a crisis dramatic is pre-cisely this unsureness, this transfusion of danger into the very artery of temporality. Each moment is no longer callously indifferent to its fellows;

each intensifies or tries to alleviate the perhaps unbearable strain they all share in common. For that reason, there are, strictly speaking, no separate moments at all in the extraordinary time of crisis; the nows which ordinarily lie beside each other so inertly are bound together into the accumulating tension of a single anguish. Usually, the present moment does not prompt the least wonder, or dread, of what will come next; rather, its very ordinariness, its lack of any exceptional quality, leads me to expect of the future only a wearying redundancy. In dramatic time, on the other hand, I can hardly bear waiting to see what will happen next, not because I am rushing time but because time itself has become, as it were, impatient, as if the future were wrestling with and rupturing every present.

Drama is never only a hurrying-up of time. If time merely quickens its pace, its moments blur under the impact of what is nevertheless a pointless momentum. Accelerated time only appears to be different from the slow pace of banality. What makes time dramatic is not tempo but that tension which is consequent upon the raising of a question that infuses each moment with its taut uncertainty. Then time itself seems to demand, with ever intensifying insistence, some kind of resolution, however tragic it might be, some climax which answers, perhaps cruelly, the question which has stretched it to such a painful extreme. The moments of time, ordinarily passive and disjointed, are joined and animated so that time itself acquires a kind of restless momentum and seems driven by a fierce and painful longing toward some culminating event, some critical occurrence on which all its passion can be rightly spent. It is too disturbing to imagine such an event not occurring, since in such a case the ardent longing which holds us in thrall would keep on intensifying, with no fulfillment or resolution in sight. From its first moment of tension, drama sets in motion a longing for its own completion. Still, this climax is no mere quieting, any more than the drama itself is a mere hurrying-up of time. The decisive event gathers together all the questions that have been realized, with their taut uncertainty, and resolves them all in one radical realization. Once such a realization occurs, there remains only the process of its reverberations, the spill-over of its consequences into all the areas of life touched in some way by the dramatic passion it has resolved. The essential completion of the drama has already occurred by virtue of the decisive event itself, whose decisiveness derives precisely from its power to make the drama a totality, a rounded whole, the tension of its beginning balanced perfectly by the serenity of its end. In retrospect, the whole of the drama seems to stand out from the skein of ordinary time with a kind of singular intensity, since each of its moments has been gathered into one consummative event that was both unpredictable and foreordained. But after it is over, the drama seems to have only momentarily interrupted ordinary time with its brief, if searing, flourish. Its meteoric rise and fall is always over, it seems, too quickly. The horrors such dramas unleash on us are remembered less for their horror than for their devastating impact, their power to rupture time with their passion. Once a crisis is over, one secretly regrets that the harsh privilege of undergoing it is also over and not to be recaptured.

There is an end to crisis. That is a factual inevitability, however much we might want to protest it. The real end of crisis does not occur simply on account of exhaustion, as if it were too draining for us to keep on being overwhelmed by it; were it to be terminated for that reason, it would be only a fragment of a drama rendered unfinishable because of human weakness. I mean, rather, that there is a critical turning point in the long route of crisis; that, once reached, this turning point deserves to have spent upon it all the passion of the heart which has been saved and readied for just this culminating horror; and that once past, and irretrievable, this one event inevitably seems, to the person who has suffered it, the last real event of his life. If the most radical of all turning points has already happened, is not one's life essentially already over, its drama already a completed whole? At that point, one adopts toward one's life a strangely posthumous perspective. New things keep happening but the drama already completed seems to rob the future of its importance and efface its claim on me. Nothing that happens succeeds in creating in me the sense of ultimacy which I felt while in the throes of the crisis that is now completed; the future seems, as it were, penultimate to what has happened in the past. One returns to ordinary time, but with the sense that it is not real time at all, only a poor facsimile. All time, all life, seems to pale and becomes superfluous in comparison to the extraordinary time of crisis.[1] While crisis seemed at first to be the rupturing of time and a radical threat to its existence, now one is tempted to think that only crisis brought real time into being; its end drops one back into the refuse-heap of nows, the excrescences of time that were not needed for its essential drama.

For this not to occur, the moments after the turning point in my life would have to possess the same significance as the decisive turning point itself; and this cannot happen. For they inevitably lack the stature which an event acquires when it culminates the gradual heightening of dramatic tension. And if the decisive event is not just the climax of one among many possible dramas but the critical moment than which none more radical can be conceived, every time which follows, not excluding the moment of death itself, will seem to be only a sorry waste of time, flaccid and perfunctory. One realizes now, all too easily, all too lucidly, how banal time is when not drawn taut by crisis. Only now, returning to it from the geography of such final suffering, does one really taste the disappointment of being ordinary. Nothing could be so anticlimactic as this return to normalcy, with all its petty cares, the waiting in line at supermarkets, the worrying over house payments; not just the enervating details of each day's trivial jobs, but the shallow pleasure of each day's leisures, the football games, the mundane conversations with one's acquaintances—all these, and all the countless trivialities attending them, encumber the heart once riven by great sufferings. Coming from crisis, one feels strangely unprepared for such trite particularities. One must be someone and do something again, in the hackneyed world; the deep truths one realized now sound like platitudes. Moreover, if, in learning to consent to the deepest suffering, one realized that the acceptance of suffering is not genuine unless it is gracious, one knows that now one should not complain about the banality of one's life but rather accept it with the same serene willingness one brought to the most extraordinary demands of crisis.

Perhaps the reader remembers these details of commonplace living from the first step of this essay, now itself in its anticlimactic stage. Then they were eagerly embraced for just those qualities which now make them so distasteful: what might be called the suction of their triviality, their quick-witted arguments on behalf of their own importance, their very everydayness. Having braved the most upsetting experiences, one deserves, it would seem, something happier or more horrifying than a return to such harmless indignities. It is exactly the easiness, the smallness of these everyday doings which makes them difficult for one grown used to the crescendos of suffering. Is not our having to face up to the very ordinariness of such demands the last ought and the slyest irony of crisis?

1. The Passing of Sacred Time and the Return of the Ordinary

For the religious person we have described, all this is no abstract generality; it is the all too palpable dilemma which unexpectedly emerges as soon as he completes the critical turning point of conversion. He has done once the one unsurpassable deed of acknowledging his nothingness before the Sacred. His heart has spilled, in one extraordinary confession, all it had secreted away in its most private chambers. He has laid before the Sacred the worst things about himself. No abasement can be more radical or more complete than this one pure moment of prostration, a consummation long prepared by all the lesser ruptures to which crisis had exposed him. That abasement consummates and consumes because it is also worship; it is not just one's giving up one's own importance but one's yes to the unconditional value of the Sacred in its very Otherness. In that moment, which I have argued is the rarest and most radical in this mortal life, one can afford to save nothing for a latter day. One keeps none of one's passion in reserve. The religious person does not just acknowledge that the Sacred *deserves* the whole of his self; he *spends* his whole self in the very yes of that consent. All that he is and has ever been is bound over and converted to this yes. It is true, of course, that this yes is a promise about the future as well as a consummation of what has gone before. For the Sacred deserves praise without end; one does not recognize its sacrality unless one promises it the unbroken holy day of one's future. But is not the very act of such a promising, in its purity and unreservedness, itself unsurpassable as an act of obedience? How can any single future equal this radical generosity which gives the whole future to the Sacred? This act seems to be both a vow and, simultaneously, its fulfillment; it is already, it seems, a living out, as radically as possible, of what it promises. The very moment it is completed, how can the religious person do anything except realize and regret that everything left to do possesses less import than the one single moment of complete oblation which seems, indeed, more definitive than ever now that it is so irreparably past? How can the details of all his ordinary days measure up to an act in which his whole being has been thus intensely concentrated?

That is no rhetorical question. It does more than express the sense of emotional let-down and disappointment. One would be glad of another death, but after the first death, no other seems possible; one has to return to the ordinary, commonplace world. Sacred time seems to annul itself. Once I consent to it, the crisis of being nothing before the Sacred is consummated. But that end, inevitably, is itself a slackening of my response to the claim the Sacred makes on me. The end of crisis is itself a crisis: the crisis of having to return to the ordinary. One wishes, devoutly, that there were some way to avoid this. Nothing would be more preferable than being permanently transfixed by the consummative moment of one's anguish: for then one would be forever dying, one would be forever nothing but this timeless wound, this passion spending itself without reserve but never spent, this sanctity. Ordinarily, one wants time to stop at what seems to be not just one's first but one's only holiness.

2. The Dramatic Bias of the Essay as a Whole

To want to freeze the consummative moment of crisis: this, we have been long prepared to realize, is the heart's final folly and, for us, the final irony. Crisis uproots me from the ordinary. But my not wanting crisis to end, my longing to suffer the death it requires—that is the disease of the ordinary which infects even the most open-hearted experience of crisis itself. Even in radically opening myself to what is most awful, I try to avoid the last thing it exacts from me: I want to be open to it always as I am this moment, to be transfixed in this prostrate surrender, not to have to let go of this experience of my unworthiness before the Sacred. This very unwillingness is a new unworthiness. Once I wanted time to be a skein of nows without exceptions, none more distinctive than any other. Now I want time to not exist except for the consummative moment of crisis itself. All other times pale beside this one radical experience, with its excruciating excellence. Would that this crystal of perfect suffering were not itself shattered! But this vain beseeching is the new voice of old avoidance. So resilient is the habit of that vice that now I do not want to have to bear the rupture of crisis itself, just as originally I did not want to let it rupture ordinary time.

That habit's hold on us is tighter than we ever anticipated. It is not just that the vice of avoidance grips the will even at the very moment of radical crisis when the will most seems to have broken free. Having grown accustomed to its cunning and tenacity, we might have expected it to survive, quietly and unobtrusively, the drama which culminates in its very death. That drama has been the theme of this long essay in the dialectic of suffering. But why were we drawn in the first place to the dramatic version of this theme? Because no other subject possesses the same compelling power, the same stirring self-importance, the same grip of radicality. This essay itself, not just in its theme but in its structure, even, indeed, in its images and its grammar, witnesses to the strange lure of the most dramatic horror; and to the almost hypnotic effect which the magic of the extraordinary has, even when one tries to be committed to the simple truth in its starkness. How could I have hoped to keep track of such truth when from the beginning I was fascinated by the dramatic? All along, I have been the cupable victim of that bias, and nothing I have said has been, I suspect, utterly free of its influence. But to think I could have reached or appreciated this very fact without undergoing the preparatory askesis of the essay itself, or some analogue of it—that, too, is an illusion inspired mainly by the will to avoid. It is not that what I have argued about crisis is wrong, but that it can occur so much more subtly than I have suggested, with none of the obtrusive flourishes that have so often raised the temperature of my description of it. The quietest crises are the most real ones. It is just such a crisis, in its very quietness, which I have from the first avoided. The one who suffers it goes about his business with such modesty that I could hardly help not noticing him.[2] But the failure to notice him is, nevertheless, the unspoken context in terms of which this text is to be understood.

3. The Holiness of the Ordinary

So the ordinary life of which I now speak seems anticlimactic only because of my dramatic bias. In fact, it is that toward which our whole discussion of crisis has been moving, as toward its radical reversal. Our understanding of crisis reaches its own crisis point only when we cease to take for granted our reasons for making it the centerpiece of our thinking. In raising this question, we both complete this inquiry and rupture it.

The "ordinary" has from the beginning of this essay meant what is normally done, what happens over and over, with rare exceptions. What is peculiar, we noted, is this: it is precisely its happening over and over, its very predictability, which makes us make the normal our norm. We want existence to be whatever it usually is, no matter what it is. It is not its particular content which holds us but only its normalcy. Indeed, our inquiry could be divided into stages only because, however deeply we suffer, we still tend to turn every rupture of our normal life into a new normality. With heroic tenacity we persevere in insisting on having our own way: and our fundamental preference is always our not having to suffer except in ways which we have already made into habits. In that sense, we always want everything to be ordinary, and so suppress the exceptional. But this means really that each of us thinks there is nothing more important than himself. "The ordinary" thus acquires a new and pregnant nuance: it means the subordinate stature, the inferiority, the lack of value I want to be characteristic of everything in comparison to me. What happens over and over, the daily routines into which I manage to coerce my life, however exceptional its circumstances, are "ordinary" because, due to their very predictability, they serve my desire for control. The heart avoids the exceptional, the rupture of the ordinary, because of the threat such rupture poses to its ability to "deal with" its life. I want my life to be ordinary precisely so that I can attain and keep my importance, my controlling stature, my superiority over it. I want myself to be the only exception to the ordinariness of everything. I want nothing to surpass my ability to prove myself above it.

But this very wanting is itself no idiosyncratic foible or occasional feint. Over and over, with more or less painful irony, I am always longing after the same ambition. Nothing, therefore, is more easily predictable, and so utterly ordinary, as my very willing to be exceptional. Usually, my will wants to be superior to everything. So constant is this fault that it follows me even into its crisis—even into the shattering discovery of my own unimportance. Even the Sacred, before whom I am nothing, does not prevent me from wanting to freeze the very moment of this encounter, so that I might live forever in its importance. Nothing, I rightly think then, can be more extraordinary than this realization of my insignificance. I conclude that no moment is more worth being in control of. Thus, I try to control even the most upsetting of all possible realizations, in my very manner of clutching its truth. To want nothing less than the most devastating proof of one's nothingness—that too, however muted, is an ambition born of the will to control. Nevertheless, there remains before one's eyes the truth of one's unimportance; it can survive the brazen manner of one's embracing it. The letdown which follows the dramatic moment of conversion occurs because, once again, I have to enter within the ordinary, to be preoccupied with its demands; I have to lose, under the sway of mundane details, the high sense of my extraordinary vocation. No more the dark ecstasy and riveting truth of nothingness, the consuming fire into which everything was thrown: now, instead of darkness, a long, listless twilight, in a landscape peopled by shadows and half-truths, that could only be charted by a geography of banality. But it is there, and nowhere else, there in the midst of just the trite particularities of the ordinary, that we find persons becoming holy. The glad doing of what once seemed the smallest acts is the liturgy of those becoming as foolish as saints. To become ordinary is the first commandment.[3]

Such a person realizes that he is himself without significance and that the inferior stature to which he has heretofore tried to reduce everything except himself rightfully belongs to him. Butler, maid, cook, janitor are the right metaphors for how one ought to live, however large or small one's public role; but one must live them without romanticizing their inverse heroism: one must stop trying to be perfectly humble, for that attempt is itself a flight from one's lack of station, one's subordinate part in the genuflection of the universe. On the other hand, to such a person, nothing in the universe seems so deserving of single-hearted passion as the small details in the midst of which he lives. What used to be experienced as ordinary is embraced as sacred in its very ordinariness, irrespective of how banal one's experience of it might be.[4] One loves others enough to be unmindful of the lack of drama in one's experience of them. The smallest gestures made by such a person are unconsciously the gestures of self-effacement. The face has slowly, gradually engraved on it the expression of its single love: the features themselves reticent, effaced, yet the face as a whole animated by solicitude, attentive and intent, shy in its very obedience. This is the face of humility, which never sees or is aware of itself. Our very describing it taints it with an attention it would prefer not to receive. If he could, the humble person would choose never to be spoken of. Radically ordinary in the sense of assuming no importance for himself, such a person is the rarest of all mortals and the utter opposite of what throughout we have called the ordinary self, the self which takes its own importance for granted. We have not travelled full circle: the end of crisis is not a return to the condition which preceded it but rather the undergoing of a daily rupture more subtle, more hidden, more demanding than those I have tried to describe. The end of crisis is its beginning.

That truth robs all I have said of its pretense to finality. I cannot, in fact, claim even to have studied the paradigm in terms of which all crisis is to be understood; I can do no more now than point to it, to that daily life of rupture whose suffering is concealed even from its own eyes. This very concealment, the hiddenness and silence of its wounds, constitute the evidence of its depth and thus the proof that it surpasses not just in subtlety but in substance the dramatic crises which have occupied my attention.

There is, I argued, an element of foolish impetuosity, a lack of constraint and discretion, within the very heart of worship. For the religious person realizes that he has no good reason to hold anything back from the Sacred. One moment of such lavish expenditure, one moment which consummates one's whole past and prefigures one's whole future, seems, at first, the most perfect way to obey the absolute claim made by the Sacred on the whole of one's being. It is just its seeming so perfect, the very extraordinariness of its oblation, which makes such a consummate act attractive. Nothing surpasses, in felt intensity, the flushed radiance of this first night of marriage. But after the first night are many others which will require the quotidian, common rites of constancy—and therefore a more subtle and demanding version of that original ardor.

Worship does demand foolish impetuosity. One ought never to take time to count the cost of one's self-abandonment. There ought to be not the slightest hesitancy, and no prudential calculation of consequences. The act of self-surrender can, in that sense, never be too instantaneous, too rushed. But, on the other hand, the religious person thinks it always sinful not to give each person, each circumstance, each with its idiosyncratic details, the time-consuming delicacy it deserves, on account of its sacredness. To be reckless with regard to what generosity costs one's self means that one lavishes on each situation in which one is placed the recklessly even pace of holy patience.

For patience does not mean that one waits, even though that is the verb it customarily modifies. Indeed, real patience never sets its eyes on some distant goal lying far ahead in the future, for such looking ahead, no matter how reserved one's appetite to get there, is itself already a sure impatience, a failure to be appropriated by the present and serve its claims. Real patience is too patient with the present to take flight from it in the distraction of the future. It never has to wait for the future to bring it something worthy of its love. It finds always and easily accessible to it a thousand demands awaiting its obedience. In the grip of such demands, one can fall all too quickly into busyness, frantically and breathlessly hurrying to finish everything at once, with not a moment's peace, because time leaves one no time for breathing. But such a burrowing into the present, cramming it full of as many deeds as possible—this, too, is all impatience, an impatience with time itself because of its refusal to let me possess all of it right now in the immediate present. I am impatient with it for not budgeting itself according to my needs. Real patience would make no such complaint. Real patience neither awaits the future impatiently nor does it throw itself impatiently into the present. Real patience is consenting to time itself, to its holy rupturing. For time is, as it were, that rupturing by which every moment is effaced and thus humbled.[5] Time is itself, in that sense, the genuflection of the now before the Sacred. The self who is truly patient adopts and does not rise from what is the posture of time itself—bowed low, bent over, subservient to what is Other than itself.

No one, however, is ever perfectly such a self, just as no one ever ceases becoming one's nothingness before the Sacred. Eventually, I must begin learning to become patient with my very impatience, to give even my own self just the time, neither more nor less, and just the mercy, neither wrath nor pity, I need if I am to succeed in losing my self-importance. Sometime, perhaps, and not a moment too soon, I will even stop hurrying toward ecstasies of self-abandonment and effacement. I will become, perhaps, humble enough not to panic when I realize that I still take myself too seriously.

And this leaves no time to count the cost of worship's generosity. It leaves no room for that kind of prudence. Worship ridicules all proverbs which caution it to be reserved. One must become blind to one's own interests: finally, we have found what deserves avoidance, if one is not to avoid the small ordeals of everyday existence. But this means, in fact, that, for the first time, one *sees*, in its particularity and intricacy, each of the reticent details of every situation. Those details demand an eye for microscopic nuance, but one which can gather its minute observations into a single insight about what one ought to do.[6] But even then, every insight into every situation is finally a submission to its elusive individuality, and an openness to the mystery of its holy darkness. Only one guided by this faint but commanding wisdom can begin to obey the subtlest truths. Only in the dictionary of self-centeredness does prudence mean keeping a sharp eye on one's interests; here it begins to mean the opposite—discerning what particular way of my becoming nothing will best serve what is sacred in this situation. So indiscrete is the prudent person with regard to his own welfare, nothing else counts, in the delicate scales of his deliberation, except this discretion toward the sacred. I hardly need add that such a person minds the inherited social conventions just insofar as they are themselves rubrics of the kind of loving sensitivity to detail which he is trying to practice. Real prudence learns precisely the unwritten etiquette of worship; it enables one to discern the exact manner of genuflecting appropriate to the particular place and time in which one has been placed.

That is why it ought not matter where one is: one would always be at home if one would bring to every place the same joyfully submissive deportment. No one living in this manner would ever claim recognition for himself. But if we want to keep in our mind an image of such reckless self-abandonment, we ought to think of one who dusts and sweeps, who makes the shopping list and lubricates the car, who pays the bills and enjoys strawberry shortcake, and all this, each day, with the same habit of grace and silence; the self to whom nothing extraordinary ever happens, who brings to the eating and clean-up of each meal, no matter its menu, the most commonplace, most unexceptional cheerfulness; in short, one who does just the things that we do, in just the way we usually do not do them.

Such patience and discretion seem, undoubtedly, too small a kind of virtue to be the final stop on the long journey of this essay. They do not, indeed, stand up well when compared to the steep ambition of the will to control, the festive and contagious joy of the will to be generous, the devastating horror of falling into crisis, the hero's willingness to embrace the most radical demands, the mortification of shame and the violence of self-loathing, the dramatic realization of one's nothingness before the Sacred. Those ways of being have, each of them, at least the excellence of their passion, the high temper of an adenture somehow wrong but at least radical. The patience and discretion just described seem, on the other hand, to be precisely a low-keyed quieting of every passion that would take us away from our vocation to the mundane; they are virtues to be practiced only in doing the small tasks at home which especially irritate our dignity. But all answers to the questions we have asked which promise more than this anticlimax prove themselves by virtue of that very promise to be false answers.

There remains to be mentioned only one last and critical reversal. The anticlimax of living at home an utterly ordinary life is anticlimactic only to those who pull back, in terror, from living it. The few, among whom I so wish I could include myself, who do not recoil from it are utterly at home with such a life, surrounded by children with their teeming demands and reckless laughter, by friends and their divorced companions, sometimes by homeless vagrants, and others of the world's delinquents. Pledged never to leave home, or its endless tasks, they have chosen the hardest road; no journey is harsher than that which leads us to live in the place we spend our lives avoiding. But, for them, suffering keeps disappearing into celebration. If they are able to work this daily miracle, it is, they tell us, because they keep receiving, in small, unnoticed ways, the harsh stroke of divine mercy. To speak more of the joys of their suffering would require an essay on the geography of a real and lasting paradise.

NOTES

Point of Departure

1. In *The Triumph of the Therapeutic* (New York: Harper Torchbooks, 1968) and *Fellow Teachers* (New York: Delta, 1975), Philip Rieff diagnoses modernity's loss of the Sacred and its attempt to find prophets who can fill the vacuum this loss created.

2. But the Platonic interpretation of the city as the macrocosm of the soul can only be carried so far; the private is never more than a partial image of the public. The private and the public each possess distinctive features which prohibit our collapsing the distinction between them, as Hannah Arendt warns us in many of her writings, e.g. *The Human Condition* (Chicago: The University of Chicago Press, 1958), 22-78. That is why I would emphasize the impropriety of extrapolating any claim about public crisis from what is said in this essay about the individual experience of crisis.

3. Cf. Robert Jay Lifton's examples of therapeutic conversions from one "totalistic ideology" to another, in *Boundaries* (New York: Random House, 1970).

4. This suggests that the very act of entering into the world of a work of art is, in a sense, itself a crisis. This would explain why a culture with more leisure time than any other in history is nevertheless characterized by the decline of pleasure in the arts, which Walter Kerr regrets: we would rush happily into the arms of such pleasures if they did not require an askesis, a self-forgetting, which must always be experienced as in some way upsetting. I think Kerr himself tends to underestimate this askesis and so must attribute our inability to participate in aesthetic experiences to the utilitarian mentality which makes us think such experiences useless. Cf. *The Decline of Pleasure* (New York: Simon and Schuster, 1968), 43-86.

5. One might say that, in the *Concluding Unscientific Postscript*, Kierkegaard accuses Hegel of exempting himself from the tear of the very dialectic he describes. He criticizes Hegel for putting existence, and es-

pecially his own existence, into his system in such a way as to rob it of its very existential character. But the charge is weakened by its ambiguity: is Hegel's philosophy being criticized for its lacking a crucial insight or is Hegel's act of philosophizing being criticized because it is an intellectual act which the thinker can perform without heeding its import for his personal life? The intellectual life is itself fraught with crises, and we are entitled to criticize a thinker's thinking only for its refusal to undergo these crises, the crises intrinsic to the process of thinking itself.

6. "The uncovering of what has been buried": this phrase has, not accidentally, both Freudian and Heideggerian resonances. Not unlike the process of psychoanalysis, becoming authentic in Heidegger's sense of the term requires that one confront what is dreadful and cease hiding from the ultimate claim which the dreadful makes on one's being. What is the "it" which is hidden? The possibility of one's own nothingness? Unrequited polymorphous desire? Or both? Or an Other which neither Heidegger nor Freud names? Cf. "Epilogue: One Step Beyond," in Philip Rieff's *Freud: The Mind of the Moralist,* 3rd edition (Chicago: The University of Chicago Press, 1979), and Martin Heidegger, *Being and Time,* trans. John Macquarrie and Edward Robinson (New York: Harper & Row, 1962), 312-82. Chapter 3 discusses whether the "It" that is hidden under our avoidances is desire; chapter 6 discusses in what sense the "it" is nothingness.

7. Both Descartes and Husserl propose methods which, they suggest, equip the mind with a kind of strobelight that illuminates obscurities. To acquire the strobelight, one must transform one's ordinary thought into the extraordinary thought of the philosopher—a transformation achieved in the one case by radical doubt, in the other by the epoché. *Then* one can start philosophizing in earnest. Contrast with this Socrates' assertion, at the end of his life as a philosopher, that the ultimate human wisdom is to know that we don't know. In other words, we never reach the "then." For Socrates, the performance of the turn, which for Husserl and Descartes seems to be the step into philosophizing, is itself the unending enterprise of philosophizing. Were we eventually to claim to know what crisis is, to grasp it in its essence, would we not be claiming to transcend Socrates' wisdom? Is the crisis which real thinking demands ever finished or healed?

Chapter One

1. Similarly, we might ask if the utilitarian's obsession with control and productivity is comparable to Nietzsche's celebration of the Will-to-Power, and if the repetitive routines of work are comparable to his idea of eternal recurrence. That such comparisons are indefensible is suggested by the fact that the utilitarians are heirs of the Enlightenment, whose principal spokesmen preferred commercial man to the heroic creator. Cf. Peter Gay, *The En-*

lightenment: An Introduction, Vol. 2 (New York: Alfred A. Knopf, 1969), 45-51.

2. I use the phrase in the sense given it by Emmanuel Levinas in *Totality and Infinity,* trans. Alphonso Lingis (Pittsburgh: Duquesne University Press, 1969).

3. Cf. Martin Heidegger, *Being and Time,* 91-148 (English pagination). I do not mean to suggest that things are first seen as things and then as tools. Rather, as Heidegger explains, we are originally workers; contemplation occurs as an interruption of the world of work. That is why the first chapter in an essay on the everyday must be about work, the second about leisure.

4. Cf. Herbert Marcuse, *Eros and Civilization* (Boston: Beacon Press, 1966) and *An Essay on Liberation* (Boston: Beacon Press, 1969).

5. Cf. Jacques Ellul, *The Technological Society* (New York: Vintage Books, 1967), 64-148 and passim. Cf. also Joseph Pieper, *Leisure, The Basis of Culture,* trans. Alexander Dru (New York: New American Library, Mentor Books, 1963), 19-23.

6. Cf. Soren Kierkegaard, *The Sickness unto Death,* trans. Walter Lowrie (Garden City: Doubleday & Company, Inc., Anchor Books, 1954), 166 and passim.

7. Cf. Rudolf Otto, *The Idea of the Holy* (New York: Oxford University Press, Galaxy Books, 1958), 12-23; and Edmund Burke, *A Philosophical Enquiry into the Origin of Our Ideas of the Sublime and Beautiful* (Notre Dame, Ind.: University of Notre Dame Press, 1968), 64-70.

8. Cf. Jacques Ellul, *The Meaning of the City,* trans. Denis Pardee (Grand Rapids, Mich.: Eerdmans, 1970).

9. Heidegger, *Being and Time,* 279-311. Just as Heidegger in *Being and Time* described death's capacity for shattering our ordinary understanding, so Thomas Kuhn describes in *The Structure of Scientific Revolutions* (Chicago: The University of Chicago Press, 1962) the way anomalies can undermine currently accepted scientific paradigms. Both are examples of the undermining of the will to control. In Tolstoy's *Death of Ivan Ilyich,* Ivan repeatedly refers to the reality of death as an "It" with which none of his ordinary linguistic techniques enable him to cope.

10. I think this attitude of reducing everything to a problem is exemplified by Wittgenstein in the *Tractatus Logico-Philosophicus,* trans. D.F. Pears and B.F. McGuinness (New York: Humanities Press, 1961), when he claims that "If a question can be framed at all, it is also possible to answer it" (6.5). This is true if one limits speech to description of facts, to the boundaries of the ordinary. But to limit speech and thought in this way is to accept the ordinary as the essence of human existence. Ultimately, it involves the refusal to question assumptions and to undergo the experience of crisis which real thought involves. Wittgenstein acknowledges in the *Tractatus* that, beside the ordinary, there is the realm of the mystical. But the latter, instead of disrupting language, merely reduces it to silence (cf. 6.44-47).

The distinction drawn here between the "nameless intruder" and a "problem" has some affinities with Gabriel Marcel's distinction between mystery and problem (cf. *The Mystery of Being,* trans. G.S. Fraser (Chicago: Henry Regnery Company, Gateway Books, 1960), vol. 1, 242-70. But I am not sure that Marcel adequately takes into account the fact that, given the nature of ordinary existence, mystery must be experienced as a nameless and upsetting rupture, not as a harbinger of joy and wonder (cf. the following chapter).

11. Cf. the "clothes" motif and the theme of being stripped which frequently recurs in tragic literature, e.g. *Agamemnon, King Lear,* in mythic literature (discussed by Joseph Campbell in *The Hero with a Thousand Faces* (New York: Meridian Books, 1967), and in ascetic literature (discussed by Dom Jean Leclercq, Dom François Vandenboucke, and Louis Bouyer in *A History of Christian Spirituality,* vol. 2 (New York: The Seabury Press, n.d.). In the classical worlds of Greek tragedy and traditional Christian spirituality, there can be neither heroism nor sanctity except insofar as one strips oneself of the ordinary and consents to the radical suffering which such a defenseless condition entails.

12. And this raises the possibility—but does not prove—that the converse is true as well: that utopian thinking is really ordinary consciousness dreaming of its own apotheosis. B.F. Skinner's *Walden Two* (New York: The Macmillan Company, 1962) is a kind of dithyramb to the ordinary. In this book there is no mistaking the fact that the father-founder-king is a technician who envisions not the reign of wisdom, or virtue, or eros, but the reign of problem solving. I will explore more fully in chapter 4 the reasons why it is impossible for a technician to be a founder.

13. While the ordinary self is necessarily a follower, this does not mean that the follower is necessarily ordinary. Obedience and following fall into disrepute as a consequence of the effort to repudiate the ordinary. But it may be that this way of repudiating the ordinary is itself a subtle mode of flight. It may be that discovery of one's obligation to obey the moral order is itself an upsetting event which does not occur unless one is willing to suffer. Cf. chapter 5.

14. The same embarrassed silence can occur among established friends—when it insinuates the possibility of a new depth of friendship the development of which will require rupture.

15. For some literary examples, cf. *King Lear,* Act I, scene II, and Faulkner's *The Bear,* section 4, in *Go Down, Moses* (New York: Random House, Vintage Books, 1973).

16. In behavioral therapy of the type practiced by Skinnerians, the individual is taught precisely how to "condition himself."

17. Heidegger has to answer this question with regard to the avoidance of death, Freud with regard to the avoidance of the erotic. The question is a modern version of the issue raised by Socrates in the *Meno:* how can we ask a

question without knowing what we are asking about? And what is the point of asking if we already know?

18. My colleague William Zak has argued in *Sovereign Shame: A Study of King Lear* (Lewisburg, Penna.: Bucknell University Press, 1984) that Lear's tragic avoidances are themselves the explanation for the difficulty we have in understanding the play. Why does the "problem" at the heart of the play and many of its scenes keep eluding us if not because a rupture always threatens and is always avoided, so that it becomes impossible for Lear and almost impossible for us to know what would be known if avoidance ceased?

19. Or, as Freud put it, "You behave like an absolute ruler who is content with the information supplied him by his highest officials and never goes among the people to hear their voice." Freud recommends as an alternative that you "Turn your eyes inward, look into your own depths, learn first to know yourself." "A Difficulty in the Path of Psychoanalysis," quoted in Rieff, *Freud: The Mind of the Moralist,* 69. But this looking into one's own depths, to be discussed in later chapters, inevitably precipitates the crisis we ordinarily spend our lives avoiding.

Chapter Two

1. This chapter as a whole can be read as a conversation, about the nature of conversation, with what might be called the literature of generosity. I would include under this rubric most of the literature of humanistic psychology as exemplified by Rollo May's *Man's Search for Himself* and Abraham Maslow's *Toward a Psychology of Being*; at least some of the literature of the Freudian Marxists, and especially Herbert Marcuse's *Eros and Civilization* and *Essay on Liberation*; some of the recent Western literature on the oldest Eastern religions, especially the work of Alan Watts, e.g., *Nature, Man, and Woman;* and last but not least, much recent Christian literature which seems to make celebration its paradigm virtue. Perhaps the most fitting epigram for the literature of generosity comes from Martin Buber's *I and Thou,* 2nd ed., trans. Ronald Gregor Smith (New York: Charles Scribners Sons, 1958): "All real living is meeting." But in saying this, I do not mean to imply that Buber is a proponent of the mode of life which I am describing here. To locate the literature of generosity historically, I think it has to be recognized as an often naive version of an earlier romanticism that desired a "holy marriage with the eternal universe, . . . a new world . . . the equivalent of paradise." Cf. M.H. Abrams, *Natural Supernaturalism* (New York: W.W. Norton & Company, 1971), 28.

2. Cf. Pieper, *Leisure the Basis of Culture*; also Pieper's *In Tune with the World: A Theory of Festivity*, trans. Richard and Clara Winston (Chicago: Franciscan Herald Press, 1973), especially 55-59.

3. I have been influenced in this description of childhood by Dylan Thomas's rendition of the child's rapport with the world in "Fern Hill."

4. Cf. Aristotle's distinction between immanent and transitive action in *Metaphysics*, IX, 6 and 8, and *De Anima*, I, 3 and III, 7.

5. Pieper, *Leisure, the Basis of Culture,* especially 69-82.

6. I think this view underlies much humanistic psychology and the modern therapeutic mentality as a whole, though not all of the practitioners of this mentality would be willing to acknowledge it explicitly. It is operative in the thought and work of any therapist who thinks that a primary purpose of therapy is to eliminate suffering. That is why the culminating achievement of the therapeutic mentality is the development of "crisis management" and specifically the development of psychological techniques for "dealing with" death and dying. Cf. Elizabeth Kubler-Ross, *On Death and Dying* (New York: Macmillan Publishing Co., Inc., 1970).

Chapter Three

1. I am using the word "world" in the sense Heidegger gives it in *Being and Time*, 91-148. The world, as Heidegger conceives it, is not a collection of objects but a horizon of meaning in terms of which we interpret everything we encounter. The end of one's world occurs, therefore, not when objects disappear but when the fundamental structures of meaning which provide one a framework for understanding everything are undermined.

2. That which brings about the end of one's world in Heidegger's sense of the term is never simply an "object" or "thing"; for the end of one's world is not one event among others which take place within one's world; it is one's loss of the world as a whole. That is why it is always experienced as a death. Cf. *Being and Time*, 279-311.

3. Heidegger emphasizes that the encounter with death is a radically in-dividualizing experience because dying is something "the they" cannot do for one. Cf. *Being and Time*, 307-08, 341-48.

4. This is, I think, the point of view developed by Albert Camus, especially in *The Plague*. I discuss this attitude at greater length in chapter 6, when I turn my attention directly to the experience of nothingness.

5. Hume raises these questions in *Dialogues on Natural Religion* (New York: The Bobbs-Merrill Company, Inc., Library of Liberal Arts, 1947), 198. In chapter 6 I try to call into question the perspective which underlies these questions and makes them plausible to us. The real issue, I would suggest, is this: on what ground are we standing when we feel justified in objecting to the reality of death? And how would our perspective change if this ground were pulled out from under us?

6. Among modern writers, Faulkner is perhaps the most effective in conveying this sense of tragic destiny. The great achievement of Faulkner's

art is that he creates a sense of tragic inevitability that has its seat in the moral character of his figures. His prose evokes a horrific sense of implacability and yet he leaves no doubt that it is the human will that has mobilized the awful powers that work toward its destruction.

7. The horrifying nature of the divine is emphasized by Burke in *A Philosophical Enquiry into the Origin of Our Ideas of the Sublime and Beautiful*, 64-70; by Mircea Eliade in *The Sacred and the Profane*, trans. Willard R. Trask (New York: Harcourt Brace Jovanovich, Harvest Books 1959), 26; and by Rudolf Otto in *The Idea of the Holy*, 12-23.

8. Cf. Sigmund Freud, *The Future of an Illusion*, trans. W. D. Robson-Scott, first rev. ed. (Garden City: Doubleday & Company, Inc., 1964), 17-35. Because Freud thought such an appeal to the Sacred for protection and/or consolation constituted the essence of religion, he was prevented from realizing that an authentic religious experience is more upsetting than the ordeal of psychoanalysis itself. Cf. chapter 6.

9. Cf. Rieff, *The Mind of the Moralist*, 76.

10. This is, of course, the central argument of *Being and Time*, where the will to control is construed as the attitude of inauthentic everydayness that is unconsciously governed by an ontology of presence.

11. Cf. Heidegger, *Being and Time*, 179-311; and "What Is Metaphysics," in *Existence and Being* (Chicago: Henry Regnery Company, Gateway Edition, 1968), 337-49.

12. Aeschylus, *Agamemnon*, 995-97.

13. Heidegger, *Being and Time*, 306.

14. Cf., for example, *The Sickness unto Death*, 159.

15. Freud himself recognizes in *The Ego and the Id* that part of the ego is unconscious, but it is not clear that this recognition is integrated into the substance of psychoanalytic theory. Cf. Rieff, *Freud: The Mind of the Moralist,* 95.

16. For a similar distinction, cf. Heidegger, *Being and Time*, 179-81 and 228-34.

17. Cf. *Being and Time*, 279-311.

18. Cf. Heidegger, *Being and Time*, 228-34 and passim; and "What Is Metaphysics," 338 and passim.

19. Camus' shift from the absurdist position of *The Stranger* to a humanist position in his later works is due, I think, to his realizing that our capacity for participating in each others' experience of despair deprives despair of its justification. The despair experienced by Dr. Rieux in *The Plague* is transformed into something meaningful by his very act of sharing it with others.

20. Kafka's stories are often parables of such pilgrimages. Cf., for example, *The Trial*, trans. Willa and Edwin Muir (New York: Alfred A. Knopf, 1960), 263-69.

Chapter Four

1. As will become clear in the pages that follow, I think Nietzsche's work offers the most profound philosophical articulation of the heroic mode of being and his Zarathustra seems as to me to be its paradigmatic individual. This chapter as a whole can therefore be read as a meditation on the heroic character as Nietzsche tried to model him in *Thus Spake Zarathustra*.

2. Throughout this discussion I am drawing on the rich existential tradition that opposes the heroic individual to the "herd" (cf. Kierkegaard, *The Present Age*, and Nietzsche's *Thus Spake Zarathustra*), "the masses" (cf. Ortega y Gassett's *Revolt of the Masses*), "the they" (cf. Heidegger's *Being and Time*). That Kierkegaard, like the others, knows that this issue is more complicated than it seems at first is shown by the fact that in *Fear and Trembling* he describes the truly religious person as someone whom it is difficult to distinguish from a completely ordinary individual (cf. *Fear and Trembling*, trans. Alastair Hannay (New York: Viking Penguin, Penguin Books, 1985), 68-70. Heidegger explains how the distinction between the herd and the authentic individual is intimately related to and, in fact, grounded in two radically different and opposed approaches to Being, the one dominated by the metaphysics of presence, the other open to the "difference" between beings and Being. Cf. *Being and Time*, 149-68 and 349-82.

3. Nietzsche's Zarathustra seems to me to oscillate between contempt and resignation, despair and rejoicing acceptance, in his attitude toward the herd. At his best moments he is aware of the fact that one of the greatest heroic achievements is to overcome the temptation to demean oneself by hating the herd for attempting to deprive one of one's greatness. Cf. *Thus Spake Zarathustra*, trans. Walter Kaufmann (New York: The Viking Press, Compass Books, 1966), 215-21.

4. In Greek tragedies like Aeschylus' *Agamemnon* and Sophocles' *Oedipus Rex,* the chorus often exemplifies such attitudes toward both their gods and their heroes.

5. Cf. Nietzsche, *Thus Spake Zarathustra*, 46-48 and passim.

6. Cf. Michael Polanyi's discussion of the attempt to justify such an inversion in *Knowing and Being* (Chicago: The University of Chicago Press, 1969). Also, cf. Hannah Arendt, *The Origins of Totalitarianism,* 2nd enlgd. ed. (New York: The World Publishing Company, Meridian Books, 1958), 305-40, for a description of a society which tried to carry out such an inversion.

7. But perhaps such nihilism is, in fact, only the will to control stripped of all generosity and carried to its logical conclusion. Indeed, the perfect plan, the final solution, for all possible problems is the murder of all by one, or the suicide of all except one. The second best plan: universal suicide, with no exceptions.

8. I am drawing here on Gabriel Marcel's distinction between hope and

optimism, but Marcel thinks the primary difference between them lies in the fact that genuine hope never fixes on a specific object of longing in the way optimism does. Cf. *Homo Viator: Introduction to a Metaphysic of Hope,* trans. Emma Craufurd (New York: Harper and Row, Harper Torchbooks, 1962), 29-67. Viktor Frankl's descriptions of concentration camp experiences provide excruciating examples of the inseparability of hope and anguish, and of the way optimism and the flight from anguish cooperate with each other. Cf. *Man's Search for Meaning,* rev. ed. (New York: Washington Square Press, 1984), especially 95-96.

9. Cf. Nietzsche, *Thus Spake Zarathustra,* 25-30, 113-116, and passim.

10. Ibid.

11. This is why Nietzsche's Zarathustra must get to the point where he embraces the beginning and end of the universe over and over again—i.e. what Nietzsche calls the "eternal recurrence" of nothingness and being. Cf. *Thus Spake Zarathustra,* 215-21.

12. Because, according to Nietzsche, the belief in immortality is motivated by an unwillingness to embrace finitude and temporality, he thinks the heroic individual would reject that belief and the entire religious perspective ordinarily associated with it. The logical thing for the heroic individual to do, once he realizes that he himself is superior to the divine as it is ordinarily understood, is to cease believing it exists.

13. Cf. Robert Jay Lifton, *Home from the War* (New York: Simon and Schuster, Touchstone Books 1973), 331-78 and passim.

14. Cf. Nietzsche, *Thus Spake Zarathustra,* 323 and passim.

15. Cf. Eliade, *The Sacred and the Profane,* 68-115. Eliade, it should be noted, describes the heroic mode of being from the point of view of its genuinely humble admirers and does not attempt to work out a phenomenological description of the heroic consciousness of the founder himself.

16. Cf. Eliade, *The Sacred and the Profane,* 20-67.

17. Cf. Nietzsche, *Thus Spake Zarathustra,* 115; and *Beyond Good and Evil,* trans. Marianne Cowan (Chicago: Henry Regnery Company, Gateway Edition, 1955), 15.

18. Eliade, *The Sacred and the Profane,* 77-85 and passim.

19. Cf. Nietzsche, *Thus Spake Zarathustra,* 215-24, and Mircea Eliade, *The Myth of the Eternal Return or Cosmos and History,* trans. Willard R. Trask (Princeton: Princeton University Press, 1971), 49-92.

20. Nietzsche, *Thus Spake Zarathustra,* 113-15 and passim.

21. C.S. Lewis discusses this debunking mentality in *The Abolition of Man* (New York: Macmillian Publishing, Inc., 1955) and B.F. Skinner exemplifies it in *Beyond Freedom and Dignity* (New York: Random House, Bantam/ Vintage Books, 1972), 175-206 and passim.

22. Cf. Hannah Arendt, *The Origins of Totalitarianism,* 389-459, and Aleksandr Solzhenitsyn, *The Gulag Archipelago, 1918-1956: An Experiment in*

Literary Investigation, I-II, trans. Thomas P. Whitney (New York: Harper and Row, 1974), 24-92 and passim.

23. Cf. James Broderick, S.J., *The Origin of the Jesuits* (Westport, Conn.: Greenwood Press, 1971), 1-33. Ignatius' case illustrates how the experience of leisure disrupts one's natural mode of being and thus creates the open space in one's life that makes the emergence of crisis possible.

24. This, it seems to me, is the moral position which Nietzsche advocates through the mouth of Zarathustra and in *Beyond Good and Evil.*

Chapter Five

1. Here and throughout my discussion of shame I am influenced by the work of Philip Rieff, whose most recently published discussion of shame is the epilogue to the third edition of *Freud: The Mind of the Moralist.*

2. Richard Rorty argues in *Consequences of Pragmatism* (Minneapolis: University of Minnesota Press, 1982) that the contemporary loss of belief in transcendent values is to be welcomed because it frees us to adopt whatever framework of meaning we find helpful to us in getting what we want. (Cf. especially xlii-xliii.)

3. The fact that only the moral person is aware of the horror of evil accounts, I think, for the banality which characterizes the evil person himself. What Hannah Arendt found most horrifying about Adolf Eichmann was the fact that he was in no way upset by what he was doing but proceeded about his business as if there was nothing out of the ordinary about murdering millions of people. Cf. Hannah Arendt, *Eichmann in Jerusalem*, rev. and enlgd. ed. (New York: The Viking Press, 1964).

4. One of the primary purposes of Kierkegaard's writing, especially in the pseudonymous works like *Fear and Trembling* and *Sickness unto Death*, is to awaken in the reader this terrible sense of the import of choices. One of his great achievements as a religious writer is that, unlike many traditional Christian authors, he is able to do so without putting any emphasis on the eternal benefits or pains consequent upon such choices.

5. Paul Ricoeur discusses the experience of evil as a contaminating stain in *The Symbolism of Evil* (Boston: Beacon Press, 1967), 25-46.

6. Gabriel Marcel, *The Mystery of Being*, vol. 1, 95-126.

7. With regard to the fact that Oedipus at one point asks to be allowed to remain in the city, one must ask whether this is a moment of weakness in which he temporarily *backs down* from the heroic ordeal of self-hatred, or a moment of saintly venturing *beyond* self-hatred to a kind of reconciliation with evil which self-hatred prevents one from envisioning. My colleagues, William Zak and Francis Kane, have helped me sharpen my grasp of this issue.

8. I am using a gnostic image here because there seems to be a profound correspondence between the tragic hero's experience of shame and

consequent self-hatred, and the gnostic view of the physical world as evil and the repressive asceticism that logically follows from it. Cf. Hans Jonas, *The Gnostic Religion: The Message of the Alien God and the Beginnings of Christianity*, 2nd ed. (Boston: Beacon Press, 1963), 62-65 and passim. Oedipus's act of self-mutilation seems to me to be the paradigmatic gesture for the kind of spirituality that a dualistic theology entails.

9. I am referring here not just to gnostic or Manichean spirituality but more generally to the kind of repressive asceticism which seems to occasionally infect all traditions of spirituality. Early Christianity has its Tertullian, Protestantism its Jonathan Edwards, and Russian Orthodoxy its Ferapont (cf. Doestoevsky's *The Brothers Karamazov*).

10. In *Beyond Good and Evil* (cf., e.g., 52-72), Nietzsche expresses his admiration for this kind of asceticism because it requires a heroic will; but he thinks it is an example of how the heroic will is perverted by the Judeo-Christian religious tradition. The question is whether this perversion occurs because, as Nietzsche argued, shame has been allowed to contaminate the heroic heart or because, as I will try to suggest, the person consumed with self-hatred does not yet take shame truly to heart.

11. There is a profoundly gnostic flavor to the metaphysical realizations which Roquentin reaches in the climactic scene of Sartre's *Nausea*, trans. Lloyd Alexander (New York: New Directions, 1964), 127:

> . . . And then all of a sudden, there it was, clear as day: existence had suddenly unveiled itself. It had lost the harmless look of an abstract category: it was the very paste of things . . . the diversity of things, their individuality, were only an appearance, a veneer. This veneer had melted, leaving soft, monstrous masses, all in disorder—naked, in a frightful, obscene nakedness.

12. In Doestoevsky's *Underground Man* and Camus' *The Fall*, the main characters, though lacking Oedipus's heroic grandeur, are like him in that each acts as his own judge and executioner. The Camus work is a psychologically profound exploration of the torturous length to which pride goes in its effort to maintain its superior position in the soul of someone filled with self-hatred.

13. The psychotic's mine of deliberate self-hatred can go so far as to include a very articulate Manichean type of theologizing. Compare R.D. Laing's *The Divided Self* (Baltimore: Penguin Books, 1965) with some of the texts in Jonas's *The Gnostic Religion* and some of the descriptions of eschatological religious enthusiasms in Norman Cohn's *The Pursuit of the Millennium* (New York: Oxford University Press, 1970).

Chapter Six

1. Cf. Heidegger, *Being and Time*, 279-311; also Tolstoy's *Death of Ivan Ilych*.

2. Cf. Heidegger, *Being and Time*, 279-311.

3. Throughout this discussion of death, we shall be reflecting on the fact that it confronts us with the possibility of our own nothingness, not with nothingness as an inevitable fact. Consequently, the discussion does not intend to preclude in any way the possibility of immortality. The same can be said of Heidegger's discussion of death in *Being and Time*. Cf. especially p. 292.

4. Cf. Kubler-Ross, *On Death and Dying*, 1-37.

5. Heidegger, *Being and Time*, 279-311.

6. Heidegger, *Being and Time*, 279-311, and "What Is Metaphysics," 338.

7. If we take Dr. Rieux in *The Plague* as representative of his own point of view, Camus finally espouses this kind of humanism, repudiating the earlier more nihilistic viewpoint expressed in *The Stranger*. Cf. also *Resistance, Rebellion and Death*, trans. Justin O'Brien (New York: Alfred A. Knopf, 1961), 1-33.

8. Cf. Frankl, *Man's Search for Meaning*, 85-90 and passim.

9. Heidegger, on the other hand, considers death the "uttermost" possibility, a possibility which is "not to be outstripped" (*Being and Time*, 294). To my knowledge, even the later Heidegger does not speak of an encounter with a reality before which and in comparison with which one experiences one's own nothingness. Even Being does not require us to identify with nothingness.

10. Cf. G.W.F. Hegel, *The Phenomenology of Spirit*, trans. A.V. Miller (Oxford: Clarendon Press, 1977), 46-58.

11. Cf. Ludwig Feuerbach, *The Essence of Christianity*, trans. George Eliot (New York: Harper and Row, Torchbooks, 1957), 1-32.

12. John Barth's *End of the Road* (New York: Doubleday & Company, 1969) is a brilliant fictional portrayal of the simultaneously arrogant and self-destructive self-criticism which is inevitably practiced by those who live in the vacuum created by the loss of belief in anything sacred.

13. This would appear to be the case with Oedipus, who thinks, when he achieves the blinding insight into his own evil, that he finally sees for sure who he is.

14. John of the Cross develops into a full-fledged mystical theology the dialectic of destitution implicit in the Socratic definition of human wisdom. Cf., for example, *The Dark Night of the Soul*, trans. E. Allison Peers (Garden City: Doubleday & Company, Inc., Image Books, 1959), especially Book Two.

15. I think Jonathan Edwards makes the mistake of confusing terror with dread. Cf., for example, "Sinners in the Hands of an Angry God" in *Selected Writings of Jonathan Edwards,* ed. Harold Simonson (New York: Frederick Ungar Publishing Co., 1970), 96-113.

16. Cf. Eliade, *The Sacred and the Profane*, 12 and passim.

17. Cf. Thomas Aquinas, *Summa contra Gentiles*, I: God, trans. Anton Pegis (Notre Dame, Ind.: University of Notre Dame Press, 1975), chapters 30, 32-34, where Aquinas argues that such terms are to be attributed to creatures only in a derivative sense. Whereas Aquinas comes to this conclusion from metaphysical arguments, I am suggesting that the religious consciousness, as focused on the Sacred in an act of worship, imposes such linguistic restrictions on itself out of a sense of radical humility.

18. Cf. Thomas Aquinas, *Summa contra Gentiles,* chapter 29.

19. This dilemma seems to me to be at the heart of the questions which Hume raises in the *Dialogues Concerning Natural Religion* and those which Feuerbach raises in *The Essence of Christianity*. For both, the issue is how can the finite conceive of what transcends it. Hume's conclusion is that we cannot conceive of it meaningfully and therefore should stop discussing it. Feuerbach's conclusion is that we can conceive of it and therefore we must be infinite. In the *Meno* and the *Apology*, Socrates shows the way to mediate between these positions by suggesting that man's ability to ask questions demonstrates his status as a being who stands in between ignorance and knowledge. Michael Polanyi discusses the nature of this "in-between" in *The Tacit Dimension* (Garden City: Doubleday & Company, Inc., Anchor Books, 1967).

20. Cf. Thomas Aquinas, *Summa contra Gentiles*, chapter 14; also the anonymous mystical work, *The Cloud of Unknowing*, ed. William Johnston (Garden City: Doubleday & Company, Inc., Image Books, 1973), and John of the Cross, *Dark Night of the Soul*, Book Two.

21. Cf. Thomas Aquinas, *Summa contra Gentiles*, chapter 17, paragraph 7.

22. Cf. Camus, *Resistance, Rebellion and Death*, 1-32.

23. Cf. Sartre, *Nausea*, p. 126-35.

24. Cf. J.P. Sartre, "The Humanism of Existentialism," in *Essays in Existentialism*, ed. Wade Baskin (New York: The Citadel Press, 1970), 40-41.

25. Cf. Plato, *The Republic*, Book VI, especially 507d-511e.

26. Immanuel Kant, *Foundations of the Metaphysics of Morals*, trans. Lewis White Beck (New York: The Bobbs-Merrill Company, Library of Liberal Arts, 1959), 47; and *Critique of Practical Reason,* trans. Lewis White Beck, (New York: The Bobbs-Merrill Company, Library of Liberal Arts, 1956), 89-91.

27. In this regard it is fascinating to compare Kant's treatment of the sublime in the *Critique of Judgment* with Burke's treatment of it in his *Enquiry*. Kant, whose whole philosophical corpus has as one of its primary purposes a defense of the intrinsic dignity of the human person, claims that sublime experience heightens our sense of our own stature (cf. *Critique of Judgment*, trans. J.H. Bernard (New York: Haffner Press, 1951), 101 and passim). Burke, on the other hand, thinks a sublime experience makes us "shrink into the

minuteness of our own nature" (*Enquiry*, 68). The present essay might be read as a long argument on behalf of Burke's position on this issue.

28. Cf. Joseph Pieper, *Leisure, The Basis of Culture*, 56-64, and *In Tune with the World*, 33-36; also, cf. Eliade, *The Sacred and the Profane*, 68-115.

29. Cf. Philip Rieff, *Freud: The Mind of the Moralist*, Epilogue to the third edition.

30. Merold Westphal makes this issue a central concern in his phenomenology of religious experience. Cf. *God, Guilt, and Death* (Bloomington: Indiana University Press, 1984).

31. This is, I think, Herbert Fingarette's view of crisis in *The Self in Transformation: Psychoanalysis, Philosophy and the Life of the Spirit* (New York: Harper and Row, Torchbooks, 1977).

32. Cf. Jean-Pierre de Caussade, *Abandonment to Divine Providence*, trans. John Beevers (Garden City, N.Y.: Doubleday and Company, Inc., Image Books, 1975).

33. Cf. Nikos Kazantzakis, *Saint Francis*, trans. P.A. Bien (New York: Simon and Schuster, Touchstone Books, 1962), 91-95.

34. Cf. John of the Cross, *The Living Flame of Love*, trans. Kieran Kavanaugh and Otilio Rodriquez, in *The Collected Works of St. John of the Cross* (Washington, D.C.: ICS Publications, 1973).

Epilogue

1. Cf. Mircea Eliade's description of the contrast between sacred and profane time in *The Sacred and the Profane*, 68-115.

2. Cf. Soren Kierkegaard, *Fear and Trembling*, 49-52.

3. Cf. Thérèse of Lisieux, *Autobiography of St. Thérèse of Lisieux: The Story of a Soul*, trans. John Beevers (Garden City, N.Y.: Doubleday & Company, Inc., Image Books, 1957), 114 and passim.

4. Dostoevsky confronts us with this truth at the end of almost every one of his novels; but, great artist of crisis that he is, he does not often attempt to depict the sacred quality of every day's small details, an aesthetic vocation of which Vermeer is one of the best representatives. Cf. Lawrence Gowing, *Vermeer* (New York: Harper and Row, 1970). Perhaps the best description of the spiritual life understood as devotion to the ordinary is Pierre de Caussade's *Abandonment to Divine Providence*.

5. To develop these intimations would require bringing Heidegger's philosophy of temporality (*Being and Time*, 349-82) under the influence of the philosophy of religious worship I have tried to develop in this essay.

6. I do not think the virtue of prudence as described by Aristotle in Book Six of the *Nicomachean Ethics* and subsequently appropriated by the classical ethical tradition can be practiced except by severing all the avoid-

ances which inevitably but often unconsciously interfere with the attempt to discern the requirements of the present moment as it erupts into the future. For that reason, I would argue that one cannot become prudent in Aristotle's sense without undergoing a crisis that severs one's deepest avoidances.